Santa Clara
County
Free Library

REFERENCE

5816

Unlikely Liberators

‹ely
Liberators

The Men of the 100th and 442nd

by

Masayo Umezawa Duus

Translated by Peter Duus

University of Hawaii Press • Honolulu

Originally published as *Buriea no kaihōshatachi*
by Bungeishunjusha, Tokyo, Japan
© 1983 Masayo Duus

English translation
© 1987 Masayo Umezawa Duus
Manufactured in the United States of America
93 92 91 90 89 88   6 5 4 3 2

Library of Congress Cataloging-in-Publication Data

Duus, Masayo, 1938–
  Unlikely liberators.

  Translation of: Buriea no kaihōshatachi.
  Bibliography: p.
  Includes index.
  1. World War, 1939–1945—Japanese Americans.
2. World War, 1939–1945—Campaigns—Western. 3. World
War, 1939–1945—Regimental histories—United States.
4. United States. Army Infantry Batallion, 100th.
5. United States. Army. Regimental Combat Team,
442nd. I. Title.
D753.D8813 1987   940.54'.04   87–6013
ISBN 0–8248–1081–3

To my parents,
the late Kiichi Umezawa
and Hana Umezawa

Contents

Preface

THIS book began as a series of eight articles which ran in *Bungei shunju*, the leading Japanese monthly magazine, from May through December 1982. The series won the Annual Readers' Prize for that year. I rewrote and expanded the articles into a book which was published in September 1983. This translation by my husband, Peter Duus, includes further revisions and additions for an English-language audience.

My interest in the Japanese American soldiers who fought in World War II grew out of a continuing fascination with the complicated relations between the two societies in which I have lived, Japan and the United States. I was born and brought up during the war years in Japan. When the war ended I was about to begin the second semester of first grade—too young to remember the rhetoric of the Greater East Asia Coprosperity Sphere promoted by Japan's military leaders but old enough to be taught the rhetoric of democracy promoted by the American occupation army. Like the rest of my generation of Japanese, which is quite different from the generations before and after, I grew up believing that a society should be organized on the principles of freedom and equality.

By the time I reached college I came to realize that in Japanese society freedom was compromised by social conformity and equality was compromised by social hierarchy. I decided to travel to the United States to see how democracy really worked. It was a journey in search of an ideal. What I found, of course, was that American society compromised the ideals of equality and freedom as much as Japan did although in different ways. In a country constantly refreshed by new waves of immigrants, everyone might be free but not everyone was equal. Latecomers had to struggle to use their freedom to acquire the same status as those who had come before. And some of those who had come before—blacks, for example—did not seem to have much equality no matter how hard they struggled.

In my earlier books I explored the gap between the rhetoric and reality of American society by looking at the U.S.–Japan relationship. Increasingly I became interested in the Japanese American community, at once the symbol and victim of that relationship. What happened to the Japanese immigrants and their children in the United States very much affected how the two nations saw each other, and in turn the vicissitudes of U.S.–Japan relations had a profound impact on the Japanese American community.

My research for this book began in 1978. Since I grew up in a country with a "peace constitution" I had to learn a great deal about the nuts and bolts of army organization and practices. And since it was the Pacific War with which most Japanese are familiar I had to read extensively in memoirs and other accounts of the American campaigns in Europe during World War II.

To trace the movements and operations of the 100th Battalion and the 442nd Regiment in the United States and Europe I used records in the branch of the National Archives in Suitland, Maryland, in the suburbs of Washington, D.C. By good fortune, just two months before I visited the archives, much World War II material had been declassified. (Parenthetically, the accessibility of public records, which are closely guarded by the bureaucracy in Japan and most other countries, is one of the unique freedoms the United States offers not only its citizens but even foreigners like me.) Since the records were not well catalogued, the archive staff allowed me to search through the record storage rooms. It was there that I found the unit narratives and journals I have relied on in this book. Personally I opened more than fifty boxes, many of them never used before, and paid for that privilege with a skin allergy brought on by archival dust. I also visited the battle sites where the Japanese American units fought in France and Italy.

My research also involved interviewing veterans and others connected with the 100th Battalion and the 442nd Regiment in Europe, Japan, and the United States. The Club 100 and the 442nd Veterans Club in Honolulu, the 442nd Veterans Association of Southern California, the Northern California Nisei Veterans Association, and the Thirty-sixth Infantry Division Associates were all cooperative and permitted me to attend several conventions. The Company K Club, one of the most active Japanese American veterans organizations, was particularly kind to me. Between 1978 and 1981 I interviewed nearly three hundred individuals. All were generous with their time and patience. Most interviews lasted at least two hours, some several days, and many interviewees consented to meet with me more than once. Fifty-two former officers who served with the

442nd also responded to questionnaires. Several interviewees were kind enough to let me use their diaries, letters, or personal papers. Sadly, at least twenty-two of those I spoke with have since passed away.

I would particularly like to acknowledge the help given me by a number of individuals. Those who helped me to understand the impact of Pearl Harbor on the Japanese American community both in Hawaii and on the mainland include Masaji Marumoto, Hung Wai Ching, the late Colonel Kendall Fielder, the late Reverend Masao Yamada, the late Reverend Hiro Higuchi, Mike Masaoka, the late Reverend Herbert Nicholson, and Dr. Clifford Uyeda. Former officers who shared their recollections with me at length include General Mark Clark, the late Colonel Gordon Singles, and Colonel Young Oak Kim. Senator Daniel Inouye and Senator Spark Matsunaga both gave me generously of their time for interviews in the midst of busy congressional sessions. In Bruyères I relied on the assistance and the recollections of Serge and Monique Carlesso as well as Dr. Raymond Collin and his family; and in southern France the Zeller family of L'Escarène not only shared their memories with me but fed and lodged me even though I came to them as a complete stranger.

I would also like to add a special word of thanks to Victor and Cleo Kobayashi, who offered me a home away from home several times when I was in Honolulu doing research. Fortunate indeed is anyone with friends so hospitable.

Prologue

THE Vosges Mountains show a gentle face to the casual traveler. Here and there the forested hills open into flat farmland or pasture dotted with small farm villages, most little more than clusters of several dozen houses huddled around a church. A few have grown into small towns. One of them is Bruyères, population four thousand.

None of my French acquaintances had ever heard of Bruyères. What brought me there in the fall of 1979 was a brief newspaper item I had read two years earlier. "NISEI GI LIBERATORS TO MEET FRENCH VILLAGERS" ran the headline.

I knew that a Japanese American regiment—a nisei unit—had fought in Europe during World War II, but this was the first time I had heard they had been in combat in the mountains of northeastern France. I was moved by the thought that thirty years later the French villagers they had liberated had gathered for a reunion with them.

What was it that brought Japanese American soldiers to Bruyères in a forest far from their home? How had their journey begun? And what kind of liberators were they for the people of Bruyères?

I had entered France at Strasbourg on the German border. Bruyères lies on the railway line that links this beautiful river city to Épinal, the capital of Vosges province. Only two local trains run on the line every day.

The one I rode panted heavily as it began the climb through the mountains. The stations grew smaller and smaller as we rode along, and the passengers fewer and fewer at every stop. The evergreen forest grew deeper and cooler too. Three hours out of Strasbourg, the train passed through a long tunnel, and the platform of Bruyères station came into view. I was the only person to get off.

The quiet streets of Bruyères have little to offer the tourist. The center of town is an intersection in front of the town hall. The post office and church are close by. Along the streets stretching out from the center are

1

the small shops where the townspeople buy their daily goods. The grandest to strike the eye is a hardware store selling farm tools. The stone and stucco houses along the street look quietly dull. Could this really have been a battleground, I wondered.

The Hotel Renaissance, the only place to stay in town, is right across the street from the town hall. It has only six rooms. When I registered, the sixtyish mistress of the house who manages the place with the help of one maid handed me a flashlight to use in the hallways after dark. During the eight days I stayed there were no other guests.

Every Friday there is a small open air market in the parking lot alongside the town hall. Farmers from nearby bring their vegetables, meat, and fruit to sell. It was market day when I arrived. It was only then that Bruyères seemed to bustle. And in the midst of that bustle I was introduced to Monsieur Henri Robert, a spry-looking old gentleman with apple-red cheeks and kneepatches that seemed to cover most of his workpants.

When I visited M. Robert's whitewashed farmhouse a few days later, he told me that it had been in the family since his grandfather's time. Around the house bloomed red geraniums and yellow gladiolas planted in an offhand way. In front of the barn a small flock of hens and turkeys cackled their greetings to the foreign visitor.

M. Robert was seventy-two, and he never missed his daily nap. His wife was off visiting a son living nearby, and when M. Robert answered the door his eyes looked still drowsy. As he slowly sipped some cooled fresh milk to wake himself up, he held out a glass. "Would you like some?" he asked. Politely refusing him I let my eye wander out the kitchen window. Beyond the rolling fields and pasture, the church spire and dull red rooftops of Bruyères shimmered under the warm afternoon sun.

"Well, the evenings get cold, you know, and the days are getting much shorter," said M. Robert, as if to urge me outside. We strolled toward the forest that began just across the road from the farmhouse. A part of the forest covering the hill still belonged to him. Hundreds of tall fir trees stretched up the slope in straight lines.

"Until that day I used to cut several dozen every year to sell, but now they're not worth a penny. The forest has been a headache to me for so many years."

With a sad look in his eyes, he shrugged his sloping shoulders. When his son and daughter were little they had played in the forest, he said, but now he was the only person to set foot there. There was a chill on my skin as we walked farther into the trees. The sun filtering through the branches drew patterns on the ground, but the light was dim and the heat was gone. M. Robert climbed up the slope, treading the soft carpet of needles and dry branches.

"It's still just the way it was that day—thirty-five years ago."

Puffing slightly he pointed here and there to traces of foxholes in the ground, each big enough for just one person. Years of wind and rain had crumbled their edges and filled them with tangles of ivy and light green ferns. Here and there fresh-looking little purple flowers peeked through the brush. Some kind of weed, said M. Robert, without much interest. Two five-gallon gasoline cans lay on the ground. They were pocked with rust, but it was still easy to read the "U.S.A." stenciled on their sides.

M. Robert sadly stroked a small fissure in the blackened bark of a tree. The shrapnel from countless shells had bitten into every one of the soaring trees, leaving scars easy to see on their trunks. But the trees were still alive, guarding their memories of battle.

"The sawmill won't take them even at a fraction of the usual price. If the saw blade hits the metal slivers, the teeth are ruined, and it's dangerous because you don't know where the metal will fly."

The shrapnel had hit more than the trees in the forest. The huge wooden door of the barn attached to the house was pitted by countless fragments. The whitewashed walls of the main house were covered with pockmarks too. M. Robert tried to cover them with plaster but it would fall out, so he had given up and left the walls as they were.

October 17, 1944. As he talked, M. Robert seemed to be reliving that day.

It was not yet dawn when M. Robert was awakened by pounding on the door. It must be a German soldier, he thought as he opened it. But to his surprise he saw Jean Drahon standing there. Jean, who had grown up in Bruyères, was supposed to be a noncom in the French army in Algeria, but instead he had joined the Resistance, and now he was back in the forest. He quickly told the startled M. Robert that the evening before the Americans had reached the forest on the other side of the hill.

As soon as he had melted back into the dark, two American soldiers came running out of the forest. Between the pasture and the garden in front of the house there was—and still is—a wire fence to keep the cows out. The American soldiers cut through it quickly. An officer and a small group of soldiers carrying communications equipment followed them and moved swiftly into the house. The officer climbed the stairs to the second floor where there was a good view of the surrounding countryside. He peered through a crack in the bedroom window shutters and began barking commands by walkie-talkie to the soldiers in the parlor below. They in turn transmitted them somewhere outside. On the wall they had tacked an aerial photograph showing the streets of Bruyères.

M. Robert was bewildered by the whirl of activity that suddenly filled his house, and he was even more taken aback to see what the American soldiers looked like. If Drahon had not told him that they were Americans he would not have believed it. His wife, Marie Louise, came up the cellar steps to see what was going on. At the top she looked around with astonishment. M. Robert turned with a comforting look to his tiny wife, then five months pregnant with a son, and whispered, "They're Americans."

No, surely that cannot be, said the look on her face. M. Robert nodded. He was sure that is what Drahon had said. He knew no English, but the soldiers used words that sounded like it. American soldiers were supposed to be so big and tall that you had to look up to them, but these soldiers were no bigger than M. Robert, who was small even for a Frenchman. Their skin was brown. It was not just suntan either, and their eyes were narrow and slanted.

M. Robert had not traveled much outside Bruyères. The soil and air of Bruyères were good enough for him. Being a simple man he did not like to pry into what did not concern him. So once he had been told that the "little brown soldiers" were American, he gave the matter no more thought. Indeed, he was quite favorably impressed by them. When they noticed the Roberts' ten-year-old daughter Jeannie standing behind her mother, they gave her chocolate and some K rations. The German soldiers often came asking for food, but M. Robert did not remember that they had ever given any away.

The region of Lorraine, whose people for centuries have worked the land, raising wheat or tending livestock, is richly blessed by nature—but not by political geography. Being near the German border, time and again it has been swept up in war. Rule over the area passed from the Gauls to the Romans, from Carolingian kings to German princes, until in the sixteenth century the French monarchs incorporated it into their realm. In 1870 it was lost to the new German empire after the Franco-Prussian War, and it returned to French control again with the German defeat in 1918. The only time when anything out of the ordinary ever happened in the drowsy town of Bruyères was in the midst of these upheavals.

In 1938, the year before the outbreak of World War II, the French government had completed the construction of the Maginot Line, a series of fortifications stretching along the Franco-German border to Belgium to repel a German attack. It was said to be impregnable, and the people of Bruyères thought they would never again be occupied by the Germans.

In May 1940, after several months of "phony war," German armies invaded France from the north across the Belgium border where the Maginot Line ended. The blitzkrieg through the Ardennes met little resistance. By June 1940 the Germans had taken Paris without a battle, and they established the Vichy government headed by Marshal Pétain in the south of France. The northern half of France was placed under direct German occupation. On June 21, 1940, German forces marched into Bruyères behind an army band, to remain until American forces drove them out four years later.

It is said that the dialect spoken in Bruyères is influenced by German. But even if words the townspeople spoke bore a German imprint, their patriotism as Frenchmen grew all the more under German control. People from all classes despised the occupying army and the Vichy puppet government. The eyes of the Gestapo were vigilant, and those suspected of opposition were arrested and tortured. About thirty Jews living in the town were sent off to concentration camps in Poland. But even in Bruyères the Germans could not stamp out the Resistance.

"Even after daybreak, it was drizzling. It was awful weather," said M. Robert.

After the signalmen set up their command post, groups of forty or fifty riflemen came out of the forest, spreading themselves out among the outbuildings and vegetable patch. A single tank slowly made its way into the pasture. Suddenly it hit a land mine, which blew off one of its tracks. As it began to circle round and round on the same spot, a brown soldier jumped out of it and came running back toward the farmhouse at breakneck speed.

It was then that the first shell landed in the field with a tremendous noise. The German artillery in Bruyères began bombarding the fields and forest with concentration barrages. Even today M. Robert finds it hard to understand why there was no direct hit either on his house or his barn, even though all the windows were shattered.

By the time the sun had begun to set, and the sky grew dim, other tanks began to make their way across the pasture toward the town. Soldiers filed out of the forest behind them. The soldiers with the brown faces moved across the pasture with no shelter or cover to protect them from the falling shells. The officer who had been giving orders and the signal troops who had been busy with their equipment all day finally disappeared after them into the growing dark too.

The Roberts hardly slept that night. When the sky grew light the next morning the soldiers coming out of the forest were unmistakably big Americans with white faces. The only day that M. Robert saw the "little brown soldiers" was the day that his farm and fields had become a battlefield.

On October 18, the day after he had pounded on M. Robert's door, Jean Drahon, clad in a huge American army coat with a rifle slung over his shoulder, guided a group of the brown soldiers from the crossroad where the road in front of M. Robert's farm met the Bruyères–Épinal road. The American column inched its way into town, moving along in two files on either side of the street, carefully searching each house for German soldiers.

Dr. Raymond Collin's residence, with his examination offices on the ground floor, is right across from the post office on a street turning off Rue Léopold at the main intersection in front of the town hall. Like the other townspeople, Dr. Collin and his family had been living in the cellar for six weeks, ever since the American air bombardment had begun in early September. As they listened to the American planes overhead and watched the food rations dwindle, they waited expectantly, hoping each day that the next would bring liberation. Dr. Collin, a man of precise habits, wore his customary English tweed jacket and a necktie every day, even in the cellar.

On the afternoon of October 18, noticing an unusual silence in the midst of the thunderous bombardment, Dr. Collin cautiously climbed by himself up to the second-floor parlor to see what was going on. In the middle of the flower-patterned living room wall, a shell had opened a gaping hole. He walked gingerly over the shattered glass on the floor. Suddenly he heard a voice downstairs.

The day before, a German soldier in a hurry to retreat had tried to commandeer Dr. Collin's Peugeot. The doctor had objected that he needed the car to make rounds to his patients. "Get one from the Americans," the soldier sneered. "They're very humane, I hear."

The voice below shouted, *"Boche?"* (That was what the French called the German soldiers behind their backs.)

It must be an American soldier looking for Germans, he thought. Trying to contain his excitement Dr. Collin rushed downstairs, his feet hardly touching the steps. He was astounded to see what he thought were two Japanese army soldiers standing there with rifles. Even Dr. Collin, a man who read the newspaper from Épinal cover to cover and knew a bit about the world, was speechless.

The Japanese are German allies, he thought. It's not the Americans at all. Have we fallen into the hands of Japanese soldiers from all the way around the world? *Mon dieu!* Is this some terrible new occupation?

Dr. Collin froze in his tracks. The two Japanese soldiers with their rifles stood still too. Their flat faces were smeared with mud and dirt. Beneath heavy eyelids their dark eyes stared warily. Then suddenly one of the soldiers flashed his white teeth. Pointing to his chest he said, "Hawaiian." As Dr. Collin stood there befuddled, not knowing what to do, the soldier grabbed his hand and, with a smile, hugged his shoulders. "Okay, okay," he said over and over again as if in reassurance.

That was the only day that Dr. Collin saw American soldiers with Japanese faces. The next day when the Collins hung from the second-story window the French Tricolor and an American Stars and Stripes that Mme. Collin had secretly made for the day of liberation, the smiling faces looking up at it were all those of white American soldiers.

If Jean-Marie Thomas, the photographer next door, had not taken lots of pictures, it might be hard to say with certainty that the townspeople had seen "American soldiers who looked like Japanese soldiers." Searching through a mountain of photographs as I sat waiting in his cluttered kitchen, M. Thomas finally found an old snapshot that showed Mme. Collin's unmarried sister, Annie, standing in front of the doorway when she had come out of the cellar that day. Beside her stand two American soldiers, grenades dangling from their field jackets and carbines cradled in their arms. Underneath their helmets the soldiers' eyes narrow as they flash happy-go-lucky smiles at the camera.

For the people of Bruyères the long humiliating occupation was over. Once again they could sing *La Marseillaise* with pride in their hearts. The townspeople did not rush out to kiss their American liberators or deck them with flowers, as so often Italian villagers did. The liberators disappeared as quickly as they had come. In their place came more and more white American soldiers. About a month after the little brown soldiers with the Oriental faces had left town, troops of the French Liberation Army arrived. It was only then that the people of Bruyères felt truly free. Dr. Collin popped the cork of a champagne bottle he had kept hidden for the day and drank a toast with his good friends, the elementary school principal and his wife. From nearby they heard M. Thomas, the photographer, picking out a Glenn Miller tune on the piano.

Several months later, according to Dr. Collin, the road that ran into town from the direction of M. Robert's farm was renamed Rue de la Libération. It was then too it was decided that the little road running west from the Rue de la Libération at the edge of town should be called Rue du 442e.

Today if you travel up Rue du 442e you will find a simple rectangular concrete memorial erected by the side of the road. The words on the plaque are in both French and English. It reads:

To the men of the 442nd Regimental Combat Team, U.S. Army, who reaffirmed an historic truth here—that loyalty to one's country is not modified by racial origin.

These Americans, whose ancestors were Japanese, on October 30, 1944, during the battle of Bruyères broke the backbone of the German defenses and rescued the 141st Infantry Battalion which had been surrounded by the enemy for four days.

This is the story of those Japanese American soldiers.

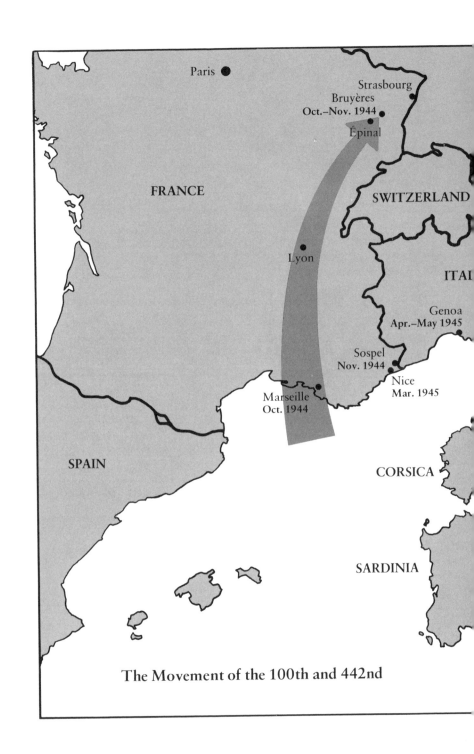

The Movement of the 100th and 442nd

I

The Destination
of the *Maui*

IN early June 1942 the troopship *Maui* zigzagged its way eastward out of Honolulu, changing course by fifteen degrees every twenty minutes to evade Japanese submarine attacks. On board were army and navy families being evacuated to the mainland. When news reached the ship that the American fleet had won at Midway, cheers went up from wives and children happy that the husbands and fathers they had left behind were safe.

A few of the passengers may have had worries about the group of American soldiers from Hawaii traveling below deck. Their faces were just like those of the fanatical emperor-worshiping enemy soldiers in the newsreels. But the soldiers—1,432 altogether, including 29 officers—were just as happy to hear about the American victory. Many of them had been worried about what might happen to their own families if the Japanese fleet had won at Midway and continued toward Hawaii.

During the daytime the troops were allowed on deck. They were kept apart from the evacuated wives and children by a rope that divided off their part of the deck. Some spent the day singing and playing their ukuleles; others killed time playing cards or shooting dice. But even though the troops had been relieved to hear the news about Midway, beneath the easygoing shipboard atmosphere was an air of glumness. When the soldiers had boarded ship, many did not believe they were leaving Hawaii. They had not even been given time to let their parents or wives and children know where they were going.

Why was it that just when a Japanese invasion of Hawaii seemed imminent, only the Japanese American soldiers were being shipped out? Rumors were bruited about even before departure. "It's relocation camp, for sure." If that were true there was not much to be done about it. Still there was a lot of grumbling. After putting out to sea, many of the soldiers were already homesick for the islands.

11

"We didn't even get leis," complained some.

It was a custom for Hawaiians to toss their leis into the sea whenever they left the islands. Eventually waves would carry the lei back to shore, a promise that the traveler too would return home someday. For troops brought up in Hawaii it was disheartening to leave the islands without leis.

How different it had been when they were inducted and sent off to Schofield Barracks. After the selective service draft system had begun to operate at the end of 1940, big farewell celebrations were held in every town where Japanese American boys were called up. Their parents saw it as an occasion to express their gratitude (*on*, as the Japanese say) to the country to whom they were indebted. Sake flowed freely, and there was plenty of good food. At the train stations or reception centers where the inductees gathered, banners waved in the breeze, each with the name of an inductee brushed in bold Japanese characters. Had there been no Stars and Stripes fluttering at the end of each pole, it might have been hard to tell that this was the United States, and not Japan.

Seeing one's son drafted is usually no cause for celebration, even in peacetime, but issei parents—first-generation Japanese immigrants— accepted the fact that their sons had a duty to serve the country of their birth. Farewell celebrations were a public gesture to show that. Now their sons would have certain proof that they were American citizens.

The strangely exotic farewell ceremonies may have surprised ordinary Americans, but no one took them amiss. As the *Honolulu Advertiser* commented when the first draft call came:

> To these homes from which Uncle Sam has picked a son, Japanese parents from far around and all the islands have come to pay honor and respect to the family so honored. Their expressions of joy at the distinction fallen upon these houses have been humble, simple and sincere. They have bowed, as is the custom of their race. They have said, many in such words, "We rejoice with you in the honor upon your home. Your son, no matter the eventuality of this world, will always honor your family name."[1]

The ocean rolled with gentle swells. Few of the troops became seasick. It was a peaceful crossing. The only regular routine was drill for abandoning ship, a prospect that seemed most unlikely. After the sun sank below the horizon, filling the sky with dazzling color, the ship was plunged into a deep blackout. Stacked in simple bunks like so many silk cocoons, the troops greeted the coming of night.

During the day Private Kenneth Kaneko was so absorbed in shooting dice that he lost track of time. But sometimes at night he just could not get to sleep. For him, as for most of his buddies, the war had begun suddenly and unexpectedly when Japanese airplanes had swooped from the skies to attack Pearl Harbor.

It had happened on a Sunday morning at 7:55 A.M. The skies of Honolulu were bright and clear as always. The city was waking up slowly, and only a few cars were on the streets. Kaneko had been in one of them—a police patrol car carrying a group of laughing and joking Japanese American youths in baseball uniforms to a baseball diamond on the outskirts of town. The young men, their skins burnt dark by the sun and their husky bodies hardened by sports, were all members of the same team. Their coach, a policeman, was taking them to practice in his official automobile.

A flight of airplanes suddenly roared over the car at an unusually low altitude. Explosions reverberated in the distance. As they drove on, the car radio repeated over and over again: "This is an emergency announcement. Pearl Harbor is under attack. Pearl Harbor is under attack." Training exercises are getting more realistic than usual, Kaneko thought to himself.

The tense voice on the radio began a new message, "This is not a maneuver. Repeat. This is not a maneuver."

The coach, who had been casually gripping the steering wheel, pulled the car to a stop. "Shall we go back?" he asked the players as if wondering to himself. In the direction of Pearl Harbor they could see heavy clouds of black smoke billowing into the air. Puffs of anti-aircraft fire dotted the blue sky. By the time they reached downtown the coach was no longer relaxed or joking. He suddenly pulled the car over to a corner and told the young men to get out. "Be careful," he said before speeding off down the street.

Was it true, or wasn't it? The young men were still not sure. They looked at each other as they turned to go their separate ways. Another wave of planes flew over their heads in the direction of Pearl Harbor. As he looked up Kaneko saw a flash of red on the wings. It was the red of the rising sun, the symbol of his parents' native land. His heart almost stopped. He quickly pressed his baseball mitt to his chest. There sewn in bold letters across his chest was the name of his team: NIPPON. He began to run as fast as he could.

The whole town had been plunged into confusion. Bombs fell not only on Pearl Harbor and Hickam Field, but in forty different places in Honolulu. In the center of town, near Iolani Palace, fires had started, and several civilians had been injured or died. (According to a list issued by the municipal hospital at 4:00 P.M. on December 7, thirty-one civilians died and sixty were injured, many with Japanese names, including a three-year-old girl who lost one of her legs. Eventually the number of dead rose to sixty-eight.)[2] The Japanese attack was concentrated in the area of

Pearl Harbor, and most of the civilian casualties were caused by stray American anti-aircraft fire.

In the midst of the confusion probably no one noticed the lettering on Kaneko's uniform. But he continued to run at full tilt, both arms still clutched to his chest. As soon as he got back to his room in the Okumura Dormitory, Kaneko tore off his uniform and stuffed it into the bottom of a trunk under his bed. He could still hear his heart pounding. Kaneko, then twenty-four years old, had lost his parents, both natives of Hiroshima, when he was little. He had been raised at the Okumura Dormitory, a Protestant-affiliated institution, and after graduating from McKinley High School he had taken a job working at the harbor. Just a month before, he had been called up for the Hawaii National Guard, and now he was in the midst of basic training at Schofield Barracks northwest of Honolulu. He had just gotten his first paycheck so he had decided to come to Honolulu that Sunday.

Even when he heard a radio announcement over and over calling all members of the Hawaii National Guard back to the barracks, he still did not think it was real. Usually so full of energy that he could hardly sit still, Kaneko lay stretched out on his bed unable to move, rubbing his long chin and staring at the ceiling. Finally he got up, slowly pulled on his military uniform, and boarded the military bus back to camp. The sun had already dyed the western sky red.

The Japanese government had planned to observe the proprieties of international law by notifying the United States of its intention to go to war just before attacking Pearl Harbor, the most important American naval base in the Pacific. The Japanese embassy staff in Washington took longer than expected to decode and type up the message, which was delivered thirty-five minutes after the attack began. That morning five American warships were sunk and three were heavily damaged; 2,335 military, marine, and naval personnel were killed, and 1,143 were wounded.[3]

To the American public this appeared a dastardly sneak attack. The United States had been stabbed in the back. President Franklin D. Roosevelt expressed this feeling when he called December 7 "a day of infamy" in his address to the Congress the next day.

Many Americans did not think that the war in Europe was any of their business. Congress had amended the Neutrality Acts so that aid could be sent to Great Britain, but the United States remained on the sideline in the European conflict, and the American public was not enthusiastic about becoming involved. "Don't send our boys to war," said many. The "sneak attack" on Pearl Harbor changed all that. The war was suddenly at their doorstep. No event could have unified the country more effectively, and public opinion quickly consolidated behind the Roosevelt administration. Fear and anger ignited fires of hatred against the Japanese enemy, a hatred that remained undiminished until their defeat four years later.

It should come as no surprise that Japanese Americans were also an easy target for national fear and anger. Although the United States was a nation of immigrants, citizenship rights were denied to immigrants from Japan—and from other East Asian countries for that matter. The children of those Japanese immigrants born in America were loyal and honorable citizens, yet the enemy's blood ran in their veins, and their skin was the same color. To Americans fearful of a Japanese invasion their faces looked no different from those of the enemy soldiers whose atrocities in Nanking and elsewhere were well known to the public.

Japanese Americans were no less victims of "the day of infamy" than other Americans. But for many of them anger toward Japan was tinged by shame and sorrow. Howard Miyake, then a twenty-four-year-old sergeant, says he can never forget his mother's sorrow as she stubbornly repeated over and over again, "A country of samurai could not have made an attack like that." She had worked hard doing everything to raise her nine children by herself after her husband had died. When Pfc Mike Tokunaga's father, a native of Hiroshima, heard the news of the attack, he slumped in front of the radio on which he so often listened to the results of the sumo matches broadcast shortwave from Japan. One soldier remembered that his father kept muttering to no one in particular, "Those idiots! Those fools!" Rage mingled with sadness.

For many Japanese American soldiers on the troopship *Maui* the voyage to the mainland was a time for reunions. They met boyhood friends, classmates, cousins who had grown up on other islands. First Lieutenant Mitsuyoshi Fukuda met junior high school friends he had not seen for years. It was strange for them to see each other in military uniform.

Twenty-five-year-old Fukuda, a handsome man with a down-to-earth manner that bespoke a warm personality, often thought about his young bride Toshiko, the daughter of a wool goods store proprietor in Honolulu. They had dated ever since Fukuda met her at the University of Hawaii. When the war broke out, they decided to speed up the wedding even though Toshiko was still in college. As their parents had hoped, they went through the formalities with a go-between and an exchange of dowry money. In the Japanese immigrant community this was natural even for the American-born second generation. Four months later Fukuda had to depart without even telling his family.

Fukuda, whose nickname was "Mits," was born on a sugar plantation at Waialua on the island of Oahu. His father, a maker of soy sauce kegs, had come from Kumamoto, and his mother followed later as a "picture bride." Fukuda was the eldest of their five children. His first clear memories were from the time when he was about three years old. The Japanese immigrant workers on the plantation had gone on a long strike, and his father could not earn enough to feed the family. They packed all their belongings and set out to hitchhike the long road to Honolulu where his father thought he might find work. Not many cars passed. They spent many hours of the day walking. Fukuda remembered following his mother, who was dressed in her sweat-stained summer kimono carrying a big cloth-wrapped bundle with his younger sister strapped to her back. His father shouldered the family *futon* (Japanese bedding). It was as though they were traveling an endless road through a sea of sugarcane with the sun burning down on their necks. Fukuda remembered his long and hard childhood well.

His father eventually got a job in a sawmill where the wages were low but the work was steady. Like Kaneko and most other Japanese Americans who grew up in Honolulu, Fukuda followed the standard course, first attending Washington Junior High and then going on to McKinley Senior High. Roosevelt High School was the English-standard high school in the territory. An English-language test was used to exclude all students but Caucasians. Education for the children of immigrant workers was kept at a minimum level. Japanese Americans who wanted an education went to McKinley High, the only other public high school on Oahu until the mid-1930s. Thus the school got its nicknames, "Tokyo High" or "Mikado High." (In fact about forty percent of the members of the 100th Battalion were McKinley High graduates.)

When Fukuda, the eldest son, became a high school senior, his father told him that he had to go to college. Fukuda had never thought about that. After graduation he had assumed he would go to work. Even a job as a store clerk somewhere would be fine. "You're the oldest. At least you should go to college," his father insisted. "I don't mind how hard I have to work to get you through." Like most of the Japanese immigrants, Fukuda's father had come to Hawaii without education or money. The dream that sustained him was to save enough money to return home as soon as he could. The harder he worked, the closer that dream should have come to fulfillment, but as children were born and the family grew, it was hard to put much money aside. The dream grew more and more distant.

Even so it was not easy for his father to decide to stay in Hawaii. Just in case the family did return to Japan it was better for the children to learn the Japanese language. Like many of his contemporaries, Fukuda, after spending the day at public school hearing about Washington, Lincoln, and American democracy, attended a Japanese-language school for another two hours. There he would work hard trying to learn how to read and write Japanese characters. But study took second place to the fun of playing with his friends and finding out what snacks his mother had packed for him.

The first generation of Japanese immigrants, whose lives were so hard, had to entrust their hopes and dreams to the second generation, born Americans. They entreated their children to become full-fledged Americans, to win the harsh struggle for existence in their place, to lose to no one. Education was the way to break down all barriers. Nearly thirty years after he had come to Hawaii Fukuda's father hardly understood the language of the United States, his son's country. He liked to eat Japanese food, even if it was only a meal of pickles and rice, and he did not feel rested after a day's work unless he went to the neighborhood public bath. No matter how much Americans might look down on him, he never stopped wearing his Japanese-style wooden *geta* or straw sandals.

This was the same father who was now telling Fukuda to go to college even if the family had to sacrifice. It was as though he were saying to his son, "I've given up on going back to Japan. My bones are going to be buried in your country." It was the first time Fukuda realized how tenacious his father had been. Fukuda studied hard and six months later he entered the University of Hawaii to the joy and pride of his father. Fukuda never forgot his father's face when he heard that Fukuda had been admitted. The creases at the corners of his eyes deepened as he looked up at the dazzling sight of his son.

Times were bad when Fukuda graduated from the university. He had a hard time finding a job. Having really nothing else to do he decided to stay in college for another year to get a teacher's certificate. (Among the twenty-nine officers in the Hawaii Provisional Infantry Battalion, sixteen were Japanese Americans, and of those all but two were junior high school teachers, reservists who had taken ROTC at the University of Hawaii.)[4]

Hawaii had worked hard to achieve racial harmony, but the Caucasians—the haoles—had economic control of the islands. This immutable reality was one of the first things that the nisei realized after they graduated from the university. On the mainland many young Japanese Americans found that even with college degrees no opportunities were open to them but to become gardeners like their fathers. In Hawaii economic discrimination was not that severe. But even in Hawaii teaching school was the only job available where there was no discrimination in pay and where the work was better than being a shop clerk or petty office worker, which required only high school education.

Fukuda had spent December 7 in Kona on the big island of Hawaii. He was listening to the radio at breakfast in a teacher's cottage next to the junior high school where he taught agriculture. There was so much static it was hard to hear. Kona was still a backwater district on the volcanic western coast of the big island in those days. It was not until evening that Fukuda was sure about the attack on Pearl Harbor.

In college Fukuda had taken ROTC. It was not easy getting up early every morning for drill before classes, but he had gotten a monthly stipend and after two years he had become a reserve officer. When he finally was sure that the Japanese had attacked Oahu, he put in a call to the island headquarters of the Hawaii National Guard at Hilo on the other side of the island. He could not get through. When he finally did make contact the next morning, he got orders to report for duty in Hilo in two days. Once again he put on his uniform.

The Hawaii National Guard was charged with the defense of the Hawaiian Islands. It consisted of the 298th Regiment, made up of Oahu residents, and the 299th Regiment made up of residents of the other islands. There were some volunteers in the guard but most were draftees.

In 1940 all young men who had reached draft age were given selective service numbers. In November, just a year before the attack on Pearl Harbor, the first number chosen in the selective service drawing belonged to a Japanese American. Fifteen hundred of the three thousand Hawaiians drafted before the outbreak of war were Japanese Americans. Half the American soldiers defending the islands, in other words, had cousins and uncles in the Japanese army.

Of the six hundred new recruits in basic training at Schofield Barracks, half were Japanese Americans like Kenneth Kaneko who had been drafted just a month before Pearl Harbor. Three days after war was declared the Japanese American troops had their rifles taken away and were assembled in tents separate from the rest of the new recruits. Until then they had been busily stringing barbed wire and carrying sandbags. Now they were kept under guard even when they went to the latrine.

Nobody gave any reasons, but there were rumors. Some said the weapons were taken away because the half-trained troops might panic with rifles in their hands; others said it was because there might be shooting if the Filipino American troops got into fights with the Japanese Americans. Not only the Japanese Americans but all the new recruits were kept isolated.

After one night their rifles were returned and the Japanese American troops began training once again. Eventually Kaneko was assigned to a defense position on the northwest coast of Oahu where he stood guard in a machine gun emplacement dug out on the beach and reinforced with sandbags. All day he sat with his eyes fixed carefully on the horizon beyond the white waves. An enemy invasion force never made its appearance. As the days dragged by, Kaneko was often drowsy at midday.

Mitsuyoshi Fukuda, who had been assigned to guard duty at the Hilo airport, also found the days boring and uneventful.

The problem of what to do with the Japanese American soldiers was a headache for Lieutenant General Delos C. Emmons, who had replaced General Walter C. Short as commander of the army forces in the Hawaiian Islands. On the mainland the Western Defence Command, under pressure from various anti-Japanese groups in California, took the position that the Japanese Americans were a dangerous security threat. On February 19, 1942, President Roosevelt signed Executive Order 9066 requiring "all Japanese persons, both alien and non-alien," to be forcibly evacuated from the West Coast for reasons of national security.

In Hawaii too there were some who wanted to clamp down on the growing power of the Japanese Americans and make sure they would stay down even at war's end. Some haole businessmen publicly said the Japanese Americans should all be confined on the island of Molokai or be rounded up and sent off to the mainland. Fortunately Hawaiian leaders in all spheres paid no heed to calls for the evacuation of the Japanese Americans. It would have been a shameful violation of the "Aloha spirit."

In the complex ethnic mix of the Hawaiian population of 420,000, about 160,000 were of Japanese ancestry, and there were also Filipino Americans, Chinese Americans, and Korean Americans. According to the 1940 census 37.3 percent of the population were Japanese American, 24.5 percent were Caucasian, 12.4 percent were Filipino American, and 6.8 percent were Chinese American. If the local authorities were not careful in dealing with this potentially volatile ethnic mix in the midst of the war situation, they might precipitate troubles that would tear island society apart. But members of all ethnic groups did their best to maintain racial harmony.

In far-off Washington few understood the situation in Hawaii. Military personnel arriving from the mainland were startled to see "yellow faces" greeting them at the harbor or the airport. They expressed their anxiety in dispatches back to the capital, so it was understandable that Washington should conclude the defenses of Hawaii were in danger. Lieutenant General Emmons was repeatedly asked to make sure the islands were secure.

On February 1, 1942, an inquiry from Washington asked Emmons whether the Japanese American soldiers should be discharged from military service or sent somewhere else. A week before—on January 23—it had already been decided that Japanese American soldiers on the mainland, including those in basic training, should all be assembled at camps in Arkansas and Alabama.

Colonel Kendall J. Fielder, who served as G-2 (military intelligence) under Lieutenant General Emmons, was absolutely opposed to putting the Hawaiian Japanese Americans in relocation camps. He later recalled that his main job was to convince the uneasy Emmons that the Japanese Americans, who made up half the defense forces of Hawaii, had been recruited according to regulations and it would be extremely dangerous to mishandle them. Fielder kept in close touch with civilian leaders too.

In May 1942, naval intelligence reported that the Japanese were planning a large-scale attack on Midway Island and the Aleutian chain. It appeared certain that if American naval forces under Admiral Nimitz lost the battle with the Japanese, enemy forces would make a beeline for Hawaii. Lieutenant General Emmons thought the possibility of a Japanese invasion rather great. According to Fielder, Emmons was extremely worried that the Japanese might send ashore troops dressed in American military uniforms. In that case how would it be possible to tell the enemy apart from the Japanese American troops? On May 12 Emmons sent a message to the War Department suggesting that the Japanese American troops in the Hawaii National Guard be organized into a battalion and sent to the mainland.

For the time being Japanese Americans were detached from the Hawaii National Guard regiments, but there was a danger that this action might intensify their discontent. On May 26 Emmons sent another message to Washington urging that the Japanese American troops be transferred to the mainland as a separate battalion as soon as possible. Already waves of B-17s had arrived in Hawaii from the mainland, and the American fleet under Nimitz was sailing toward Midway. Two days later Washington gave its assent to Emmons's request. Orders were issued immediately to send the Japanese Americans to the continental United States. For convenience the newly formed Japanese American unit was designated as the Hawaii Provisional Infantry Battalion. Lieutenant General Emmons arranged to have the new unit put on the next boat leaving for the mainland—the S.S. *Maui.*[5]

Mits Fukuda remembers suddenly being relieved from guard duty at the Hilo airport and then being put on a boat to Honolulu with Japanese American soldiers from other islands. The next day was to be the Hilo city festival. A festive mood was already in the air. Parades wound through the streets. James Maeda, then a private first class, remembers hearing the junior high school band playing marches in the distance. The army wanted to get the Japanese American soldiers under way with as little public attention as possible. The only people who came to see them off were a few wives living in Hilo, who rushed down to the docks when they heard the news.

There was only one person to say good-bye to the soldiers departing from the harbor at Ahukini on Kauai—Sergeant Shukichi Sato's wife. For some soldiers the last memory of their homeland was the figure of Mrs. Sato, in her ample maternity dress, waving her handkerchief endlessly as the ship sailed out to sea. Sergeant Sato was never to hold the son born several months later. He was to die in Italy.

In the boat to Honolulu the sole topic of conversation was the rumor that the men would be sent to a relocation camp somewhere. As if to confirm the rumor, when the Japanese American troops arrived at Schofield Barracks they were put in tents in a corner of the base at some distance from the regular barracks. The tents were surrounded with barbed wire, and rifles were taken away from the soldiers. If they were angry, they contained their feelings. There was little they could do.

On June 5 the S.S. *Maui* loaded the Hawaii Provisional Infantry Battalion and set sail. There was no report of the departure in local newspapers or on local radio broadcasts. Everyone in the islands was interested in only one thing—the outcome of the big battle at Midway. No one knew whether the entire Hawaiian population might have to be evacuated. On June 6, the day after the S.S. *Maui*'s departure, Admiral Nimitz announced the outcome of the battle. The United States had won the greatest victory in its naval history, and half the American objective in the Pacific had been achieved.[6] Across the United States the press and radio carried the news. The danger of a Japanese invasion of Hawaii had passed, and with the American victory at Midway the Pacific War had reached a turning point.

On June 12, a week after its departure, the S.S. *Maui* sailed into San Francisco Bay under the majestic span of the Golden Gate Bridge. It was the first time that either Lieutenant Mits Fukuda or Private Second Class Kenneth Kaneko had seen the American mainland. Oblivious to what might be waiting on shore, the men were stirred with excitement as the elegant silhouette of San Francisco passed in front of their eyes. Visiting the mainland was a dream for Hawaiians born and raised in the islands.

When the ship finally docked at Oakland, the sun was still high in the sky. The military dependents who had shared the voyage disembarked, but no orders came for the Hawaii Provisional Infantry Battalion to land. The men were told to stay below deck. It was only after dark that they finally disembarked and were hustled onto waiting trains. The window blinds were drawn, and orders were issued not to open them.

San Francisco long had been known as a center of anti-Japanese feelings in California. For example, the San Francisco school board had precipitated an international crisis with Japan a generation before by putting the children of Japanese immigrants into segregated schools. The army, worried about possible trouble with the local residents, had taken every precaution to ensure that no one would see the Japanese American troops passing through. Even if they had been told it was for their own safety, the Japanese American soldiers at the time probably could not have accepted that explanation at face value.

From the moment of their landing in Oakland, the Hawaii Provisional Infantry Battalion was officially designated as the 100th Infantry Battalion. Although everyone was headed for the same destination the unit was divided among three separate military trains, each traveling in a different direction. One train took a circuitous southern route through Texas; another went on a central route through the Midwest; the third went on a northern route. The army was anxious to attract as little attention as possible. Even officers like Mits Fukuda did not know their destination.

Fukuda's train went by the central route. Only when the train crossed the border from California into Nevada were the black window blinds finally raised at a little station where the train stopped for a while. Railroad workers, unable to contain their curiosity, put down their picks to take a look at the train's passengers. "Must be Chinks," said one of them.

Fukuda was just as curious about the workers as they were about the trainload of Japanese Americans. At Oakland he felt the same surprise. The first thing that struck his notice when he disembarked was the white faces of the dockworkers. Caucasians did not do that sort of work in Hawaii.

The train stopped several more times after leaving California. At each station Red Cross volunteers served hot coffee and doughnuts. As the journey wore on, the Japanese Americans began to relax, falling into an easygoing Hawaiian mood. The strumming of ukuleles carried soft melodies through the train. Even the Caucasian train conductors had to smile as the sound welled into a chorus. Kaneko, who was riding the same train as Fukuda, got so involved in his crap game that he forgot the passing time.

On June 16, four days after the men had landed in Oakland, the train arrived in Wisconsin. Forests and lakes just like the pictures in school geography books flashed by outside. Here and there silos and herds of cattle dotted the flat landscape. To the Hawaiians it all looked very exotic.

As evening fell, the train finally stopped. Kaneko, joking with his friends as usual, suddenly noticed that on one side of the train was a high barbed-wire fence punctuated by what looked like watchtowers stretching off into the distance.

"They've done it! They've tricked us!" someone blurted out.

It certainly looked that way to Kaneko. It must be one of the relocation camps he had heard the mainland Japanese Americans had been herded into, he thought. A shiver went through his whole body. Some soldiers sat with tears of sorrow and anger welling in their eye. Had their own country betrayed them? Mits Fukuda felt his heart tighten with indignation.

The train stopped for twenty, perhaps thirty, minutes. Then quietly it slid backward, changed tracks, and moved forward again. When it stopped a short time later, there were no barbed-wire fences or watchtowers to be seen. The train had arrived at Camp McCoy, where the 100th Battalion was to train for the next six months.

II

One-Puka-Puka

CAMP McCoy sits in the southwest corner of Wisconsin not far from the Minnesota border. Originally a training camp for the Wisconsin National Guard, it sprawled over fourteen thousand acres of fields and forests, gullies and low hills. When war broke out in 1941, it was taken over by the Second Division but there had been no usable buildings on the base. At the time the 100th Battalion arrived construction crews were still hurrying to put up new wooden barracks. The troops had to live in field tents for three months until the work was finally completed in September. There were no other units on the base except an MP battalion, and they were off in another corner of the camp so the 100th Battalion troops rarely saw them.

The barbed-wire enclosure the men had seen from the train was actually a temporary internment center for persons regarded as a threat to national security, principally Italian and German nationals. The first boatload of 172 issei arrested in Hawaii by the FBI on the day of the Pearl Harbor attack had also been detained there since March 1942. Kenneth Kaneko recalls hearing that one of the issei detainees was the father of a 100th Battalion soldier. The first assignment of the 100th Battalion was to guard the issei when they were allowed out for exercise.

The morning after the battalion arrived, training began in the unfamiliar rolling countryside. The brisk morning air pierced their lungs even though they could hear the cry of cicadas, the metallic sound of summer.

Usually a battalion is divided into four companies together with a headquarters company. The 100th was overmanned, however, so it had six companies (A, B, C, D, E, and F) in addition to the headquarters company. A battalion also normally is part of a regiment made up of three battalions—usually designated First Battalion, Second Battalion, Third Battalion. But the 100th belonged neither to a regiment nor a division. It was a "bastard battalion" without a legitimate parent.

The unit's designation as the *100th* showed that the army did not know quite what to do with it. The Japanese Americans did not hide their dissatisfaction and anxiety at the strange-sounding battalion designation. Being a bastard battalion really meant that no one wanted them. The army, many felt, was discriminating against them. Wryly the troops began calling themselves the "One-Puka-Puka." In Hawaiian *puka* means "hole"—and also the zero in a telephone number.

Wisconsin, as everyone knows, is famous for its dairy farms. Immigrants from northern Europe—Germans, Swedes, Norwegians, and Danes—found there a landscape and climate like the old country. There were hardly any Asian immigrants in the state. The story goes that when one startled old farmer saw some troopers from the One-Puka-Puka marching down the road, he jumped into his truck and headed off to tell the state police, "The Jap army has landed by parachute!" The police wouldn't believe him if he phoned, he thought. Even after an explanation arrived from the MP battalion at Camp McCoy, it was hard to calm the old farmer down.

The town of Sparta was about five miles from the camp. Even today its population is a little under six thousand. Some 100th veterans recall that only when they went there on pass for the first time did they really feel sure they had not been confined in an internment camp.

It was a Saturday. A crowd of townspeople stood at a distance, looking on curiously, but no one tried to approach the men of One-Puka-Puka. Eyes peered suspiciously from behind window curtains watching every move made by these soldiers with enemy faces. Not wanting to upset anyone, a number of the men got right back on the bus to return to camp.

The remaining soldiers wandered down the street without much to do. Finally one smiling young woman approached them. "The USO is over here," she said. "Come right in and make yourselves at home." The USO was in the meeting hall of a church. Miss Alice Kelly, the middle-aged spinster who ran the club, did her best to get the community to accept the Japanese Americans. She arranged weekend dances at the Episcopal Guild Hall and bus trips to nearby towns. Soon the ice was broken, and families in town began calling the USO to invite the soldiers to dinner. Army uniforms made friends.

The Japanese Americans were delighted. They went to dinner carrying as gifts leis made from candy and fresh flowers. Though many of the soldiers came from poor families, they had grown up in the generous atmosphere of the islands and felt at ease wherever they were.

More than ninety percent of the Hawaiian troops had lived on isolated plantations. Their immigrant parents did not know much about Western-style manners. Though the soldiers were open and friendly, they must have seemed rough-edged even to the smalltown people of Sparta. Many spoke a pidgin mixture of English, Japanese, and Hawaiian completely alien to the Midwestern ear that made them sound uncultured, but those who listened long enough had no difficulty understanding that the Hawaiian soldiers were well educated. The majority were high school graduates. Twelve percent had attended college, and five percent had graduated. In fact the average IQ score on the induction intelligence test was 103. To get into officer training one had to have a score of 110. There must have been many men in the unit who could have qualified.

It was only after the troops reached Camp McCoy that they were able to let their families know that they had gone to the mainland. After that all their letters were censored. The soldiers never spoke anything but pidgin among themselves, but their letters were written in good grammatical standard English. That came as a surprise to the Caucasian officers in charge of censorship.

The local bookstore did a booming business with the Japanese American soldiers. The manager sold more books and magazines the first month after their arrival than he had during any month since the store had opened. The townspeople also noticed that the Japanese Americans were kind to the elderly. Their parents had taught them to respect older people, and that made a good impression.

The soldiers seemed to have had an easier time making friends with the German Americans in town. Their attitude seemed to be—our fathers' country has become an enemy too, and we understand how you feel. The townspeople who befriended the soldiers found themselves deluged with gift packages from grateful parents who sent jars of pineapple and guava jam, Hawaiian handcrafts, and the like. The issei parents were moved that people had been so kind to their far-off sons. Some of them invited nearly two hundred Wisconsin boys stationed on Oahu to a big luau as a way of showing gratitude.

Since the Hawaiian soldiers were outgoing, good-humored, and always generous with money, they were popular with the young women of the town, who found them interestingly exotic too. There was bowling and dances. When the weather got cold some soldiers went skating for the first time in their lives, laughing heartily as they slid and fell on the ice.

Seven years after the war a group of 100th Battalion veterans invited sixty-three-year-old Nellie Kiefer to Hawaii as a Christmas present. She had been their "mother in La Crosse," or simply "Ma." La Crosse was a dozen or so miles west of Sparta, on the banks of the Mississippi, and the Japanese Americans often went there since it had more of a big town atmosphere than Sparta. Because the town was larger it was also less hos-pitable. One of the few townspeople to befriend the Japanese Americans was Nellie Kiefer, then a widow in her mid-fifties. One day her son John had brought home a lonesome-looking Japanese American soldier he had met in town—Private Kazuo Mito, who later died in Europe. From then on the hefty "Ma" got to know the Japanese American soldiers very well. "I never cooked so much rice and fish in my life," she later reminisced.[1] Some citizens of La Crosse cut off Nellie and her son for taking the Japa-nese Americans into her house.

There was a popular nightclub in town, the Trocadero, where the Jap-anese Americans often went. A private's monthly pay was $21, and a Pfc's was $36—with food, clothing, and shelter taken care of—but beer was only five cents a glass at the Trocadero. It was not hard for the sol-diers to go there several times a month to drink beer, stuff themselves with the oysters for which the club was famous, and dance till their feet were sore. Good-natured, yet not wanting to be made fun of either, they were free with their money. The female dancers at the club were always glad to see them, but many local boys were not, and there were often fights on the weekend.

The battalion's "Old Man," forty-seven-year-old Lieutenant Colonel Farrant L. Turner, had been executive officer of the 298th Battalion when the war broke out. When Colonel Fielder had called him in to ask what he thought about organizing a battalion made up of Japanese Americans, he immediately volunteered to serve with the unit. During his long years with the National Guard he had gotten to know many Japanese Ameri-cans, and he was well acquainted with how Hawaiian society worked.

The "Old Man" often assembled the entire unit for a Monday morning talk. "Isn't this the most important time in your life?" he would ask. "Every one of you is being watched. Don't forget that the future of your families rests on your shoulders. This is the chance you've been waiting for—the chance to go to the front." If they risked their lives on the battle-field and returned home triumphant, they could be sure of acceptance as full-fledged Americans. But first they had to be given the opportunity to fight. The Japanese American soldiers well understood what the "Old Man" was trying to tell them. Major James Lovell, the assistant battalion commander, thought to himself that they understood it in their guts.

Lovell had been Turner's right-hand man since the days of the National Guard. When he heard that Turner had volunteered for duty with the new Japanese American battalion he followed him without a second thought.

Turner and Lovell did their best to make the local people near Camp McCoy get a better understanding of the 100th Battalion troops. Whenever they had a chance they made speeches before local Chambers of Commerce and Lions Club meetings. They told their audiences how loyal the Japanese American soldiers were. They tried to talk as much as they could with local newspaper reporters too.

The soldiers, of course, were young and hot-tempered. If anyone did something that reflected badly on the battalion he got the silent treatment from his buddies. But that did not put an end to fights in town. There were a few hell-raisers who always seemed to be getting in trouble. Everyone knew who was going to start a ruckus after a few drinks.

It was Lovell's regular Saturday duty to collect the troublemakers from the local police in La Crosse. He became very good friends with the sheriff. There were also times when he had to deal through the sheriff with the pleas of parents whose daughters had fallen in love with one of the soldiers. Since the battalion commander had to give permission for marriages, none of the troopers got married to girls from Sparta or La Crosse until after the war. (The one exception was Second Lieutenant Ted Ebata, twenty-six, who died in Italy, leaving behind a wife and son.)

James Lovell, then thirty-five years old, was a man of few words. Even today in his seventies he seems taciturn. He looks straight at his listener with gentle eyes as he talks. His left leg was severely wounded in the Italian campaign, so he walks with a noticeable limp, and his legs seem barely able to support the heavy torso of a once strong and muscular body, but there is power in his jutting chin. Lovell, born in a farmtown in Nevada, had worked his way through the state college. After graduation he got a job as a physical education instructor in Honolulu. For more than a dozen years he taught physical education at McKinley High School ("Tokyo High"), where he eventually became vice principal. He was well known as a baseball and football coach. Many of his former players were in the 100th.

On December 7, 1941, Lovell was on coastal guard duty near Makapuu Lighthouse on the eastern coast of Oahu. The final game of the National Guard football team was to be played that Sunday. Just before he was about to leave for the game, as he was playing with his five-year-old daughter, he heard the news of the Pearl Harbor attack. He hurried back to his post. When he got there, the sighting of a disabled Japanese midget submarine was reported. Orders came from the navy to take the enemy alive. The captured occupant became the first Japanese POW of the Pacific War.

Major Lovell was not the only regular Saturday visitor to the police station. First Lieutenant Mits Fukuda, assigned to Company D, also remembers going to retrieve some of the unit hell-raisers from jail. The Japanese American officers always kept a sharp eye out to make sure their men did not cause any disgraceful episodes. The officer who probably did the most to keep the men from getting into trouble was Captain Katsumi Kometani—known as "Doc" to the men. There were two doctors attached to the 100th Battalion, Isaac Kawasaki and Richard Kainuma, but usually the staffing of a battalion does not include a dentist. Doc Kometani, a dentist in civilian life, joined the battalion with special duty as morale officer. At Camp McCoy he never once took a look at soldiers' teeth. He spent his days instead listening to gripes and talking problems out with the men. No one seemed to understand the feelings of the Japanese American troops better than Doc Kometani. Whenever parents wrote a letter that they hadn't gotten any recent news from their son, the letter was addressed to Doc.

Immediately after the Pearl Harbor attack nisei leaders had formed an organization called the Emergency Service Committee. They hoped to lead the Japanese American community through the difficult time ahead, keeping in close touch with agencies responsible for internal security, the FBI and the military intelligence. Prewar issei leaders of the Japanese American community did not think they could rely on the nisei, but when the war broke out most of the issei leaders were rounded up as enemy aliens. The burden fell on the nisei shoulders. It was time for a change in generations.

Kometani was a member of the Emergency Service Committee. When he heard that a Japanese American battalion was being organized, he immediately visited military intelligence to ask Colonel Fielder that he be allowed to join the unit as a go-between for the Japanese American soldiers and the Caucasian battalion commander. The request was unusual, but Kometani was given the go-ahead. Many sons of his patients were in the 100th Battalion. It made sense to set the minds of the Japanese American community at ease by having Kometani in the unit as a kind of representative of the home folks. Kometani was then thirty-six years old, the father of three children.

The Japanese American troops were surprised and happy to see their dentist in military uniform. Many of them had sat in his dentist chair. Having him with the unit was like having a strong older brother around. Even today the veterans never tire of telling stories about Doc.

Israel Yost, who joined the 100th as chaplain when it was at the Italian front, always worked with "Kome" (or "Komi" as he pronounces it) on the battlefield. Yost today lives near the Pennsylvania town where he was born. When he first met Kometani he remembers thinking that Komi had a face like a bulldog. Kometani, whose immigrant father had come from Fukuoka on the island of Kyushu, was a big man, well fleshed out, unlike many Japanese Americans who were smaller than the average Caucasian. His thick neck seemed to grow out of a thrusting barrel chest. Deep lines creased his cheeks. He was a good listener, always nodding his head and murmuring "Uh-huh, uh-huh." Whenever someone told him a joke, his face became a mass of wrinkles and his whole body shook with an explosive guffaw. The soldiers loved him.

In Hawaii Doc Kometani was well known for activities in baseball. Football was popular in the 1930s, but most Japanese Americans were too slight in build to play, so baseball was the favorite sport among young Hawaiian nisei. The plantation owners encouraged baseball as a healthy sort of recreation that would provide entertainment for young men on the plantation—and keep them out of trouble making, such as union activities. It provided a distraction from plantation life, and it taught nisei the teamwork they needed to survive and to improve their lot in the world.

There was a Japanese American league on every island and frequent interisland games. Many teams were "semi-amateur." The players did not get paid, but the teams charged admission to pay for equipment and other expenses. Doc was one of the owners of a semi-amateur team, the Azuma, then the Asahi. He was good at sports himself. He had gone to the mainland on a college athletic scholarship as a swimmer. While working as a houseboy he eventually got into the dental school at the University of Southern California.

In June 1940 the Far Eastern Olympics—with participants from Japan, Manchukuo, the Philippines, and other Asian countries—was held in Tokyo. Kometani led the Japanese American team representing Hawaii. Japan then was in the midst of preparations for war, and the government was organizing a "new order." Everywhere were wartime slogans like "Luxury Is the Enemy" *(Zeitaku wa teki)*. The political atmosphere was oppressive. While the team was in Japan, the secret police *(tokko)* kept the team members under surveillance constantly, even searching their belongings while they were out. The experience of these young Japanese Americans in the army-dominated "old country" was not at all pleasant. For many the experience made them feel even more American than before.

After the war when the defeated Japanese in 1947 petitioned to be allowed to participate in the 1952 Olympics at Helsinki, they did not have enough money to send a representative to the meeting of the International Olympic Committee at Rome. Doc quickly got together funds from the Japanese American community in Hawaii to help them out. Later he often had dealings with Japan through sports and Boy Scout activities. In fact his first heart attack came in 1972 while he was attending the Winter Olympics in Sapporo. Doc Kometani always thought of himself as an American, but he was concerned about Japan as the homeland of his ancestors. In him one can see the heart of the nisei Americans, who stood between two countries, Japan and the United States, yet embraced them both.

Most players in the Japanese American baseball league were drafted and eventually assigned to the 100th Battalion. Doc knew many of them well. Soon after he and Lovell settled in at Camp McCoy, they got some former players together to start practice once more. It was a way of keeping their spirits up in face of uncertainty about where the unit was to be sent. Kometani and Lovell wanted to use sports to get the local people to know the Japanese Americans better. The first battle fought by the men of the 100th Battalion was against the prejudice of other Americans. The baseball team was on the front line.

By chance nearly all the stars of the semi-amateur Hawaiian teams were in the 100th. Most had been friends from high school days. They had gone on to play ball not only in the Hawaiian League but also in the National Guard. Many players were in Company B, Kenneth Kaneko's unit. Among them was Joe Takata, a center fielder, the hero of the McKinley High team that won the all-island high school baseball tournament in 1937. After graduation Takata played on the Azuma team, but when Kometani moved to the Asahi, Joe went with him. He batted right-handed or left-handed equally well, and he often hit homers.

Joe Takata was a boyish-looking young man. He had a serene personality. Despite his prowess on the ball field he was not at all conceited, and his buddies liked him. Joe had gone to Japan as a member of the team Kometani led to the Far Eastern Olympics. Like Kaneko he had been drafted just a month before the war began. At the time of Pearl Harbor, he was in basic training at Schofield Barracks.

Masaharu Takeba had joined the army four months earlier than either. He was already a corporal. Takeba had made his name in baseball but he was also known as a football player, and he had won a black belt in judo, a sport he had practiced since he was a boy. At a glance it was easy to see he had the sturdy legs and back of a good judo man. Before going into the army he had played with a baseball team from the Moiliili section of Honolulu while working at a pineapple cannery.

Apart from games of catch with other men in their unit after daily training, the 100th team practiced only once a week, every Wednesday, with Kometani and Lovell coaching. No matter how tired they were when drill ended at 4 P.M., the players would be waiting happily at the field to start. Every now and then they played games with the MP unit stationed at the camp. But most fun were the friendship games on Saturdays. At first they played at towns near the base like Sparta, but eventually they traveled all over Wisconsin. Lieutenant Colonel Turner went along with Kometani and Lovell to cheer his boys on the field.

The players wore white uniforms with "Aloha" printed on the chest but no numbers on the back. They advertised themselves as soldiers from Hawaii. Wherever they visited, the exotic team was almost as sought after as movie stars.

Years later, sitting in the living room of his friend and former teammate Yozo Yamamoto overlooking Pearl Harbor, Kenneth Kaneko happily reminisced about his good old days on the 100th team. Whenever the team arrived by army truck in a new town, the local kids would always ask the same questions.

"Are you Chinese?"

"Yeah, yeah."

"Are you from the Philippines?"

"Yeah."

Most Americans in 1942 got their image of what a Japanese looked like from the newspaper cartoons. The cartoon Japanese wore round black glasses on his sneaky slanted eyes. He had buck teeth, and his stubby nose turned up so sharply it seemed to be only nostrils. It was hard for those who knew that caricature to believe that the members of the Aloha Team were Japanese Americans in whose veins ran the same blood as the "ugly Japs."

It was a nuisance to answer all the questions in pidgin English. Usually there was not much time before the game, so the players just answered "Yeah, yeah" to all questions.

"Can you pick pineapples in your garden?"

"Yeah."

"Do you own a banana plantation?"

"Yeah."

Even if you had only one banana tree in your yard, recalled Kaneko chuckling, you just said "Yeah."

Yozo Yamamoto, the third baseman, was the third son in a family of nine children. He had been born on a sugar plantation near the Akaka Falls on the island of Hawaii where his father, a native of Hiroshima, worked before he went into business delivering ice in Honolulu. After Yozo graduated from McKinley High he helped his father. In the National Guard he had been on the football team that Lovell had coached.

The players on the local teams were usually much older than the Hawaiians. All able-bodied young men had been drafted, so only the older men were left behind for the baseball teams. Of all the towns the team visited they best remembered Black River Falls where they bought roast corn on the street corner, Green Bay where they played a hotly contested game on the shores of Lake Michigan, and Madison where they divided up in pairs to stay overnight in the houses of local citizens after they played the University of Wisconsin team.

Wherever the team went, they were accompanied by a band, the "Hawaiian Serenade," who played Hawaiian music before the games. The soldiers even put on grass skirts and winningly danced the hula for the audience. The leader of the band was Sergeant James Kaholokula, whose father was Hawaiian and whose mother was Japanese. His younger half-brother Eddie, who had been with him in the National Guard, had no Japanese blood, but since he wanted to stay with James and play in the band, he pretended to be Japanese American and joined the 100th Battalion.

There were about twenty mixed-blood soldiers in the battalion beside the Kaholokula brothers. Some had Hawaiian surnames like Kaleialoha or Kealoha, and some Japanese surnames. There were also soldiers with Japanese-Portuguese, Japanese-Chinese, or Japanese-Filipino parents. Issei who succeeded financially often took mistresses, as was common for well-to-do businessmen in Japan, so a number of the soldiers had been born out of wedlock.

Winter came early to Camp McCoy. The baseball team's season lasted about three months. They had played a big role as ambassadors to the local civilian population. After the baseball season ended, Kometani and Lovell put their energies into winter indoor sports and recruited basketball and boxing teams which were also popular with the nearby townspeople.

The temperature fell. After a day of hard training the soldiers gathered round the barracks stoves as soon as evening chow was over. They tried to drive away the unaccustomed cold and homesickness by watching the brightly burning coals. Someone always got a ukulele out. The strains of soft tropical songs often floated through the icy night air.

One evening Doc Kometani was startled to hear a chorus of voices singing *"Shina no yoru"* ("China Night"), a favorite of Japanese Imperial Army troops occupying China. He raced from his quarters over to the barracks. Lieutenant Colonel Turner had made his orders clear. It was absolutely prohibited to sing Japanese songs. If the soldiers sang in Japanese, the local people might get the wrong idea.

"I never saw Kome move that fast," recalled Lovell later with a smile.

Kometani did his best to make sure the orders were kept, but the strains of Japanese songs were heard again after that. The one luxury many issei parents allowed themselves was a short-wave radio to listen to broadcasts from Radio Tokyo and some bought phonograph records too. The latest hits in Japan were often as familiar to the nisei as they were to young people in Japan. Even though they did not consciously try to learn the words or music of popular ballads like *"Sake wa namida ka tameiki ka,"* somehow they remembered them. One of the officers, Lieutenant

Masao Koga, had the same surname as one of Japan's most popular songwriters. In fact they were second cousins. Koga remembered their playing together at their grandfather's house during a trip to Japan when he was five years old. When I visited Koga at his house on the outskirts of Hilo he showed me an old samurai sword which had belonged to his uncle, a former major general in the Imperial Army. His uncle had sent it to him when he heard that Koga was in the army, but during the war the family hid it in the closet.

The Japanese American soldiers at Camp McCoy were not as interested in Hollywood movie stars like Betty Grable or Jane Russell as other American GIs were during the war. When American troops landed on the islands of the Pacific, they often found among the belongings of the Japanese battle dead smiling photographs of Hara Setsuko and Ri Koran (Yamaguchi Yoshiko), two of the most popular Japanese movie actresses at the time, clipped from gravure magazines. If the Hawaiians at Camp McCoy had been allowed to, they might have picked these enemy beauties as pin-up girls too.

The nisei soldiers had grown up not only with Japanese songs but with Japanese movies and plays too. Even in the smallest towns in Hawaii there were Japanese movie theaters, and nearly every year on the plantations there was a staging of *Chushingura,* the famous Japanese play about the vengeance of forty-seven loyal samurai whose lord was tricked into pulling his sword at the shogun's palace and then forced to commit suicide for his breach of conduct. When the audience applauded at the end, it was not only the issei but their nisei children who were cheering the dedication and loyalty of Oishi Kuranosuke, leader of the samurai band and hero of the drama.

Even today nisei veterans still living in the Kona District can speak fluent and natural Japanese in the regional dialects learned from their parents. Often they use expressions common in Japan at the turn of the century but not today. It was common practice on the plantations for managers to group immigrants from the same regions of Japan together. Not only did this give the plantation workers stronger cohesion, but it bound them together with the same ties of duty and obligation common in rural communities at home. This made it easier for the plantation owners to deal with them. As a result many words and expressions scarcely heard in Japan today remain alive in Hawaii.

Even though the nisei were ordered not to speak in Japanese, it was natural that they mixed in Japanese words when they talked with their friends and buddies. Most nisei in the unit had six to eight years of formal training in Japanese. Since Army Intelligence was looking for recruits to train for intelligence and propaganda work in the Pacific, the soldiers at McCoy were given Japanese-language tests, but the results were unexpectedly poor. Like Fukuda many nisei kids went to Japanese-language school mainly to play with their friends. They had really not mastered textbook Japanese.

Even so ninety-two of the men passed the test and were assigned to study at the Japanese-language school the army had established at the University of Minnesota. According to one of them, Donald Kuwaye, who later saw duty as an interpreter in Burma and Chungking, the group left Camp McCoy by army truck in early December 1942, about a week after taking the test. Though their chances of surviving the war were better as interpreters in the Military Intelligence Service (MIS) than as infantry foot soldiers, most of them were sad at leaving their friends behind. Many thought that if they were going to be fighting their parents' countrymen, it would be better to carry rifles and risk their lives directly than to do spy work.

Among the 100th troops were kibei—Japanese Americans who had been born in the States, gone back to Japan several years for education, and then returned home. ("Kibei" literally means "return to America.") Most kibei could speak Japanese as fluently as native Japanese. But by the same token some could hardly read or write English. Few of them from the battalion were selected for intelligence work.

Some kibei had returned only recently to the United States to avoid conscription in Japan. Ironically, the kibei found themselves facing the draft once they got to Hawaii. In fact, however, in January 1941 a law went into effect requiring those who had spent more than six months in Japan to provide proof of their citizenship on their return to the States. If they could not prove that they had not served in the Japanese army, voted in Japanese elections, or served in official posts restricted to Japanese citizens, they would lose their American citizenship. Many kibei had been studying in Japanese universities but had hurried home to avoid losing their citizenship.

Not only did the kibei prefer to speak Japanese, but they seemed to the other Japanese American soldiers rather stiff. The cook in Mits Fukuda's Company D was a kibei, a fisherman from Maui, with the brawny build and the sun-blackened face of a man of the sea. He said he had been a fisherman in Japan. Just why he had come back was not clear. He turned out to be Mits Fukuda's big problem at Camp McCoy. No matter how often Fukuda ordered him not to, the cook spoke only in Japanese.

"This is the American army! You are an American soldier!"

The cook pretended not to understand Fukuda's orders in English, or at least Fukuda thought he was pretending, and he always spoke Japanese at the top of his lungs. While cooking, or even when he was in the latrine, he would croon sentimental Japanese folk songs. What he seemed to love most was singing off-color lyrics to the tune of the Imperial Japanese Navy March.

The cook, a hard drinker, began tippling in the morning. He played dice with the flair and pluck of a traditional Japanese gambler. He rolled up the money he won, tied it with a string attached to his belt, and stuffed it into his Japanese-style stomachband. Every Saturday, with the regularity of a bank clerk, he took his role of bills and went off to visit a whorehouse in nearby Winona. Early in the Italian campaign, while resting in the midst of a forest, the battalion was surprised by a German tank which began firing indiscriminately. One bullet got Fukuda's cook between the legs, and he lost a testicle. Fukuda, knowing the cook's chief pleasure in life, could not help thinking how ironic that was.

By late 1942 the tide of war had turned in the Pacific. Japanese forces were fighting desperately to recapture Guadalcanal, and battles were raging in the Solomon Islands. The Japanese government announced that it would punish or execute American fighter pilots who attacked the Japanese homeland. It created the Greater East Asia Ministry to supervise the activities of local Japanese officials in the occupied territories.

For the Japanese American soldiers the end of the year was their first experience of winter. The evening of the first snowfall, everyone dashed barefooted out of the barracks. Turning their faces toward the sky, they stuck out their tongues to catch the falling snowflakes, frolicking like little children as they discovered how snow felt. Some got out their cameras to take snapshots, or pelted their friends with snowballs.

At the end of November Texan soldiers of the Second Division arrived in Camp McCoy. On the first Saturday after their arrival, trouble began. The Texans did not seem to like seeing yellow men who looked like the enemy wearing American uniforms. Some of them shoved a group of Japanese Americans off the pavement as they were walking by and started calling them names.

"Jap!"

"Yellow belly!"

No matter how many times Turner and Kometani told the men to expect this sort of thing, the Hawaiian-born Americans were not used to hearing insults like that. Those were fighting words, all the harder to accept because the soldiers insulting them were wearing the same uniform.

There were fifteen thousand men in the Second Division. Clearly the Texans enjoyed the advantage of numbers, but that did not stop the 100th Battalion from taking up the challenge. Shove led to push. Some Texans, dressed in civilian clothes for their first weekend pass, took off their heavy-buckled cowboy belts and began swinging them ominously.

Being bigger than the Japanese Americans they were not worried about taking on the "Japs."

They underestimated the small-statured nisei. Even though short, the Japanese Americans were fast. Before they knew it the big Texans found the little "Japs" jumping all over them. A few moments later it was the Texans who were being thrown around.

Judo was popular among Hawaiian Japanese Americans. Before the war judo teachers often came from Japan to teach. Many men in the 100th, like Corporal Masaharu Takeba, had practiced judo since they were small, and many had black belts. In fact some companies at McCoy set aside an hour in the afternoon for judo training taught by black belts in the company. It is said that the Texans picked as their first target Private Satoshi Furukawa, who was later killed in battle. A kibei with a black belt, Furukawa had taught judo and had also been the teacher at Yozo Yamamoto's Japanese language school.

There were many Mexican American soldiers in the Texas division, but the Japanese Americans did not make any moves against them. They had heard that whenever a fight broke out the Mexican Americans would pull knives. And since the Japanese Americans were a colored minority too, the Mexican Americans did not want to fight them either. They watched, smiling broadly, as the little soldiers from the 100th flung the big Texans helter-skelter with judo throws.

In later years, whenever 100th Battalion veterans talk about their encounter with the Texans, someone starts singing, "One little, two little, three little Indians, . . . Thirty-eight little Indian boys."

"Thirty-eight" was the number of the injured soldiers hospitalized at the Camp McCoy infirmary that evening. There were Texans with broken arms and legs, but only one Japanese American required hospitalization. His skull had been fractured by one of the Texan MPs who should have tried to stop the fight but instead came at the Japanese Americans flailing their billy clubs.

Since there were no married quarters at Camp McCoy, Lieutenant Colonel Turner, whose son was away at prep school in the east, lived with his wife in a house they had rented in Sparta. Usually he left home early in the morning, but he liked to have breakfast with his wife on Sundays at least. "That Sunday," recalled his wife with a smile, "was different." Turner left for battalion headquarters very early in the morning. Orders had already been issued confining the soldiers to quarters, but they had gotten up early too, waiting expectantly to find out what was going to happen to them. Those with black eyes and cut lips would have no alibi if anyone looked at their hands and knuckle joints swollen from punching. Even though the Texans had goaded them, that was no excuse. They had still gotten into the fight. It was awkward for the battalion. The Hawaiians had been training continuously but still had no orders to go to the front. There were unsettling rumors that the 100th was going to be kept on the mainland as a labor battalion. Even before being chewed out by their company officers, the troops felt sorry they had let things develop into a fight.

It was about ten o'clock in the morning. The battalion headquarters was a rather unprepossessing wooden barrack building. A smart-looking car was parked in front. The brusque figure who had gotten out of the car and gone into the headquarters was the commanding general of the Second Division. One nisei soldier watching from a nearby window turned to his buddies and said, "Look, they came to see us." It was a very Japanese way of looking at things. In fact the Texan division commander strode into Turner's office demanding to know who was going to take responsibility for the incident. It was Turner, not the division commander, who was supposed to do the bowing and scraping.

Turner, a member of the haole elite in Hawaii, was a wartime civilian soldier, not a professional. He knew that once the war was over he would be going back to his job as an executive with a big lumber company. That gave him an advantage. It allowed him to say what needed to be said.

"I guess both sides ought to be punished for the fight," said Turner. "But after all it was a division of fifteen thousand that took on a battalion of twelve hundred. If it had been one battalion against another, I guess you wouldn't have stood a chance of winning."[2]

James Lovell was impressed at how Turner stood up for "his boys." It was part of Turner's pride as commander of the Japanese American battalion. The Second Division commander left without making any more of the incident. After that there were no more fights between the Japanese Americans and the Texans, who now had a kind of respect for the little nisei who fought with such crazy courage. The Japanese Americans were to meet Texans again on the battlefield, but under different circumstances.

Lieutenant Colonel Turner kept reminding the soldiers of their special mission, but if outsiders showed the least bit of prejudice toward his men, he displayed a dogged toughness. When the battalion was transferred to Camp Shelby in Mississippi, he went to pay his respects to the division staff with whom they were to train.

"Did you get your Jap's here all right?" asked one of the officers.

"Sir, my men are not 'Japs.' That is a term of opprobrium we use for the enemy. My troops are Americans of Japanese ancestry serving in the American army." Turner made clear that he was prepared to take the matter to the War Department if necessary.

Near the end of the year transfer orders came for the 100th Battalion. On January 6, 1943, they left Camp McCoy by train. The icicles hanging from the barrack roofs sparkled in the morning sun.

The train carried them south for two days. On January 8, 1943, they arrived at their destination, Camp Shelby, Mississippi, in the forested region south of the state capital, Jackson. The camp, one of the largest in the United States, is still used by the army for training and maneuvers. When the camp was in full swing during World War II, several divisions with about 100,000 troops trained there.

In the first week of February, about a month after the 100th had arrived, the camp bus pulled up in front of Building 180. The last passenger, a slender-looking second lieutenant, stepped out into the evening dusk. As he looked around he could see the flat rows of hastily built wooden barracks. The camp road was not even completely paved. It was a quagmire in the rain.

The lieutenant, his posture smartly erect, stood for a moment clutching his suitcase in one hand. His flat face was expressionless. Finally he dashed across the wooden board laid over the mud to the building marked with a wooden signboard: "100th Battalion." Inside he noticed a large puddle of water on the floor, evidently from a leak in the roof. There was only one soldier on duty. "I would like to report to the commanding officer," the lieutenant said. "I have been assigned to the unit."

The soldier looked at him and replied brusquely, "The battalion is out on field training. They won't be back for two days."

The barracks were dim and unlighted. A look of confusion played over the lieutenant's face. Suddenly he realized how quiet the barracks were.

"Captain Kometani is still here though," the soldier added helpfully.

Winter is the rainy season in Mississippi. The steadily falling rain makes everything clammy. In the evening the chill sends shivers through the body. The thin plywood walls of the barracks were covered with tarpaper to seal them against the wind. Even so a cold draft seemed to be coming in from somewhere.

When the lieutenant introduced himself at the officers' billets, Captain Kometani rose slowly, holding out his hand in greeting. His face showed no surprise to hear that the newly arrived lieutenant's name was Kim.

"Where've you come from?" asked Doc.

"Fort Benning."

Fort Benning, Georgia, was the base for Officer Candidate School. Second Lieutenant Kim, then twenty-four years old, had graduated just two weeks before. He told Kometani that he was the only graduate who had not gotten an assignment right away. At the time the only officers of Asian extraction in the army were a handful of technical officers, and it was rare for them to be assigned to an infantry unit. It looked as though the army had not been able to decide where to send him.

His orders finally came five days after all his other classmates had left. He was to report to the 100th Battalion. There was no division nor even a regiment mentioned. Not until the day before he arrived at Camp Shelby did he learn from a friend in Arkansas that his new unit was made up of Japanese Americans. He did not even know they were all from Hawaii.

To judge from his name, the young lieutenant was a Korean American. Casually Kometani asked, "Where were you when they attacked Pearl Harbor?"

He had been on leave in San Francisco, the lieutenant replied. He was stationed for training at Fort Ord, about three hours to the south. He was supposed to spend the day with his girlfriend, a childhood playmate later to become his wife. She was working as a nurse in San Francisco. When Kim heard news of the attack on the radio he returned to camp. Early the next morning he was hurrying north again to guard duty on the coast above the Golden Gate Bridge.

There were a few Japanese Americans in Kim's regiment, which was made up mainly of recruits from California. They were assigned to guard duty too. Four months later, while the unit was on field training in the desert, the relocation of the Japanese Americans living on the West Coast began.[3] The Japanese American recruits were taken out of Kim's unit and sent off somewhere.

After a pause Kometani, who had been listening intently to Kim's recollections of that Sunday, said in a deliberate tone of voice, "The motto of the 100th Battalion is 'Remember Pearl Harbor.' "

It was a slogan heard often during the war. The government used it to stir up hatred for the enemy. The 100th Battalion had chosen it as a motto despite its strong anti-Japanese connotations. That was interesting, thought Kim.

Two days later, when the battalion returned from the field, Lieutenant Colonel Turner called Kim in.

"You're Korean American, aren't you?"

"Yes sir."

"The War Department seems to have made a mistake. They can't tell the difference between Japanese Americans and Korean Americans. I'll get to work on a transfer for you right away."

"What for, sir?"

"You should know. This battalion is made up only of Japanese Americans."

"Yes sir, I understand."

"You know that Japanese and Koreans don't get along together, don't you?"

"Yes sir. But I am an American, and the Japanese Americans are too. We all have the same reason for going to war. I think I'd like to stay in the battalion, sir."

He spoke out of one side of his mouth. His tone was flat and quiet, but his voice had strength and an undertone of tenacity.

Lieutenant Colonel Turner peered steadily at Kim from behind his rimless glasses. A number of Chinese Americans and Korean Americans had been sent to the unit before, but all of them had asked to be transferred out right away.

"Well, if that's what you say, then let's try it out for a while. But you'll have to get along well with the troops."

"Yes sir."

As he was leaving, Kim added with a slight smile, "They will have to get along with me too."

That day Kim took command of the Second Platoon in Company B. He dealt with the men bluntly. He minced no words. It was as though he were trying to show them that there was a clear line between officers and troops. Pfc Kenneth Kaneko was platoon messenger, and Sergeant Masaharu Takeba, who played with Kaneko on the Aloha Team, was assistant platoon leader. Kim did not let down his guard even with Takeba. He never raised his voice. That was even more unnerving.

From the first day Kim also seemed bent on correcting everything the troops had learned from the beginning of their training. The commander of Company B, a Caucasian captain who had been with the unit since Hawaii, was a plain and honest fellow, but he was an older man who had been promoted from the noncommissioned ranks. He was aware that he was not well acquainted with infantry battle tactics. When Kim asked whether he could try infantry training his way, the captain had agreed readily without any objections. None of the other officers complained either when Kim took it on himself to draw up a training plan. That made their job easier.

The Japanese American soldiers were smaller in physique than the army average, but their average age—twenty-four—was higher. Kim realized from the start that their physical conditioning was superb. They were also agile and quick. Indeed so unusual did the Japanese Americans seem that they were constantly inspected by officers from other units.

When the 100th first arrived at Camp McCoy the troops had carried wooden rifles during close order drill. Many soldiers, still uncertain over their future status, thought they knew why. But they worked as hard as they could, driven by their uncertainty, hoping that if they did well in training they would be sent to the front. Lieutenant Colonel Turner and the rest of the officers constantly reminded them how important it was for them to perform well.

According to army manuals it was supposed to take an average of sixteen seconds to set up a heavy machine gun. At Officer Candidate School at Fort Benning the average was eleven seconds. In their tests at Camp McCoy the soldiers of the 100th Battalion did it in an astonishing five seconds.

Although the average height of the 100th Battalion troops was five feet three inches, they did extremely well in the obstacle course that required them to climb eight-foot fences in full gear. The heavy machine gun squads in full gear managed to cover 3.3 miles in an hour during an eight-hour march. That was much better than soldiers with longer legs. The usual average was 2.5 miles an hour.

During their second week at Camp Shelby the commander of the Eighty-fifth Division inspected the battalion. It was a cold day and the rain was pouring down. The troops had to crawl through mud under live fire. The test made a strong impression upon the division commander. It was then that Lieutenant Colonel Turner was sure for the first time that the unit would be sent to the front.

The day Kim arrived the battalion had been in joint training with supporting artillery units in preparation for major training maneuvers in Louisiana. After the battalion returned from the field, most units spent their days practicing marksmanship and doing maintenance on their weapons.

It was just at this point that Kim started to retrain his troops, who were full of confidence about their fighting skills, in the techniques he had just learned at Officer Candidate School. All the other companies were taking it easy before the big maneuvers. Kim was confident of what he was trying to do. He was all fired up, in fact. It may have been the first time he realized who he was and what he wanted to do.

Young Oak Kim had grown up in the Bunker Hill section of Los Angeles, near Chinatown and Little Tokyo. Now the site of the Los Angeles Music Center, it then was a ghetto inhabited by a mixture of blacks, Japanese, Mexicans, and Koreans. Kim's father ran a small grocery and variety store. After high school Kim had commuted to junior college, but he had to stop because his family needed to have him go to work. It was easy to quit, he later said. He knew that even if he studied hard he would not be able to get a decent job later on, so he went to work cutting meat at a wholesale house owned by a Chinese American. The job did not interest him at all, but he continued for several months. When the first draft call came in January 1941, Kim's number was among the first selected.

At a time when the public regarded Asian Americans as second-class citizens, it was conventional wisdom in the military that men of Asian extraction would not make good combat soldiers. Filipinos were used as cooks, and Chinese and Japanese Americans were used as mechanics or in other noncombatant work. Asian Americans were ordinarily treated as unfit for fighting on the front lines.

Kim finished basic training with an outstanding record. His instructors were the first people to notice that he had special talents. After basic he was sent to school to learn automotive repair, but his company commander arranged for him to be sent to Officer Candidate School at Fort Benning. For Kim, who was repairing jeeps and trucks, the chance to go to OCS was completely unexpected. He had just married his childhood friend, the nurse.

Kim received an exceptionally high grade on the intelligence test he was given the day after he arrived at Benning. Kim was probably more surprised than anyone else. He realized for the first time that he was not all that stupid. It was a turning point in his life.

Everything he studied at OCS fascinated him. He seemed to have a special gift for map reading, and an exceptional sense of direction. In a night map reading exercise he reached the target area in a fraction of the time the other trainees took. The instructors were a bit suspicious of his speed. But at the end of the course he graduated with distinguished grades.

At first the soldiers of Company B did not much like this new OCS graduate scarcely older than themselves. They resisted him at every turn, displaying their Hawaiian-born stubbornness. They got tired of hearing the name Kim. Kim could not have been unaware that he was the only Korean American in the midst of Japanese Americans. He does not like to admit that, but awareness of his position must have expressed itself unconsciously in his behavior.

Kim's mother spent her final years in an old people's home for Japanese Americans, but Kim says that when she heard her eldest son was going to be assigned to a Japanese American unit she just could not accept it. Not once in her life had she invited a Japanese American to her house. She did not even like Kim and his three brothers to play with Japanese American children in the neighborhood. Kim's father, who had died two years before, hated the Japanese with a passion.

His father had been the son of a small landholder in the Han River valley near Seoul. While he was growing up Korea had come under the colonial control of the Japanese who instituted a harsh and brutal regime. There were complications at home too. Kim's father did not get along with his stepmother, his father's second wife. Together with a cousin he stowed away on a ship and escaped to America when he was sixteen.

The field maneuvers which were to be the culmination of the 100th's training began on April 6. They continued in the swamplands of Louisiana until early June. It was hot, but the heat was different from Hawaii. It was a heavy damp heat that clung to the skin. The beautiful bright-colored little coral snakes living in the swamp were poisonous, but worst of all were the ticks and the chiggers that dug their way under the skin. It was useless trying to avoid them. And if they bit you, the itching was enough to drive you out of your mind even though you scratched till the blood came.

Even under these extreme conditions Kim drove his men as hard as ever, barely giving them a chance to catch their breath. "G.I. Kim" they called him, not with affection.

A Chinese American officer assigned to the unit about this time immediately transferred to another unit. Lieutenant Colonel Turner kept waiting for Kim to ask for a transfer too. Doc Kometani, who was hearing complaints from the troops, did his best to get to know Kim better. Jim Lovell thought that Kim was just overconscious of his position. But he had no quarrel with Kim's training methods, and he liked Kim's personality.

Kim was well received among his fellow officers. When the battalion arrived at Camp McCoy it had been understaffed. Gradually new Caucasian officers were assigned to the unit. Many had been promoted from the noncommissioned ranks and did not feel quite at ease with the Japanese American officers. But Kim was able to move easily back and forth between the two groups.

In early May the battalion was given a day and a half of rest. Many of the officers went off on pass to a nearby town. Some like Mits Fukuda went to meet wives who had come in from Hawaii. The rest—mostly lieutenants—stayed in their tents drinking beer, playing poker, and shooting the breeze to pass the time.

As the humid evening shadows grew longer and the young officers tipsier, the conversation became freer and franker. The Japanese Americans reminisced about growing up on plantations at first, but before long the talk drifted to how society in Hawaii was divided between the haoles and the non-haoles. The usually close-mouthed First Lieutenant Sakae Takahashi, twenty-four, had the strongest things to say. He spoke slowly, with power in his words.

"We're fighting two wars. One for American democracy, and one against the prejudice toward us in America. That's a fact even in Hawaii," he said looking at the other young nisei officers.

It was the "Big Five" representing the haole society who controlled Hawaii. You could even say it was the descendants of the white missionaries who had taken over the islands. They ran the plantations; they owned the only shiplines that connected Hawaii with the mainland; they dominated the business community; they held the economic power in Hawaii. The nisei were up against a discouragingly high wall. But, said Takahashi, it might be possible to make a hole in that wall.

"If the nisei want to take on the haoles, then it has to be in politics. There's no other way. At least it's the fastest way. You're dreaming if you think you can catch up with them economically. There's only politics."

The Democratic Party hardly existed in Hawaii then. The white leaders who made the important decisions and carried them out were all long-standing Republicans. They did not intend to let the Democrats get the slightest foothold on the islands. Sakae Takahashi thought that the nisei ought to get behind the Democrats in Hawaii. The Japanese Americans outnumbered the haoles, and it might be possible to make a political breakthrough with the backing of Japanese American votes.

"We ought to use this war. We ought to make it into an opportunity. The only chance we have to turn Hawaiian society around is after the war when we come back with our war service behind us. After the war, we ought to use the 100th to pull together some political organization. If we don't, going to the front and risking our lives doesn't mean anything."

Takahashi, a graduate of the University of Hawaii, had taught agriculture at a junior high school at Aiea near Pearl Harbor. His bushy eyebrows looked as though they had been drawn with a heavy brush stroke, and his eyes were small under puffy eyelids. His face was expressionless, and his manner was blunt. Some took his stubborn toughness for arrogance.

Takahashi says that even when he was a poor kid growing up on the Makaweli plantation on Kauai, he never once considered himself a bit inferior to the haoles. He did not make much of his own ethnic heritage either. When his parents decided to take their six children back to visit their hometown in Niigata, it was only Sakae, the second son, who stubbornly refused to go to Japan. He tried to think of himself only as an American. Perhaps the other side of that feeling was in fact a sense of inferiority.

At the Okumura Dormitory in Honolulu where Kenneth Kaneko had grown up, nisei from other islands studying at the University of Hawaii could stay cheaply and supervise the younger boys. Sakae Takahashi had been one of them. The head of the dormitory was Takie Okumura, a Christian minister from Kochi prefecture on the island of Shikoku. He had built the Makiki Church, modeled on a Japanese castle tower, still visible in downtown Honolulu today. Okumura, who had come to Hawaii in 1891 at the age of twenty-nine, tried early on to develop in the nisei a strong sense that they were "new Americans." He was influential in the hundred percent American movement after World War I. The loyalty of the nisei as Americans was often questioned because many issei parents did not cut ties with their homeland. Many nisei held their dual nationality because of their parents' insistence. Okumura was one of the issei Christian leaders to argue that the only way for the nisei to gain recognition by other Americans was to think of themselves as one hundred percent Americans.

At the New Americans Conference in 1927, Okumura told the issei, "The nisei have become the adopted children of America." To the nisei he repeated over and over, "I think that the American conscience will not let the nisei be deprived of their rights as citizens, but it is not clear if something like that will happen. The nisei must prove that they are splendid American citizens."[4]

Okumura hoped that the bright young Japanese Americans at the dormitory would become the future leaders of their generation. In fact, many did go on to make a career in politics, including Sakae Takahashi. When Takahashi knew him, Okumura was already in his seventies with a reputation for being shrewd and manipulative. Many issei were suspicious of him since he was too close to the Hawaiian Sugar Planters' Association and tried to ingratiate himself with the haole elite. But there is no doubt that Okumura's "New Americanism" movement contributed to the political consciousness of young nisei like Takahashi, who came to think of themselves as Americans.

In the heavy heat of the Louisiana night the young nisei officers talked enthusiastically about their dreams and hopes—always in pidgin. They were going off to fight for their future, and if they fell in battle they could pass on the torch to others. Kim, listening silently, remembered how when he was little he had been thrown out of the YMCA pool because of his yellow skin. Japanese Americans, Korean Americans, and other Asian Americans who had been born on the mainland did not think of that kind of prejudice as anything special. They had been brought up to accept it. Every word Takahashi and the other Hawaiian-born officers spoke shook Kim's own sleeping consciousness awake.

First Lieutenant Ernest Tanaka, Kim's fellow officer in Company B, was usually a listener whenever these discussions took place. His father ran a small Japanese confectionary shop in Waialua, so his nickname was "Candy." He had been a friend of Takahashi since their days together in ROTC at the University of Hawaii. Just before the maneuvers Tanaka had gone for five months of "special training." One night, after getting back, he told his fellow officers what he had been doing.

The "special training" epitomized the position of the nisei in the American army. In the fall of 1942 while the battalion was still at Camp McCoy Jim Lovell had received orders from the War Department to report immediately to Fort Myer, Virginia, a base for special training of ski troops, mountain troops, and underwater operations.

Two days later Lovell was told that a Swiss captain who formerly had worked as a hunting guide had recommended to President Roosevelt that special dogs be trained to attack Japanese. It was hoped that if the dogs learned how to recognize the body scent of Japanese they would be very useful in the Pacific battle zone. Orders had been issued that a squad of Japanese American soldiers be detached to help train the dogs.

Under confidential orders twenty-six men from the Third Platoon of Company B headed by Lieutenant Tanaka left Camp McCoy on October 31, 1942. As far as the other soldiers from the 100th were concerned, they simply "disappeared suddenly" with swimsuits and fishing poles. Until they returned safe and sound five months later their whereabouts remained a mystery.

No one explained anything to Tanaka or his troops before they left. Jim Lovell, who accompanied them, just smiled and said, "You're going to a nice warm place like Hawaii for training." They traveled by plane to Kessler Field on the Mississippi Gulf Coast. The landing area had been cleared of other people, and the men were loaded onto covered trucks. At an isolated pier they got into a motorboat to Ship Island, about twenty miles offshore in the gulf.

What first struck their eye on the long narrow island was Fort Massachusetts, built at the time of the Civil War. They were to live in a wooden building to one side of the fort. Once the motorboat departed they were the only people on the island. The clear blue sea reminded them of Hawaii, and so did the fine white sand beach. Yelling with delight the soldiers plunged into the water. They lost track of time as they rode the waves. Later they took a look at the subterranean prison of the fort which was said to have housed Yankee prisoners. There was also said to be pirate treasure buried somewhere on the island, but they were not much interested in looking for it.

For two days it was as though they were having a vacation back home. Then they again boarded the motorboat to travel to a small neighboring island, Cat Island, where the military dogs were being trained. Quite unlike Ship Island, it was covered with swampy jungle brush and crawling with alligators. Swarms of mosquitoes attacked them.

They were met by the Swiss captain, who spoke a heavily accented English and looked as though he was getting on in years.

"After the war I'll be going back to Hawaii with them. Think about my position," pleaded Lovell to the captain. "It makes sense for you to tell them about the training."

"No, that's the only thing I won't do," refused the captain.

Having no choice, Lovell explained to the men what the "special training" was, and then left to return to Camp McCoy.

At first the Japanese Americans trained scout dogs. That was interesting. All they had to do was hide in the jungle with containers of horse meat. When the dogs found them the dog trainer fired a shot from an air rifle. The Japanese Americans, putting the horse meat on their throats, lay down pretending to be dead. The dogs would grab the meat and then lick the soldiers' faces, perhaps because they smelled the meat or perhaps because they "smelled Japanese blood."

The training began after nine in the morning and continued past three in the afternoon. The Japanese Americans returned to Ship Island by motorboat. After they got back they went fishing for evening dinner with handmade bamboo poles. The sea was as full of fish as Hawaii. They caught white salmon trout which they smoked and sent in two big boxes back to Company B at Camp McCoy. They gathered oysters and roasted them on the spot. They wanted to marinate octopus in vinegar, too, but no matter how hard they tried they could not catch any. The men even got hold of a skiff to row out to shrimp boats in the middle of the bay where they bought bucketsful. Lovell made sure that they had lots of rice too.

In the afternoon Lieutenant Tanaka had to censor the letters the soldiers wrote. Their participation in the "special training" was top secret. They were not allowed to write about either "dogs" or "islands." For fun some soldiers tried to get around that by writing in Japanese, or even in Latin, so Tanaka's afternoons would be more challenging.

When the fishermen on the shrimp boats asked who they were, they replied only that they were Hawaiians. Someone reported to the authorities that there was a strange group on the island. Two government agents who came to investigate were the only guests to visit the island.

When the soldiers landed on the island they were allowed to keep their rifles but were not given any ammunition. They did not stay on Ship Island long. For some reason, perhaps to speed up training for the dogs, the soldiers were moved to barracks on Cat Island. The dogs were divided into groups according to breed, and the training changed. The soldiers now had to train attack dogs. The animals used were hunting breeds like German shepherds, Labrador retrievers, Doberman pinschers, and Russian wolfhounds.

In the first stage the dogs were trained to hate the Japanese American soldiers. They were chained to trees and the soldiers beat one dog at a time with knotted burlap sacks. Before long the dogs bared their teeth and growled whenever the soldiers approached.

In the second stage the dogs were trained to bite the burlap sacks. Clad in helmets, with protective masks on their faces and necks and hockey gloves on their hands, the soldiers would place the sacks against their throats. At the trainer's command "Kill!" the dogs would leap at them. Sometimes the dogs would lunge not for the neck but for the unprotected feet and legs. The only thing to do then was to punch them or kick them away. It was like having fighting dogs as boxing partners.

In the third stage of training the soldiers wore thick cotton-padded protective garments on their upper bodies and burlap sacks covering their right arms. The dogs were trained to bite their arms. Finally the soldiers put on padded protective garments covering their whole bodies, and the dogs were trained to attack them in pairs. The dogs' teeth never touched their skin, but every bite hurt. It was like being pinched with a pliers through the protective padding.

What the soldiers feared most was walking in front of the chained dogs on their way to training in ordinary fatigue uniforms. Stretching at their chains, the dogs would growl and howl as they went by. The soldiers broke out in cold sweat even thinking about what would happen if the chains broke.

Suddenly one day the Swiss captain left the island. He had asked for a little more time, but the War Department decided to end the "special training." Perhaps the Japanese Americans from Hawaii had eaten too much hamburger and ice cream instead of rice gruel and pickled *daikon*, and so had entirely lost their "Japanese scent."

In any case, the Japanese American soldiers drank up the entire three months' supply of beer allotted to them on Cat Island in three weeks. The reason, they said, was that the drinking water on the island smelled like rotten eggs. They were probably reacting to the tension of their dog training sessions too. By the time Tanaka and the Third Platoon from Company B returned to the 100th Battalion, by then at Camp Shelby, they all had beer bellies. And instead of telling about their "special training," all they wanted to talk about was the delicious fish they had eaten on the island.

At the end of May, Major General Leslie J. McNair, chief of army ground forces, visited the Louisiana maneuver on a personal inspection tour. It was a chance for the 100th to be examined on the results of their year of training. The general gave Turner some strong words of commendation and returned to Washington. On June 9, 1943, after stopping for two days to practice weapons firing at Camp Polk on the way, the 100th Battalion arrived back at Camp Shelby.

III

Go for Broke

LIKE many veterans Richard Kumashiro, a Honolulu-born artillery veteran with a dental practice near Disneyland, tried to push aside memories of events that had happened forty years before, but eventually he had to confront his past.

"Sometimes I would feel that I was responsible in getting many of the boys enlisted and eventually being killed on the battlefront," he wrote recently. "But then again, with or without my picture the combat team would have been formed."[1]

Kumashiro had been drafted before Pearl Harbor. When war broke out he was one of a few Japanese Americans assigned to a quartermaster unit. The only nisei soldiers not sent to the 100th Battalion were these quartermaster troops and the last draftees recruited on February 6, 1942. Kumashiro remained in Hawaii for work duty. A Signal Corps cameraman came to his barracks one day, and without any explanation asked Kumashiro to pose for some photographs.

After deciding to accept Japanese American volunteers, the army distributed recruiting posters to towns all over the Hawaiian Islands. The posters showed a nisei soldier with his arm pulled back about to throw a grenade. The model was Pfc Kumashiro, then twenty-five years old. Above his photograph the poster read in big bold letters: "It is my right to fight for America."

A few hours after the attack on Pearl Harbor the governor of Hawaii ordered the organization of a Hawaii Territorial Guard to replace the National Guard units called into federal service. The core of this new guard was to be the ROTC units on the islands, and the first contingent called up was the one at the University of Hawaii. By 10:00 A.M. on the morning of December 7 ROTC students from the university reported for service to the Honolulu Armory. From the first day, they were posted at key points in Honolulu such as the territorial governor's mansion, the waterworks, the power stations, and the airport. Half the ROTC students were nisei. Like the haole students, the Japanese Americans were given rifles and assigned to various units. On January 19, 1942, they were suddenly released from duty. The reason, they were told, was top secret. The action had been taken on orders from Washington.

On the mainland the decision to put the Japanese Americans into relocation camps was finally taking shape.[2] According to Colonel Kendall Fielder, who served as G-2 under Lieutenant General Emmons, the Hawaiian authorities may have been trying to avoid the establishment of relocation camps in Hawaii by going along with Washington's wishes. The Japanese immigrants and their families constituted a major element of the labor force in the islands, and interning them would have crippled the economy.

It is not hard to imagine how shocked the young Japanese American students were when they got the news. There were bull sessions every day in the dormitories and on the broad campus lawns. With the outbreak of war, classes had almost completely come to a halt. Over and over the students insisted they wanted to fight for their country.

The nisei students knew that if they did not make clear that they were willing to fight, their position would be very difficult after the war. Hung Wai Ching, director of the university YMCA, was impressed by how well the young men had thought it through. The son of illiterate Cantonese immigrants, and today a prominent Honolulu business leader, Ching was much trusted by the young nisei. Even though Chinese American he played an active role immediately after the outbreak of war, mediating between the Japanese Americans and the other ethnic groups on the islands, including the haoles.

The students came to Ching's YMCA office every day, often in tears, asking him to do something. The nisei had been excluded from the selective service system. It was the same as being told, "Your country has attacked us." It was a humiliation hard to accept. Even today nisei veterans are pained when they talk about it. The best way for Japanese American students to show their loyalty had been denied them. To make matters worse, the nisei were classified 4C: "enemy aliens."

Some 169 of the 317 Japanese American students who had been released from the Hawaii Territorial Guard sent a petition to Lieutenant General Emmons. It was a heartfelt plea. "Hawaii is our home, the United States our country. We know but one loyalty, and that is to the Stars and Stripes. We wish to do our part as loyal Americans in every way possible and we hereby present ourselves for whatever service you may see fit to use us."[3] Ching took the petition himself to Colonel Fielder, who thought that if the nisei met with any further rejection, discontent would grow in the Japanese American community and that would affect the security of the islands.

On February 23, 1942, Lieutenant General Emmons, persuaded by Fielder's views, gave the Japanese American students permission to form a unit of their own. They called themselves the VVV (Varsity Victory Volunteers). Officially designated the Corps of Engineers Auxiliary, the unit was placed under the Hawaiian Department of Army Engineers. For the next eleven months the Japanese American students were used for manual labor, mainly working to construct roads essential to the military defense of the islands. But that was not the same as being real soldiers.

On the mainland too some nisei wanted to be allowed to volunteer for military service. The movement was led by the Japanese American Citizens League (JACL), today the most influential organization of mainland Japanese Americans. In the early 1940s, however, the JACL was a small group composed mainly of young nisei. It could hardly be said to represent the whole Japanese American community. But as in Hawaii, internment removed mainland issei from positions of leadership, and unexpectedly the young organization found itself in the forefront of the nisei community. One of the leaders of the organization was twenty-seven-year-old Masaru "Mike" Masaoka, a native of Salt Lake City and a lecturer in public speaking at his alma mater, the University of Utah.

When the Japanese Americans on the West Coast were ordered to relocation camps by presidential executive order on February 19, 1942, the JACL cooperated positively with the move. It neither protested the order nor stood up for the civil rights of nisei as American citizens. JACL leaders were leery of embarking on a fight they had little chance of winning and feared that resistance or protest might make things worse.[4] Mike Masaoka later said that it was the duty of the nisei to cooperate with the government, not to fight it.[5] But until the executive order was finally issued, the JACL sought desperately to find ways of avoiding compulsory internment. Masaoka came up with a plan himself.

"We were driven to desperation," he now says of his proposal. "We wanted to gather nisei volunteers into a special attack force to fight against the Japanese army." He called it a "suicide battalion." To guarantee the loyalty of the nisei soldiers, their parents were to be kept as "hostages" by the American government. The proposal was a response to anti-Japanese groups calling for the compulsory internment of the Japanese Americans who invariably pointed to their lack of a war record as proof that their loyalty to the United States was doubtful. To be sure, some issei had served in World War I but the number was too small to be consequential. The plan to form a special nisei attack force—"suicide battalion"—was a pathetic attempt by the mainland nisei to establish such a record in the most spectacular way possible, by showing grim determination to shed their own blood if necessary.

When rioting led mainly by kibei broke out at the relocation camp at Manzanar in California, Masaoka was burned in effigy. His aging mother, an immigrant from Kumamoto, was removed from the camp for her own safety. Some Japanese Americans regarded the JACL leaders, Masaoka in particular, as traitors to their community. Clearly his idea for a Japanese American suicide brigade did not represent the views of most mainland Japanese Americans. (All five Masaoka brothers, however, including Mike, later volunteered for military service, and his second brother died in battle.)

In any case, the American military authorities did not pay much attention to the JACL proposal. They took the position that it was not the American army's policy to organize racially segregated military units— "except for Negroes." If the nisei were used in the Pacific theater, there would be the problem of how to tell them apart from the enemy soldiers. Besides, the notion of "suicide units" was alien to a democratic country, and no one was going to go along with the idea of keeping anyone's parents as "hostages."[6]

According to Masaji Marumoto, nisei leaders in Hawaii held back from making any positive efforts to organize Japanese American volunteers into a unit. Marumoto, a Harvard graduate and lawyer, later to become the first nisei on the Hawaiian Supreme Court, was a central figure in the Hawaiian Emergency Service Committee (ESC), which worked to get the Japanese American community behind any activity that would demonstrate their loyalty to the United States. Immediately after the war broke out the ESC moved quickly to shut down Japanese-language schools all over the islands, and it threw its effort into war bond and blood donation drives.

When Marumoto heard about the discontent among the University of Hawaii ROTC students, he went to the campus to help his friend from McKinley High School days, Hung Wai Ching, to defuse the situation and get the VVV organized. Marumoto never forgot what Robert Shivers, the local FBI representative in the islands, had told him. "I hate to say it, but for you persons of Japanese ancestry war with Japan might be the best thing that could happen because then you can prove what you've been saying."

Both Shivers, who was responsible for internal security in the islands, and Colonel Fielder understood how important it was for the nisei to establish a record of wartime military accomplishment, and Ching worked hard to build support for the idea of a Japanese American volunteer force among haole community leaders. But the nisei leaders of the ESC were reluctant to make any direct move. It is clear from War Department documents that they did not begin to lobby for a nisei volunteer unit until after the battle of Midway. By that time Washington showed less concern about whether or not the Japanese Americans in Hawaii should be relocated, and the nisei draftees organized into the 100th Battalion had been shipped off to the mainland. Lobbying from the Hawaiian side began with appeals by the boys in the VVV and military authorities in the islands.

At first the authorities in Washington seemed unwilling to change their policy. On June 17, 1942, at about the time the 100th Battalion arrived in Camp McCoy, Secretary of War Henry L. Stimson sent a memorandum to Major General Lewis B. Hershey, head of the National Selective Service System in Washington. "Except as may be specifically authorized in exceptional cases, the War Department will not accept for service with the armed forces Japanese, or persons of Japanese extraction, regardless of citizenship status or other factors," Stimson wrote. The exception, of course, was Japanese-speaking nisei who could be used for intelligence work.

Ten days later, on June 26, however, the Army Chief of Staff G-2 Section recommended the formation of a small committee—a Board of Military Utilization of U.S. Citizens of Japanese Ancestry—to consider the proposal to form a small unit made up of Japanese Americans to be sent to the European front.[7] The War Department had begun to wonder what to do about the Japanese American soldiers already training on the mainland—and the problems they were causing.

On July 21, 1942, the Office of the Chief of Staff sent a memorandum to the Commander-in-Chief, U.S. Fleet, on the question of inducting Japanese Americans from Hawaii. "Our efforts to absorb even small units with the army," said the memorandum, "have been quite unsatisfactory. Serious difficulties have arisen where these troops were stationed and minor difficulties in others. For this reason, the War Department is not accepting Japanese-Americans for enlistment."

When the relocation camps finally went into operation, most of the mainland Japanese American soldiers had been assembled at Camp Robinson in Arkansas. Local citizens in nearby Little Rock were upset at their presence. In March 1942 a delegation led by the manager of the Chamber of Commerce met in Washington with Brigadier General F. B. Mallon, chief of the Army Ground Forces Replacement and School Command, to express their complaints.

Local leaders were disturbed that "901 Japs" had already arrived at the camp and more were bound to come. "Very grave social problems" were likely to arise, they said. The majority of the soldiers were Buddhists, and there were even Buddhist services held inside the camp.[8] What effects would this pagan religion have on the area? Then too there was the possibility that the families of the Japanese American soldiers might come to live in the area.

But the main worry of the local leaders lay elsewhere. What they feared most was the impact the Japanese Americans might have on the local color line. The delegation reported that some local parents were alarmed at the prospect of their daughters associating with the Japanese American soldiers who attended USO dances. Even worse, there were reports of the "commingling of Japanese soldiers and negro women." After talking with the Little Rock delegation, Brigadier General Mallon concluded, "It appears that the fear on the part of the local residents of Little Rock lies in their belief that any equality shown to the Japanese by white people may result in the negroes in this vicinity increasing their demands."[9]

This may have been one of the reasons, even if not the main reason, why the 100th Battalion was sent to Camp McCoy even before barracks had been built for them. Lieutenant General John L. DeWitt, commanding general of the Western Defence Command, one of the main movers behind the relocation camp policy, requested that the War Department curtail news reports about the Japanese American battalion at McCoy since it might stir up a public fuss.[10]

The army's staff committee set up to consider the problem of Japanese American volunteers began its work on July 1, 1942. It consisted of five colonels from the Army Chief of Staff office together with Dillon S. Myer, director of the War Relocation Authority. The committee solicited opinions from various concerned or knowledgeable parties in the army.

One of those consulted was Colonel Moses W. Pettigrew, a former military attaché at the American embassy in Tokyo serving as head of the Far Eastern Group in G-2. Fluent in Japanese and long involved in Japanese American problems, he had been quite shocked by the relocation policy. Pettigrew told the staff committee that "if we did not make use of such citizens we would be passing up a considerable quantity of very good manpower." He emphasized that "the great majority of second-generation citizens of Japanese ancestry were unquestionably loyal." His opinion was shared by Colonel Rufus S. Bratten, who had served as military attaché in Tokyo too. Dillon Myer, the man in charge of the relocation program, thought that the Japanese Americans ought to be given the opportunity to show their loyalty to their country.[11] On the other hand, Colonel Martin J. Haas, who had about three months' contact with Japanese Americans during the evacuation, testified that he did not trust them and did not recommend their use for military service.[12]

The army committee gathered the views of top army and navy brass. Both Admiral Nimitz and Lieutenant General Emmons, citing the successful training organization of the 100th Battalion, expressed agreement to the formation of a volunteer Japanese American fighting unit. The committee also asked the views of Lieutenant General DeWitt. On July 14 he replied that at a time when the country must make use of all available manpower, the Japanese Americans should be allowed into the military service. But he added that since their loyalty was doubtful they should not be sent to the front. The Japanese Americans, he wrote, should be kept "within the continental United States only"; they should be "removed from areas subject to sabotage of a character that would interfere with the war effort"; and they should be placed in "service units only, unarmed."[13] The committee attached great importance to DeWitt's views.

In the committee's estimate there were about 36,000 Japanese Americans of an age eligible for military service, of whom 18,000 would be acceptable for induction. About 4,000 were already in the service, leaving 14,000 to be considered. The committee asked the commanding general, Services of Supply, if they could be used in noncombatant jobs. His answer was that it would be "impracticable." There would be too many problems with local citizens if that many Japanese Americans were used for labor service within the United States.[14] Some Japanese Americans at Camp Robinson had been sent to other installations to work in laundries or as cooks, but the G-2 Division of the Army Ground Forces reported that "there is some evidence which indicates that Japanese residents of this country are promoting anti-white sentiment among Negroes." The Services of Supply command suggested that Japanese Americans could best be used in Iceland, Africa, or even the British Isles.[15]

On September 14, 1942, the staff committee reported its conclusions. The Japanese Americans, they said, were "a distinctive class of individuals, so marked by racial appearance, characteristics and background, that they are particularly repulsive to the military establishment at large and the civilian population." The "lone fact that these individuals are of Japanese ancestry tends to place them in a most questionable light as to their loyalty to the United States." The committee opposed the formation of a Japanese American unit "because of the universal distrust in which they are held."

Autumn winds were blowing in Camp McCoy. The men of the 100th Battalion were putting even more effort into training, unaware that the possibility of their going to the battlefront was close to nil at that point.

The decision handed down by the War Department staff committee did not stop Mike Masaoka and the other JACL leaders who continued to work for the organization of a nisei volunteer unit. Moreover, protests began coming into the War Department from American Civil Liberties Union branches on the East Coast.

The decision did not stop activities on the Hawaiian side either. When Assistant Secretary of War John J. McCloy visited Hawaii to inspect its defense system, Colonel Fielder made a special point of routing his trip through the Kolekole pass. There McCloy could see the young Japanese American members of the VVV hard at work breaking rock. Fielder later visited McCloy in Washington as Lieutenant General Emmons's representative. He pointed out that if the army did not use Japanese American manpower skillfully there was a danger that their injured pride might turn to hostility and alienation. This was probably the real reason why the military authorities in Hawaii were so enthusiastic for the organization of a nisei unit. As Admiral Nimitz pointed out, "the induction of approximately 10,000 eligible Japanese Americans in Hawaii would remove many dangerous characters from the islands."[16]

In the latter part of October McCloy received a copy of a letter from Elmer Davis, head of the Office of War Information, dated October 15, 1942. Roosevelt had asked Secretary of War Stimson for his view of Davis's letter, and Stimson had passed the inquiry on to McCloy. Davis had written that Japanese army propaganda in Southeast Asia stressed that the war was a racial war caused by racial discrimination. Indeed the Japanese often pointed to the relocation camps as evidence of that. Davis urged Roosevelt to give personal recognition to the importance of the Japanese Americans' loyalty. An extremely effective way to counter Japanese propaganda in Southeast Asia, he said, would be the organization of a nisei unit. "I believe the propaganda value of such a step would be great," he wrote, "and I believe they would make good troops."

McCloy immediately supported Davis's argument. So did Chief of Staff George C. Marshall. It is sometimes said that Marshall gave in to Lieutenant General DeWitt's argument that the relocation of the Japanese Americans was essential to the security of the West Coast, but he wrote a memo strongly supporting the formation of a nisei unit. "I don't think that you can permanently proscribe a lot of American citizens because of their racial origin," he wrote. "We have gone to the full limit in evacuating them—that's enough." Marshall thought that a nisei unit would not only be useful in the propaganda war with the Japanese but it would also be very significant in shaping the image the United States presented to its allies. It would bear out the principles stated in the Declaration of the United Nations signed earlier that year in Washington.

In the face of these pressures from above, all involved agencies in the War Department at once fell into line. The recommendations the staff committee had presented a month before were completely overturned.

A plan was proposed to form a new Japanese American regiment with the 100th Battalion at its core. G-3 opposed the idea since it had already planned to send the 100th to the North African front. It wanted a completely separate new regiment to be organized. At the beginning of 1943 the 100th, knowing nothing at all about these discussions in Washington, moved from Camp McCoy to Camp Shelby.

On February 1, 1943, President Roosevelt announced from the White House that the 442nd Infantry Regimental Combat Team consisting of Americans of Japanese ancestry was to be organized. The president, who little more than a year before had indicted the attack on Pearl Harbor as a "day of infamy," now used his elegant rhetoric to answer the call for a nisei volunteer unit. And more than 110,000 mainland Japanese aliens and Japanese Americans confined behind barbed wire in ten relocation camps heard his words:

> No loyal citizen of the United States should be denied the democratic right to exercise the responsibilities of his citizenship, regardless of his ancestry. The principle on which this country was founded and by which it has always been governed is that Americanism is a matter of the mind and heart; Americanism is not, and never was, a matter of race or ancestry. A good American is one who is loyal to this country and to our creed of liberty and democracy.

The 442nd Infantry Regiment was to be made up of the following units: Regimental Headquarters Company, a medical detachment, First Battalion (Companies A to D; after the unit was sent abroad the 100th Battalion was assigned as the First Battalion), Second Battalion (Companies E to H), Third Battalion (Companies I to M), 232nd Engineer Combat Company, and 552nd Field Artillery Battalion. The War Department organizational plan for the unit (dated January 22, 1943) specified that all officers down to the company commander level were to be "white American citizens." (The only exception was Captain Pershing Nakada, commander of the 232nd Engineer Company.) Most of the platoon leaders were also to be Caucasian. In other words, the majority of the officers in the nisei battalion were white.

On March 28, 1943, the Honolulu Chamber of Commerce held a farewell ceremony for the 2,686 nisei volunteers from the Hawaiian Islands in front of the Iolani Palace, then the territorial governor's office. On March 30 the *Honolulu Star-Bulletin* commented:

> No scene in Honolulu during World War II has been more striking, more significant, than that at the territorial capitol grounds on Sunday. It was not alone the size of the crowd, somewhere between 15,000 and 17,000, and said by oldtimers to be the largest that ever massed within the gateways to

old Iolani Palace. . . . It was, most significantly, the evident pride of the families and friends of these young Americans—their pride that the youths are entrusted with the patriotic mission of fighting for their country and the Allied nations.

The Japanese American leaders in the ESC, who had worked so hard to bring about the formation of the 442nd Regiment, had been worried about just how many young men would volunteer. The local ESC branches on every island worked hard to drum up interest. The poster with Kumashiro's photograph went up everywhere. There was no need for worry. The original plan called for 1,500 volunteers from all the islands, but more than 10,000 men volunteered right away. The Japanese American community was in a mood to celebrate. Not only had Roosevelt not put them in relocation camps, but he had allowed the Japanese Americans to volunteer for military service as full-fledged Americans.

Many issei parents must have had mixed feelings. They wondered if this were to be a last parting. Some were upset at the designation of the battalion—442. In Japanese the word for "four" *(shi)* is pronounced in the same way as the word for "death" *(shi),* and a double four was particularly ominous. But most issei, even though reluctant as most parents to see their sons go to war, accepted the situation as inevitable. They knew that their sons wanted to show devotion to the land of their birth. "The foster parent is dearer than the real one," goes an old Japanese saying. And so, as the *Honolulu Star-Bulletin* reported, the issei hid their fears and concern as they made a show of proudly sending off their sons.

Since the nisei response was so overwhelming, the number of volunteers authorized was increased to 2,600. Many volunteers were eliminated in the physical examination. This meant shame for their families at the time, and after the war they felt they had been left out of something important. Only about one out of every five volunteers was accepted. Following Japanese custom, those so honored were showered with farewell gifts of money. Haole plantation owners gave going-away parties for the volunteers too.

As the volunteers marched through the streets of Honolulu on their way to the ceremonies in front of Iolani Palace, thousands of Japanese American spectators lined the sidewalks, waving American flags and cheering "Banzai" as their sons and husbands, their brothers and boyfriends, marched by in their grand new American uniforms. The volunteers had taken "Go for Broke" as the rousing battalion motto. They marched along smartly, garrison caps perched at a snappy angle on their very short new GI haircuts. Around their necks all wore leis made of small white jasmine flowers. Probably some of the nisei soldiers already had blisters from wearing shoes too large. Their feet were much smaller than the army average, and also unusually wide. When the unit finally reached the battlefield, one of its biggest logistical headaches was that the quartermaster forces did not have boots to fit the men. Their boots had to be ordered specially.

Not all the men who marched that day with proud and happy faces had volunteered for the same reason. Their motives were many and mixed.

The 169 members of the VVV, who had continued to perform labor service duties with the army engineers, were overjoyed at being given the first chance to volunteer. In the photographs of the parade it is easy to see their hands raised in "V for Victory" signs. The University of Hawaii president had sent them off with words of strong encouragement.

Japanese American students in the premedical program at the university volunteering as a group had asked to serve as regular infantrymen, not as medics. One of them, Daniel Inouye, now the senior senator from Hawaii, says that most of the premed students were wartime casualties and not one of them later became a doctor.

Among the marching troops was Richard Kumashiro, the unwitting poster model. Two hundred or so draftees like Kumashiro who were not shipped out with the 100th Battalion had been put to work fixing roads, loading trucks, and performing other labor service like the VVV. Many were dissatisfied with the way the army treated them, so only a few volunteered for the 442nd.

One of the marchers, Tom Tanaka, had been working at Pearl Harbor on the day of the Japanese attack. Though he had spent the whole day and night helping with the wounded, a marine had chased him off the base at bayonet point when dawn came the next day. Until the day he volunteered for the 442nd he had worked tending the fire at the public bath his father operated.

Another volunteer, Yutaka Yoshida, was a former policeman who had accompanied FBI agents when they went to arrest a priest of the Nishi Honganji Buddhist sect on the day of the attack. Even though it was his job, he still cannot forget how sad it was to point his gun at the tiny old issei priest.

The father of two marchers, Katsuaki and Katsugo Miho, was the principal of a Japanese-language school who had been sent off to an internment camp in Texas. His sons had volunteered together.

A kibei born in Honolulu, Takao Hedani, had returned to the islands after going to school in Hiroshima. He worked as a *kendo* (swordsmanship) instructor and Japanese-language teacher before volunteering for the 442nd.

The brother of one volunteer, Lyman Harada, had been the local manager for the Robinson family on the tiny island of Niihau near Kauai. Immediately after the Pearl Harbor attack a Japanese fighter plane had made a forced landing on the island and Harada's brother had tried to help the downed pilot escape. Eventually both men were cornered and committed suicide. Since the incident cast doubt on their loyalty, the Japanese American community was upset, and the Harada family was ostracized afterward. Even though Raymond Harada was over thirty and had a wife and children, he volunteered for the 442nd to retrieve his family's honor.

The driver for the president of the *Honolulu Star-Bulletin,* Moon Saito, had joined to show his pride at being an American.

One volunteer, Don Seki, whose father had left Hawaii to return to his native province of Fukushima two months before war broke out, said, "I wanted to show that I was full of the Yamato spirit [*Yamato-damashii,* the spirit of Japan]."

Another volunteer, Roy Kobayashi, signed up because he had nothing to do at home in the evening after wartime curfew was imposed. "I was feeling kind of blue," he told me. "I thought that even going into the army would be better than this. I wanted to enjoy myself while I was still alive."

Another, Larry Kukita, was simply tired of being in Hawaii and thought he would never have an opportunity like this again. He volunteered so that he could leave and see some of the world.

And still another, Noboru Kimura, said he wanted to see the Mississippi River more than anything else.

One marcher, Sanji Kimoto, later recalled, "I only knew about war as something fantastic that I saw in Hollywood movies. It even seemed romantic to me."

A close buddy of one volunteer, Tadao Miyamoto, kept urging him to sign up. Since Miyamoto was nearsighted he did not worry much about taking the army physical, thinking he would not be accepted. He was shocked to discover that he had qualified but his friend had not.

Like Miyamoto, most volunteers had signed up because their brothers or cousins or boyhood friends, lured by the adventure of leaving the islands, had joined. Seniors at Baldwin High School on Maui ran through the sugarcane fields to see who could get to the recruiting station first. One of them, Eiichi Oki, always a good student at school, says that the first thing he bought at the PX after he got into the army was a buckram-bound Webster's dictionary he had been longing to have; he carried it in his knapsack throughout the war.

Four Japanese American teachers at Baldwin High also volunteered. One of them, Saburo Maehara, was the son of a well-known Japanese school principal interned on the mainland.

Thirty-six-year-old Toshio Anzai from Maui spoke as representative of the volunteers at the farewell ceremony. Active in local politics, he was one of the ESC leaders on Maui. He did not feel he could face parents whose sons were enlisting unless he himself volunteered before calling on younger men to sign up.

Even the ESC leader in Honolulu, thirty-eight-year-old Masaji Marumoto, volunteered. He failed the physical examination because of a clubfoot and nearsightedness, but he later volunteered for the Military Intelligence Service and did duty in the Pacific theater.

On April 13, 1943, two weeks after the farewell ceremony, the Hawaiian volunteers entered their barracks at Camp Shelby as full-fledged American soldiers. On just that day General DeWitt was speaking before the congressional subcommittee on naval affairs in San Francisco. "A Jap's a Jap," he said. "They are a dangerous element. There is no way to determine their loyalty. It makes no difference whether he is an American citizen; theoretically he is still a Japanese, and you can't change him. You can't change him by giving him a piece of paper."

DeWitt was responding to a recommendation by Dillon S. Myer, director of the War Relocation Authority, to Secretary of War Stimson that the ban prohibiting Japanese Americans from the West be lifted. His words reveal that anti-Japanese sentiments were still strong in the United States.

Rudy Tokiwa was a volunteer from the mainland. His parents had urged him to postpone induction until he had finished high school. By the time he got to Camp Shelby the Hawaiians already had been training for two months.

"You where from? You a Kotonk?"

It was his first day in the barracks. One of the soldiers had come over to him and asked the question with a peculiar kind of hostility. A footlocker was sitting on the bed Rudy thought was his. It was supposed to be at the end of the bed.

"Whose is this?" Rudy asked. No one answered.

Instead he heard again, "You a Kotonk?" He looked around to see himself surrounded by several soldiers.

After they had glared at each other for a few moments, Tokiwa picked up the footlocker and heaved it in the direction of the door. One of the other soldiers, a look of surprise on his face, asked, "Hey, you a Buddhahead? You Hawaiian?"

Tokiwa, making no answer, stretched out on his bed. The owner of the footlocker, perhaps thinking that anyone with guts like that must be a Buddhahead, quietly moved it over to his own bed.

Tokiwa's head was splitting with pain. The day before in New Orleans he had had his first beer with a Caucasian boy about his age whom he had met on the train. One bottle followed another, and soon they had drunk themselves into a stupor. The next morning the MPs had loaded the two of them back on the train. Tokiwa had not quite reached his eighteenth birthday.

The first thing he had found awaiting him in his new life was the "war" between the volunteers from the mainland and those from Hawaii. The Hawaiians called mainland nisei "Kotonks." When a coconut with no meat inside it falls to the ground, that is the sound it makes. The Hawaiians said that if you knocked a mainland nisei on the head, it would go "kotonk." For their part, the mainlanders called the Hawaiians "Buddhaheads." They looked more Japanese, the mainlanders said; and "Buddha" sounds like *buta,* the Japanese word for "pig."

Even though all were in the same boat together, during the year the 442nd spent training at Camp Shelby the internal "war" went on day after day. Some say the war started when the regiment was first organized. Most of the original noncommissioned officers were mainland nisei. None were volunteers. They had been drafted before the war. After going through Camp Robinson they had been dispersed all over the country in a variety of duties.

When the Hawaiian volunteers arrived at Camp Shelby, full of energy and raring to go, they found that the cadre ordering them to do this or that were all draftees from the mainland. That was the big reason why there was such a barrier between the two groups.

The first personnel assembled when the regiment was organized were the Caucasian officers. Then came the mainland nisei noncoms. It was they who had busily made preparations for the arrival of the Hawaiian volunteers, repairing the leaking roofs and sagging floors of the temporary barracks. Once training began, the mainland noncoms were not especially harsh on the enlisted men nor did they try to throw their weight around, but the Hawaiian recruits still made them targets of resentment.

Often a group of Hawaiian soldiers, ganging up all at once, would ambush a mainlander unexpectedly or jump him even if he were lying quietly on his bunk. That was said to be the Hawaiian style of fighting. Some mainland veterans claim that as they walked along, minding their own business, they might suddenly find themselves surrounded and dumped on the ground by a group they had never laid eyes on before. They have only unpleasant memories of their days at Camp Shelby, and for that reason they do not like to attend veteran reunions even today.

Fights could be set off by anything. It was an inevitable ritual by which the young men got to know each other by testing their manhood. Even so, it was troublesome business, like a fight among brothers a family does not want outsiders to know about.

Two Japanese American chaplains were attached to the 442nd, Masao

Yamada and Hiro Higuchi. Both were well-known Christian ministers in Hawaii. Their job was much like that of Doc Kometani. Although a majority of the men in the unit were Buddhist, the two Christian chaplains were trusted and respected. But even they were caught up in the confrontations between the Hawaiians and the mainlanders.

The thirty-six-year-old Yamada, the second oldest nisei minister in Hawaii, was the son of an immigrant carpenter from Niigata. He had grown up on Kauai. He came from the same home town as Sakae Takahashi, and their families were good friends. Yamada had stayed at the Okumura Dormitory and gone to the University of Hawaii more than ten years before Takahashi. After the war broke out he was one of the leaders of the Emergency Service Committee on Kauai. In dealing with the soldiers he was very serious and very straight, unlike Higuchi who was always joking and acting like a buddy. The mainland soldiers seemed to trust him a little better than they did Higuchi. But it was only natural that Yamada looked at the mainland soldiers with the eyes of a Hawaiian-born.

In one of his letters home Reverend Yamada compared the two groups. "It seems to me that [the mainlanders] don't have the initiative like the Hawaiians. They seem to lack vision. Their heart is small and they don't fight hard enough. . . . They worry about their personal future, but they don't take vital interest in the questions of the good of all or the whole Nisei problem."[17]

Rudy Tokiwa had the broad shoulders of a man, and he planted his short legs firmly on the ground. Only his face was still that of a boy. Rudy was tough for his age, maybe a little too tough. He had grown up with a reputation for being a mischievous "bad boy," but even he found the Hawaiian soldiers a surprise.

When the day's training ended, the Hawaiians would take off their fatigue tops and go bare-chested. They wore zori sandals or often simply went barefoot. Rudy was not very confident about his spoken English. At school people had made fun of him when he spoke as his parents did, using "me" instead of "I." But the Hawaiians spoke a strange English even more broken than his and never gave it a second thought. Without the slightest embarrassment some of them peppered their talk with four-letter words.

Most mainland soldiers looked down on the Hawaiians because they lacked Western-style manners. "They were like barbarians from the jungle," said one. Some mainlanders were ashamed to think that the same blood ran in their veins. They weren't really Japanese Americans at all, they were Hawaiians. Secretly mainlanders called them "Kanaks," a word for native Hawaiians.

But the mainland soldiers often looked down on one another too.

Nisei from Los Angeles regarded those from Seattle as country bump-kins, and city-born Japanese Americans had a low estimate of those from isolated farm communities.

Rudy Tokiwa had grown up in the farm country around Salinas, California. His father, an immigrant from Kagoshima, grew lettuce there. Rudy was the youngest of six children, three girls and three boys. He had no memories of helping his father in the fields from dawn to dusk as his older brothers did. The family pampered him, and he grew up without the reserve characteristic of many mainland Japanese Americans. He was a country boy not so different from the Hawaiians.

The thing that Rudy noticed right away about the Hawaiians was their unity. They had a strong sense of comradeship the mainlanders lacked. They spoke their minds freely to each other and gave each other comical nicknames. A soldier with dark skin became "Shadow," a timid one "Chicken," a short one "Big man," a fat one "Skinny."

The Hawaiians went everywhere in groups. When they went to drink beer in the PX, whoever had money in his pocket would pay. Even if someone offered to treat, the mainland soldiers did not drink if they did not have money, and they would not pay for anyone else's drink but their own.

If a Hawaiian soldier wanted to buy a candy bar but had no money of his own, he would simply ask, "Hey, someone give me a dime." And whoever had a dime in his pocket would hand it over. The Hawaiian rule for borrowing and lending was: whatever is mine is yours and vice versa. It was a carryover from the strong community spirit of their parents' plantation days when people helped each other out in hard times. Hawaiians who went to eat chow mein at the Chinese restaurant in nearby Hattiesburg would always order extra for their buddies back in camp. No matter how little there was, everyone would sit around and share it. Naturally the Hawaiians always invited the mainlanders to join them too.

Unlike the Pacific Coast states Utah had not been included in the relocation zone for Japanese Americans. Japanese Americans there continued to live and work as they had before the war broke out. One day a package full of Japanese delicacies—pickled plums and pickled radish—arrived in the barracks for a soldier from Utah. It had been a long time since his Hawaiian barrack mates had tasted Japanese food, but the soldier from Utah did not ask if anyone would like a taste. By the time he got back from the shower, the contents of his package was inside the stomachs of the Hawaiians.

"The Kotonks are all *manini*," the Hawaiians say even today with some contempt. The *manini*, a beautifully striped Hawaiian reef fish with a very small mouth, nibbles at its food with little bites. In Hawaiian it means someone extremely stingy.

The Hawaiian soldiers were generous, openhanded, and optimistic. In their own view of themselves, they would never think of stepping on other people to get ahead in the world as the mainlanders seemed to. The Hawaiians represented a sizable ethnic group in a small island community, but the mainland soldiers were part of a tiny minority in a vast continent. They had grown up amid prejudice the Hawaiians had never encountered. The Hawaiians, however, had neither the inclination nor the experience to understand that.

The solidarity of the Hawaiian soldiers had been nurtured in small communities. There was an element of exclusiveness or cliquishness about them. Rather than being aware of their own islander provincialism, the Hawaiians became impatient with the mainlanders' lack of comradeship. They decided the mainlanders might be clever at toadying to Caucasians but were basically chickenhearted and lacking in self-confidence. The mainlanders seemed strangely timid, always worrying about what people would think of them. Few Hawaiians knew that many mainland soldiers sent money from their small paychecks back to their families in relocation camps.

Soon after he arrived at Camp Shelby, Rudy Tokiwa developed a passion for shooting dice. He was surprised at how the Hawaiians gambled. They played with thick rolls of bills, winning and losing big. The Hawaiians always seemed to have cash. According to Reverend Yamada, their parents often sent money, and a gift of a hundred dollars was regarded as a trifling amount. A soldier had only to write that he had a once-in-a-lifetime chance to see a bit of the mainland on leave and his parents would scrimp together money to send him. More than once Yamada saw soldiers whose parents had sent five hundred dollars at one time.

At the time a regimental commander's monthly pay was $250. The Caucasian officers were astounded to see the amount of money the soldiers received. They were unacquainted with the Japanese custom of giving money to travelers going off on a long journey, and they were not used to parents who sent their full-grown sons this much spending money. Almost all the money was staked on dice games. Even after word went back to the soldiers' parents through the Emergency Service Committee, the money kept coming. Reverend Yamada was completely fed up. He thought it only widened the gulf between the Hawaiian and mainland soldiers.

The Hawaiians had left their hometowns as heroes, sent off with cheers of "Banzai." The mainlanders, far from being hailed as heroes, were often abused as traitors or foolish sons when they volunteered. No matter how hard Yamada and the other officers tried, the gap between the two groups remained deep.

Even today some mainlander veterans in the same company with Rudy Tokiwa still think of him as a "Buddhahead." Tokiwa himself says that since people thought of him that way he did not much feel like identifying himself as a "Kotonk" on his first day in the company. It was easier to get along at Shelby letting people think he was a Hawaiian. His character was rather close to the "Buddhaheads," but even so his experience was typical of the mainland soldier.

Four days after the war began the FBI rounded up a large number of mainland issei. One of them was Rudy Tokiwa's father. Rudy says he cannot think why except that his father was active in the Kagoshima Prefecture Association, an organization for natives of the prefecture. A former schoolteacher in Kagoshima, Rudy's father was already several years past his sixtieth birthday. He had crossed the Pacific full of ideals and dreams, but since he did not know English well, the only work he could do was to shoulder a hoe. He had no regrets though. He was not just a sojourner. From the beginning he had staked his fortune on life in America.

Because he so much wanted to acquire American citizenship, Rudy's father volunteered for military service during World War I. He was one of a handful of issei who saw service at the front in France. Even so, he did not get citizenship rights. In 1935 a movement to give citizenship to the Asian American World War I veterans finally moved Congress to pass legislation, but no one got in touch with Rudy's father.

When word got around that influential Japanese in the Salinas area were to be rounded up, Rudy's father seems to have realized that he might be one. He greeted FBI agents at the front door in his old World War I army uniform, which he had gotten out of the trunk for the occasion. The FBI agents merely gave him a quick glance before taking him away.

The rest of the family tried to follow the government's appeal to the Japanese Americans to disperse voluntarily into the interior. They decided to move with several other families in Salinas, also of Kagoshima origin, to central Idaho and start all over again, but they hesitated to travel to an unknown place by themselves. In the meantime Executive Order 9066 was issued ordering relocation of all Japanese Americans on the West Coast.

The family sold everything they had except their hand luggage and their bedding. Even their treasured farm tools went at ridiculously low prices. The family was sent first to a hastily built assembly center at a rodeo ground near Salinas. Three months later they moved to the relocation camp at Poston, Arizona, officially called Colorado River Camp, in a former Indian reservation in the middle of the desert near the California border.

Rudy remembers that his father never raised his voice or his hand.

About four months after the family was sent to Poston, his father, who had been confined in a prison in Texas, finally rejoined them. He was even more taciturn than before. He said not a word about the kind of interrogation he had undergone or what his life in jail had been like.

Rudy worked as a cook's assistant in the camp mess hall in the early morning and in the evening. The camp was managed by personnel from the War Relocation Authority, but it was kept together as a community by the Japanese Americans incarcerated there. Those working for the camp administration were given a wage, but since the camp inmates were provided food, clothing, and shelter free of charge, the maximum pay was quite low, much less than the $21 a month an army private received.

Teachers and doctors got $19 a month, the highest pay. Rudy earned only $12 a month, the lowest end of the pay scale. Even so, that was enough to buy cigarettes for his father and a few other things at the camp canteen. There was a high school in the camp, but at first there were few qualified teachers. It was difficult to get proper schooling. In any case Rudy did not like to study.

According to the official WRA definition, a "relocation center" was a "pioneer community, with basic housing and protective services provided by the Federal government, for the occupancy by evacuees for the duration of the war."[18] Rudy's family was assigned a single room in one of the tarpaper-covered camp barracks. One bare light bulb hung from the ceiling, and the only pieces of furniture were army cots to sleep on. Desert sand constantly blew into the room. Sweeping it out was his mother's main occupation. But that at least was a light job compared to the heavy farm work she had done in order to survive since she came to America.

Even though the camp was big and free to move around in, the hurt and shock a teenager like Rudy felt at suddenly being thrust into such a confined environment expressed itself in psychological strain and rage. It was smothering to live day after day in the same small room face-to-face with his elderly parents. Whenever he had free time he would pass the day hanging out with friends his own age. He flirted with girls, and he stopped listening to what his parents told him. Rudy still dreamed about what was beyond the barbed wire. He wanted to walk out beyond the barbed wire fence into the great open spaces, to be liberated from everything, able to do what he wanted.

At first he thought about going to work as a day laborer during harvest time on farms near the relocation camp. Neighboring farmers were shorthanded because of the war, and they were eager to hire the hardworking Japanese Americans. Adult males in the camp were allowed temporary leave to work as farmhands.

It was about then that the government launched an investigation to determine the loyalty of the Japanese Americans.

When the army announced its plan to organize the 442nd, it also began to administer loyalty tests at all the relocation centers to ascertain the loyalty of all adults over seventeen years old whether or not they held American citizenship. In Hawaii where both the FBI and the army had adequate information about the volunteers, it was possible to investigate all the Hawaiian soldiers quickly. The problem came with volunteers from the relocation camps. It was necessary to make absolutely certain that they were loyal, and perhaps also to dispel public misgivings about them.

Dillon S. Myer, director of the War Relocation Authority, agreed to the loyalty test for other reasons. He wanted to get the Japanese Americans out of the relocation camps as fast as he could. He could see their morale declining before his eyes. Because of wartime manpower shortages, defense plants in Chicago and other areas wanted to hire Japanese Americans who had a reputation for being hard workers, but the clearance investigations necessary to move them out of the camps took too much time. Myer thought a general loyalty test could take care of the problem all at once. The real purpose of the loyalty test, then, was to determine whether or not adult males wanted to volunteer for military service and to facilitate clearance for adult females who wanted to work in war plants.

The loyalty test, however, provoked rioting and disturbances that resulted in death or injury for a number of the Japanese Americans. The relocation camps became divided into factions: those who opposed the loyalty test and those who did not. Families were divided too, with children turning against parents and brother turning against brother. What caused the trouble was the last two questions on the loyalty questionnaire:

Question 27: Are you willing to serve in the armed forces of the United States on combat duty, whenever ordered?

Question 28: Will you swear unqualified allegiance to the United States of America and faithfully defend the United States from any or all attack by foreign or domestic forces, and forswear any form of allegiance or obedience to the Japanese emperor, to any foreign government, power or organization?

Let us remember that the nisei were all natural-born American citizens who had been placed in official detention for more than a year. The loyalty questionnaire forced them to make the same pledge of allegiance to the United States required of foreign nationals who wanted to be naturalized as American citizens. They were asked to forswear an allegiance to Japan that they had never pledged. To the nisei this was more than a shock, it was a profound insult. The older the nisei, the better he understood the logic, making the loyalty test even harder to accept.

Their issei parents, who were aliens, were asked the same questions. If they answered yes to either question, then what would happen to them as Japanese? If they were to deny their loyalty to the emperor, would they become stateless persons? If the nisei were to volunteer for military service, then who would guarantee the safety of their parents? If they were to lose their lives on the battlefield, then who would protect the civil rights of their parents? Would their loved ones be able to leave the camps and return home?

The reaction of the internees at each relocation camp depended on the attitude of the officials in charge of the investigation. The worst situation developed at Tule Lake, California, where disturbances were so intense that troops with tanks were called in to bring them under control. The WRA officials, it is said, did not give an adequate explanation of the last two questions on the questionnaire. The colonel in charge was a Southerner who seemed clearly prejudiced against the Japanese Americans, and the head of the camp was also an authoritarian type. Taro Tsukahara, a kibei draftee in the Japanese-language school at Minnesota, who was sent to Tule Lake as an interpreter for the issei, says the attitude of the two men exacerbated the conflicts raised by the loyalty test. Administration of the test, originally scheduled to be done in three weeks, took twice as long.

Many issei who listened to Tsukahara's explanation reacted negatively. How could they offer up the sons to whom they had entrusted their dreams of the future to a country that treated them like this? It was difficult to see their sons taken away from them.

The nisei were caught between their parents' feelings and their concern over what would happen to their status as American citizens if they answered no to the last two questions on the questionnaire. In every family parents and children thrashed over what to do late into the night. Parents who thought that someday they might return to Japan put strong pressure on their children by making clear that they did not want their families to break up.

There were 23,606 nisei of draft age (between eighteen and thirty-seven) among the mainland Japanese Americans incarcerated in the relocation camps. Many of them answered yes to the loyalty test. But of those only 1,256, or about five percent, volunteered for military service (as of March 23, 1943). About 800 passed the physical examination.[19]

The number of volunteers was much lower than the army had anticipated. The large increase in the number of Hawaiian volunteers inducted was made possible by the small number of volunteers among the mainland Japanese Americans.

At Poston the volunteer rate was much better than average, but even so only 228 of 3,405 eligible for military service signed up. One of them was Rudy Tokiwa.

Only he and an older brother lived with his parents in their room at the camp barracks. The rest of his brothers and sisters were married and had children of their own. Rudy's father told his two sons that even if they replied yes to both questions on the loyalty test, they should not volunteer for military service.

The day Rudy came home from taking his loyalty test he could not look his parents in the eye. He turned his back to them and mumbled, "Me, volunteered."

His father's face, always so calm, darkened.

"You'll be lucky if they use you in a labor battalion. They're leading you on, you young fool! When you get to the front they'll use you as a shield for the white soldiers. That's what everyone is saying."

Just then his older brother came home. With averted eyes he too reported that he had volunteered. His father's voice quavered.

"So we have two fools in the family!"

The room was separated from the neighboring room by only a thin plywood wall. Everyone on the other side could hear what was going on. There was no privacy at all. Rudy's mother tried to stifle her sobbing. Rudy was often annoyed at his mother, who always told him, "Do your very best." But even today he says he cannot forget his mother's fingers, gnarled from years of hard work in the fields, as she covered her tearful face.

Fumiko Karatsu, now nearly eighty years old, lives by herself in Los Angeles. She is still lively considering her age. A devout member of *Seicho no ie,* a "new religion" that sprang up in the 1920s, her memory is still clear and sharp. She emigrated to the United States at the age of twenty-three with her husband, the second son of a farm family from Chiba prefecture where her family lived. After being sent to the assembly center at the Santa Anita racetrack, she and her family were relocated to the camp at Amache, Colorado. Here too during the summer dust storms blew up so suddenly the grit even got into your mouth if you didn't close the window fast enough. During the winter the cold was so sharp it cut through the body. Fumiko's husband worked as a porter cleaning toilets for $16 a month, and she worked as chief waitress in the mess hall for $19 a month. A year and a half after the loyalty test was given, the War Department sent official notification that her third son, Saburo, had died in battle in Europe. It was January with day after day of relentless cold.

"I was worried that people might hear so I couldn't even let myself go to pieces. When evening came I couldn't stand it any more so I went outside. The snow was piled up about three feet deep. I walked through the snow to a corner of the camp where people said it was dangerous to go because of the coyotes. I leaned on the wire fence and cried as hard as I could."

The evening Saburo came home after volunteering for the army he stood in front of his mother with tears of excitement in his eyes. It was his duty, he said, to do his utmost for the country of his birth. "Sabu-chan," an amiable young man whose cheeks dimpled when he smiled, seemed completely changed when he came home on leave eight months later just before he was to ship off overseas. After five days at home, he seemed strangely subdued as he boarded the evening bus to return to camp, a dufflebag slung over his shoulder.

"Next time I come I'll stay with you a long time, Mom."

That was their final farewell. Every night Fumiko said a special prayer for victory and survival in war, but she was startled when she received a package Saburo sent home just before he departed overseas. It was full of clothing he would not need at the front. In one pocket she discovered the talisman she had given him before he left.

Sitting in front of a photograph of her baby-faced son, she murmured, "They say that even strong Japanese soldiers call out their mothers' names when they die in battle."

Even though her son died in battle she felt ashamed. No one praised his volunteering as a heroic act. Pro-Japanese issei and kibei in the camp even complained openly that she and her husband had not brought up their boy properly. Other mainland veterans recall how their parents were mortified and abused as "traitors" when their sons volunteered for service.

Rudy Tokiwa understood his parents' misery and bitterness, but it was not just a simple yearning for freedom that made him volunteer. If someone had asked him how he felt, this seventeen-year-old would probably have said that his feelings were sad rather than complicated.

When Rudy was thirteen, the year he graduated from elementary school, his parents had sent him to stay in Kokubu, their hometown in Kagoshima. His father thought he would like one of his sons to inherit the land still registered in his name there. Of all the children only Rudy, the youngest, still had dual citizenship.

About three hundred Japanese American families lived in the fertile farming area near Salinas. All worked hard, even late into the night. Other local inhabitants, mainly Italian American or Portuguese American immigrants who arrived there ahead of them, were hostile toward their competitive Japanese American neighbors. Rudy's father may have been disheartened about the future.

Rudy says he was so happy he could hardly sleep the night that his father asked him whether he would go to Japan by himself. His heart pounded at the thought that when he went back to Japan no one would call him a "Jap," and everyone would have a face just like his. As Rudy had grown up his father told him time and again, "As a Japanese don't do anything shameful." Rudy thought that he was Japanese. When his boat arrived in Yokohama, tears came to his eyes when he saw Japanese faces everywhere he looked.

None of his classmates at school in Kagoshima called him a "Jap." Instead they called him "America-jin" and threw stones at him. Once they get used to me, thought Rudy, they will accept me as a Japanese. But that day never came, even after he had been in Japan for two years. After the death of his grandfather, who had lived alone with Rudy to take care of him, Rudy boarded a ship for home. The easygoing child became a wild and mischievous teenager whom nobody could control. By the time his closely cropped pate had grown out again after his return, the war began.

Although Rudy had been told he was Japanese when he was brought up, no one in Japan had thought so. He did not seem to be an American in America either. Still it was much harder to be discriminated against by people with yellow faces like his own. Even though he was rejected by some Americans there were openhearted white Americans who defended him too.

There was no hesitation in the heart of the seventeen-year-old volunteer. He left camp early in the morning while the sky was still dark. To avoid any trouble, the army had picked an early hour when few were up and about. There were only six volunteers in the truck. It was hard for Rudy to bear his mother's tears as she saw him off. His father, who had said nothing until then, spoke to him as the truck was leaving.

"As a Japanese don't do anything shameful."

The experience was much the same for all the mainlander volunteers. They left for war as if in flight, no cries of "Banzai" ringing in their ears or little American flags waving to send them off.

After the 100th Battalion returned from the Louisiana maneuvers, the fighting between the Hawaiian and mainland soldiers in the neighboring 442nd barracks began to escalate.

"Aren't you fighting the wrong enemy? What did you volunteer for?"

Many 100th veterans remember chewing out their young brothers from Hawaii. Most were fed up with the youthful rawness of eighteen and nineteen-year-olds suddenly freed from their parents' influence, able to get drunk, visit red light districts, and shoot dice for the first time in their lives.

"What soldiers do is the same all over," explained one veteran. "They drink, they gamble, and they buy women."

Life in the 100th was probably no exception. Even so, many 100th soldiers, being older and more mature, were upset by the life-style of the 442nd soldiers, whom they still thought of as children. Some disliked the regimental motto—"Go for Broke"—because it was too hotheaded. And perhaps they did not care for the gung-ho attitude of the 442nd soldiers, all of whom were volunteers, not draftees.

The streets of nearby Hattiesburg (population forty thousand), where the soldiers went on pass, were lined with bars, nightclubs, and entertainment places catering to GIs. Jim Crow still prevailed in the town. Blacks and whites sat in different parts of the bus, used different toilets, and drank from different drinking fountains. Black people were not even allowed to use the sidewalks. They had to walk in the street.

Although mainland Japanese Americans had grown up in the midst of white prejudice against people of color, their encounter with Southern racial discrimination was deeply shocking. It was all the harder for the Hawaiians to pretend not to notice. But the Hawaiians were irritated at what they regarded as the passiveness of the mainland soldiers.

Japanese Americans were treated as "white men" in Hattiesburg just as the mainland soldiers had been at Camp Robinson in Arkansas. All too clearly this was a convenient hypocrisy adopted to keep trouble from starting. Not a few of the nisei soldiers remember feeling anger at suddenly being turned into haoles. On the first Saturday Hawaiians from the 442nd went into town, duty officers at regimental headquarters were overwhelmed with complaining telephone calls from the police, city hall, and the chamber of commerce.

A number of soldiers lined up to drink from the "colored" drinking fountains. Here and there they were going into colored toilets wondering aloud whether blacks and whites defecated in different ways. And there was a group who sat in the back of the bus in seats reserved for blacks. When the bus driver angrily told them that he would not start the bus until they moved to seats reserved for whites, one Hawaiian soldier jeered, "Look at my face. It's not white, you know. It's close to black, you know."

Alcohol made some Hawaiian soldiers bold. One slugged a driver, threw him out of the bus, and then started to drive it back to camp himself. Other Hawaiians spent the night in the Hattiesburg jail after getting into fights with white soldiers.

The 100th soldiers had never caused this kind of trouble in Hattiesburg. As soon as Colonel Turner had found out that the unit was moving to the Deep South, he assembled the men and warned them about what they would face.

"If you get friendly with the Negroes the white people will be antagonized," he told them. "There is no way that you boys are going to break down the southern way of doing things for so many years. It's not a question of right or wrong. Just don't forget what you're aiming for right now."

The 100th soldiers were sorry to leave the people of Sparta.

Even though it had been agreed that the Japanese American soldiers would use the white USO Club in Hattiesburg, almost no white girls would dance with them. The relocation camp closest to Camp Shelby was Camp Jerome (also called Camp Denson), about two hundred miles to the northeast in Arkansas. When the YWCA staff at Camp Jerome heard about the problem of the Japanese American GIs at the Hattiesburg USO, they decided to organize a Camp Jerome USO.

Buses were chartered so some of the nisei girls could visit the Japanese American soldiers at Shelby, but when the call went out for volunteers only eight young women showed up. Their parents, used to the stricter morals they had learned in Japan, were reluctant to allow this kind of American-style mixing of young men and women. It was not unusual to find issei who expected their daughters to return to Japan for marriage or who did not let their daughters date at all. And many were even more worried at the prospect of exposing their daughters to roughnecks brought up on the plantations of Hawaii. The more conservative said the girls who volunteered for the USO trip must be delinquents.

Leaflets distributed by the YWCA appealed to patriotic sentiments: "The young Japanese Americans who volunteered to go to war are doing it for our families staying behind at home. Isn't it our duty to give them encouragement?" After repeated appeals the YWCA finally managed to get eighty-three volunteers. On June 19—a Saturday—they boarded two buses at seven o'clock in the morning, had lunch at Jackson, Mississippi, and arrived at Camp Shelby at two thirty in the afternoon. Dinner was to be at five thirty, followed by a dance at the service hall. Showing no fatigue from their long trip, the girls danced the night away with two hundred or so lucky Japanese American soldiers, selected by lot, each of whom had paid ten dollars to cover the cost of the trip.

Several days after the dance the 100th Battalion returned to camp. During the next two months many 100th soldiers made the trip to Camp Jerome. Among the camp inmates were the families of issei who had been arrested by the FBI when the war broke out. There were also some issei who had been held for a time at Camp McCoy.

Kenneth Kaneko, Joe Takata, and the other members of the 100th Battalion baseball team accompanied Doc Kometani on a trip to play an exhibition game at Camp Jerome on the Fourth of July. They left Shelby by bus at three thirty in the afternoon, and it was already past two in the morning by the time they arrived at Jerome.

As Kenneth Kaneko drowsily looked at the high wire fences lit by searchlights he thought to himself that it was just like an army base. The top of a wire fence around an army base, however, faced outward to protect against intrusion, while the top of the fence at Camp Jerome seemed to point inside—or at least so it seemed in the dark. Kaneko did not notice the guards armed with machine guns in watchtowers overlooking the camp. At the main gate a soldier dressed in the same uniform as the soldiers inside the bus checked them through. Inside Kaneko saw the silhouette of long low barracks stretching off into the distance.

Camp Jerome was divided into forty-six blocks, each with its own leader. There were two sections in each block, each with twelve barracks, a mess hall, toilet facilities, community bath and shower facilities, and a recreation hall. In each barrack were six units divided by plywood walls, and each unit housed one family. At its largest there were 8,497 internees in the camp. Camp Poston, where Rudy Tokiwa's family was interned, had a population of 20,000, so Jerome was somewhat smaller.

Nearby the bus carrying the team stopped in front of what looked like a large warehouse, the only lighted building in the camp. It was the camp recreation hall. Despite the lateness of the hour a group of young women rushed out of the gym to greet them as they came off the bus, shaking hands with each of them. They were the Camp Jerome USO volunteers. All at once the team members forgot their drowsiness, so happy at the friendly reception that they did not much feel like turning in to sleep on the army cots laid out in the gym.

After the game on Saturday morning, the team visited several blocks where families from Hawaii were living. They were overjoyed to see the players, including Joe Takata, who was well known from his days in the Hawaiian "semi-amateur" leagues. Many recognized Doc Kometani as a familiar face, and some broke into tears and called out greetings.

In the doorway of one barracks Yozo Yamamoto unexpectedly ran into his old Japanese-language school teacher, a strict martinet, quick to call a laggard student "Idiot!" or rap him on the knuckles. The teacher looked at Yamamoto, dressed in his U.S. Army uniform, from head to toe. Without a word of greeting, he turned away with a tight expression on his face and disappeared into his own room.

The majority of the issei had words of encouragement for the soldiers. "You're risking your lives for your country. That is your Japanese blood showing." In the mess hall the soldiers found a meal of painstakingly prepared sushi, Japanese pickles, and miso soup with homemade bean curd. For some of the teammates it was to be the last taste of home cooking.

The Japanese issei inmates broke out bottles of homemade sake hidden away under the floor and exchanged cups with the soldiers. "Keep up the good work!" they toasted. "Do your best!" As the sun began to sink, the soldiers made their way back to the recreation hall. Masaharu Takeba, whose strong legs were toughened by years of judo training, was feeling wobbly. He slipped as he crossed a plank across a ditch. Immediately the team members christened it "Takeba Bridge."

In the early evening the sky was lit up with a fireworks display. At nine o'clock there was a dance. In contrast to Camp Shelby, there were a dozen or so girls for every soldier.

On Sunday morning came a playoff game with the Camp Jerome All Stars. The crowd was even bigger than the day before. Almost four thousand people, nearly half the camp population, attended. The Jerome team, made up of young players from all over the mainland, proved to be unexpectedly tough competition. At the beginning of the game they pulled ahead with a five-run lead. Joe Takata, responding to cheers of encouragement from the Hawaiians in the crowd, hit a home run. But the young men from the camp, pouring all their cooped-up anger and energy into the game, won against the Aloha Team by a score of 19 to 10. Doc Kometani, the Aloha Team coach, was content that the crowd, cheering every movement of the players, seemed to have forgotten for a moment where they were and why.

As the players boarded their bus to return to camp after the game ended, someone began to sing *Aloha-oe,* the famous song written by Queen Liliuokalani. Strains of the sweet sad melody, a traveler's farewell to a lover before leaving on a journey, lingered as the bus pulled away.

Shortly afterward the 100th Battalion received its colors. The design combined two Hawaiian symbols—the helmet of yellow feathers worn by Hawaiian chieftains and a leaf of the *ape* tree which Hawaiians were said to have planted at their gates to ward off evil spirits. Washington suggested that something like "Be of Good Cheer" might be a better battalion motto than "Remember Pearl Harbor." But Lieutenant Colonel Turner, the battalion commander, insisted the unit would stick with the motto the troops had chosen themselves.

Washington also requested that the Japanese American soldiers be given special identification tags, but Turner refused. The Japanese Americans ought not to be treated any different from other American soldiers risking their lives in battle, he said. And when it was suggested that several kibei of questionable loyalty be removed from the unit, Turner once again refused, saying that he would take full responsibility.

On August 13 the 100th Battalion arrived at Camp Kilmer in New Jersey. Mrs. Turner and other officers' wives who had been living in Hattiesburg followed their husbands east too. They silently bade farewell to their men through the fence at Camp Kilmer.

Early on the morning of August 21 the 100th Battalion left the United States on the *James Parker,* which had once carried tourists and bananas through the Caribbean. As the ship sailed out of Staten Island, they gazed at the Manhattan skyline. It was a beautiful sight to the departing soldiers, each watching with separate thoughts, moving closer and closer to the war front. The last thing the soldiers could see was the outline of the Statue of Liberty, the symbol that had greeted a generation of immigrants arriving from Europe. Her majestic face looked down on the Japanese American soldiers of the 100th Battalion now going there to fight.

ral Mark Clark, commanding general of the Fifth Army, reviewing the troops in Italy *(courtesy of*
nal Archives)

an soldiers surrendering in Italy *(courtesy of National Archives)*

Bruyères after liberation *(courtesy of Jean-Marie Thomas)*

Townspeople of Bruyères with one of their liberators *(courtesy of Jean-Marie Thomas)*

Left, The author and Serge Carlesso at the 442nd monument, Bruyères. *Below,* Before the move into the Vosges *(courtesy of National Archives).*

Planning the attack in the Vosges *(courtesy of National Archives)*

A trooper from Company B, 100th Battalion, in the Vosges forest *(courtesy of National Archives)*

Facing another day of battle in the Vosges *(courtesy of National Archives)*

...e Vosges with members of the French Resistance *(courtesy of National Archives)*

...xhole in the Vosges *(courtesy of National Archives)*

Bivouac in the Vosges forest *(courtesy of National Archives)*

A salute to comrades killed in the rescue of the lost battalion *(courtesy of National Archives)*

:ome for a safe homecoming; Sgt. Howard Kiyama with his father, Iuemon Kiyama
rtesy of Honolulu Star-Bulletin)

Parents of a fallen Hawaii soldier in front of the family altar *(courtesy of National Archives)*

Gold Star Mothers in Honolulu *(courtesy of National Archives)*

IV

Guinea Pigs
from Pearl Harbor

THE transport carrying the 100th Battalion arrived at the port of Oran on the coast of North Africa on September 2, 1943. In the Pacific theater American forces began their island-hopping campaign with landings on the Solomon Islands and the northern coast of New Guinea. In Europe it was the eve of the Allied invasion of Italy, and tension was high.

On September 3 the British Eighth Army, which had already occupied Sicily, moved across the narrow Straits of Messina to land on the southern tip of the Italian boot. Five days later the Italian army surrendered unconditionally to the Allied forces.

On September 9 the Allied Fifth Army, made up of British and American units under the command of Lieutenant General Mark Clark, began an amphibious assault on the beaches near the port of Salerno south of Naples. Anticipating little or no resistance from the enemy, Allied leaders were confident that their Operation Avalanche would work. The German high command, however, had expected a landing at Salerno, the only beach suitable for an amphibian landing within range of Allied fighter support. Field Marshal Kesselring, the German Commander in Chief, South, concentrated his smaller force and launched six divisions in a heavy counterattack against the Allied invasion force. Contrary to Allied expectations the Salerno landing was not an avalanche but a hard-fought struggle that inflicted severe casualties on Allied forces.

At such a critical moment in the war few took special notice of a single battalion entering the port of Oran, especially an orphan unit assigned to no regiment or division. Having crossed a vast ocean the Japanese Americans found no one to take care of them.

With some difficulty the 100th finally managed to set up camp at Goat Hill, a rock-strewn mound near Fleurus, a few miles south of Oran. During the day the hot African wind blew sand into their tents and grit into their rations. At night sand fleas left bites that itched no matter how hard they were scratched. The 100th soldiers could do little but spend their days in anxious waiting. No matter how long they waited, nothing happened.

Turner and Lovell made several trips to the Mediterranean Base Section Headquarters in Oran to negotiate an assignment for the unit. One proposal was to have the 100th patrol the rail line that carried supplies from Casablanca to the Tunisian army. It was said that nearly half the materiel loaded on the train was stolen or pilfered before it reached its destination. Turner rejected that idea. After coming this far how could his boys hold their heads up back in Hawaii if they did not have an opportunity to go to the front lines?

Word soon spread among the ranking Allied officers in Oran about the battalion that wanted to go to the front. The 100th troops had a much better chance of returning home alive if they guarded supply trains against marauding Arabs. It made no sense for the battalion to refuse the offer.

Major General Charles W. Ryder, commander of the Thirty-fourth Division, thought the story interesting. He called Lieutenant Colonel Turner in to ask one question.

"Do you think you can trust them to fight?"

"Absolutely," said Turner.

The Thirty-fourth Division was a National Guard unit made up of men from Iowa, Minnesota, Nebraska, North Dakota, and South Dakota. It was the first American division sent to the European front. It had taken part in the invasion of North Africa and had won a name for itself in the attack on German-occupied Tunis. The division was nicknamed the "Red Bulls." Its shoulder patch was a red bull's head against a black background. The division motto was "Attack, Attack, Attack." The Japanese American soldiers would be proud to wear the division shoulder patch.

The day after Turner met with Ryder the 100th moved into the Thirty-fourth Division's bivouac area in the midst of a cork tree grove. They were attached to the 133rd Regiment. Major General Ryder called together all the battalion officers and noncoms. He told them that they should take the lead in battle and that the key to the safety of the troops would be their leadership.

Ryder, a West Point graduate, had combat experience as an infantry battalion commander in World War I. Even though the gray-haired general was in his fifties, his tall muscular build and personal vigor belied his age. He had the kind of leadership that seemed to say, "You want to fight? Fine, then follow me."

The reception of the 100th Battalion by the men of the 133rd Regiment was not unfriendly. Their baseball team won them quick acceptance, as it had before. With the troops cheering them on, members of the Aloha Team played for the Thirty-fourth Division in the playoffs to determine the best team stationed in North Africa. With the Thirty-fourth's lead-off hitter on second base, and Pfc Hide Yamashita on first base, Pfc Yoshinao Omiya (twenty-four years old) stood in the batter's box. Omiya seemed nervous, his narrow eyes blinking as if dazzled by the sun. In reality he was a very relaxed person, always last to leave the shower after a game. His teammates nicknamed him "Turtle." Like Masaharu Takeba, Omiya had been born in the Moiliili section of Honolulu, where his father ran a small grocery store. He had been catcher and captain of the McKinley High School championship team.

For Turtle the championship game in North Africa provided memories of glory that he never forgot the rest of his life. As he stood at bat, his brow knitted, he squinted as though he could hardly see the ball in the glare of the North African sun. The bat cracked as he swung with his powerful arms. He touched first base and kept on going. Turtle, who everyone said was the slowest member of the Aloha Team, ran as fast as he could. Happily he got the double that led the Thirty-fourth Division team to the North Africa championship.

The Allied strategy for the invasion of Italy was divided into four stages: landing at Salerno; securing the airport near the harbor at Naples; capturing key points on the roads and rail lines to Rome; and advancing north to occupy key points on the routes of retreat from Florence and the port of Leghorn.

The Salerno landing was intended to open the way to the port of Naples. It would also allow the Allies to cut off retreating German forces as they were pushed back by the British Eighth Army moving up from the south.

The Fifth Army attempted an all-out advance across the steep passes of the Sorrento peninsula to seize adjacent routes but met with heavy German resistance. The Allies were almost forced to the sea, but eventually they managed to push the enemy back. When the Germans realized that they could not drive the Allied invading army into the sea, they retreated to a line cutting across the Italian peninsula at the Volturno River about twenty miles south of Naples.

The unexpected German counterattack changed the timetable of the Thirty-fourth Division. The division moved from North Africa to join the Allied forces in Italy, arriving in Salerno on September 22 just as the Germans were destroying the harbor at Naples to gain time for their retreat north.

During the short voyage to Italy the 100th Battalion troops listened intently to the BBC broadcast about the war situation. They heard the clipped voice of the British announcer report that the Salerno coastal area had finally fallen to the Allies the evening before their landing. It had taken three weeks for the Fifth Army to capture Naples at a loss of about fifteen thousand casualties. Offshore at Salerno the troops could see the deceptively tranquil coastal hills. The sea was calm. The Thirty-fourth Division was fifteen thousand strong.

The 100th Battalion had to wait several hours for their turn to land. When it finally came the soldiers clambered down rope ladders from the troop transport to the waiting landing craft. It took several hours of more waiting until the entire battalion was loaded. As the landing craft rocked back and forth soldiers became ill from seasickness, tension, and anxiety.

The several hundred landing craft finally began to move toward the shore. As each pulled near the beach its front landing ramp went down with a resounding thud. The troops, lined up in two columns with knap-sacks on their backs and their rifles at the ready, plunged off the ramp one by one into the water.

Landing craft that made the shore without mishap were lucky. Many struck hidden rocks or sandbars. Jim Lovell's landing craft ran aground. Mindful of General Ryder's admonition to show leadership, Lovell jumped into the water without hesitation. When he discovered that the water was up to his chest, he pulled his pipe tobacco out of his breast pocket and held it above his head along with his rifle to show it was safe to move forward. Lovell was addicted to his pipe. It was hard for him to get his favorite brand from the quartermaster, so he treasured his stash of tobacco.

To soldiers still in the landing craft, the men following Lovell off the ramp suddenly seemed to disappear into the sea. Most were barely able to keep their heads above water, gasping for breath as they made their way ashore. One soldier, a full head shorter than Lovell, grabbed Lovell's arm as though his life depended on it. Together they stumbled through the surf toward the beach. Another soldier coming behind them threw himself on the beach with a sigh of relief. "What a shame for my family if I drowned here without ever seeing the enemy," he thought.

Trucks and tanks followed the men into the foaming surf. Lieutenant Colonel Turner's jeep, its motor roaring, sped forward off the landing ramp—and sank sputtering into the water. Momentum carried it forward toward the beach. The driver had cleverly provided himself with a snor-kel to breath through.

The officers and men of the 100th, water dripping from their uni-forms, marched inland about six miles to a bivouac area where they finally pitched their tents that evening. During the next two days war correspondents and journalists swarmed over them.

The 100th was only one battalion among the 190,000 Allied troops landing in Italy after the Salerno invasion. Even so it attracted journalistic curiosity. Not a few of the correspondents who came looking for stories about the battalion were clearly taken by surprise. It was hard for them to see any difference at all between the soldiers in the One-Puka-Puka and the enemy troops they had seen in the Pacific theater.

JAPANESE-AMERICANS: THEY BATTLE THE AXIS IN ITALY [*New York Times*, October 3, 1943]

AMERICAN BORN JAPS FIGHT WITH 5TH ARMY [*Washington News*, October 4, 1943]

JAPANESE HELP ALLIES TAKE BENEVENTO [*Washington Post*, October 12, 1943]

AMERICAN-BORN JAPS ENJOY WAR ON NAZIS [*St. Paul Pioneer Press*, October 20, 1943]

Newspaper reports at home sometimes quoted Sakae Takahashi, who seemed to be softening the shock for the journalists by pointing out the realities himself.

"It's more practical that we fight in the European theater, because we look so much like Japanese," he said. "There cannot be any confusion here in Europe."[1]

War correspondents covering the battalion were often surprised that these Japanese American soldiers were unconcernedly happy even on the front line.

"Their smiles brought expressions of blank amazement from veterans and officers accustomed to seeing men enter combat with tense, drawn faces," reported an Associated Press story. "These troops acted like they were going to a baseball game."[2]

Lieutenant Colonel Turner tried to use the correspondents' curiosity to do some public relations work. He emphasized to reporters that the Japanese American soldiers wanted the opportunity to show their loyalty as Americans.

"The men would rather be in the Pacific fighting the Japanese than Germans," he said.[3]

On the evening before the battalion moved to the front lines, Lieutenant Colonel Turner had Jim Lovell assemble the officers. He asked them to remember once more what it meant for the troops to be going into combat so far from their native Hawaii. Take care of "my boys," he asked them. There were a few Japanese American officers, but Turner was making his appeal to the Caucasian officers, especially the lieutenants and captains newly assigned to the unit before it left for North Africa.

On September 25 the 100th troops were loaded onto trucks. Following the rest of the division, they rode south for a while and then turned northward. As each day passed, there was less and less sunshine, more and more rain. The roads became muddy quagmires, slowing down the Allied advance. The rainy season had begun a month earlier than Allied planners had anticipated. Soldiers wrote home wondering if they were really in "Sunny Italy." The damp autumn cold, cutting through their army jackets, wrapped itself around these troopers from Hawaii.

The trucks bounced around as they moved along. The roads were full of shell craters. The convoy passed through village after village reduced to mounds of rubble. Trees were burned to their roots, the carcasses of dogs and horses lay strewn about. There was a strange smell in the air. It also came from the burned-out German tanks abandoned by the side of the road.

It was as though scenes from a movie were flashing in front of the men in the trucks. Between each grim scene came the sight of gentle green slopes and plains, vineyards intermingled with olive and orange groves. Cheers went up at the sight of ripening persimmon trees. The fruit was the color of autumn their parents missed so much. Many picked the fruit when the trucks stopped.

There was little destruction in villages in mountain valleys or on high ground. With picturesque churches at their center, they seemed pristine and untouched. But in the distance the soldiers could hear the muffled rumble of artillery fire. They could smell the gunsmoke of battles fought the day before.

It was October 25, about a month after the 100th Battalion moved north. Florence Takata, then working in the Waialua branch of the Bank of Hawaii, remembered that Monday morning well.

"I remember distinctly that it was just 8:15. As I opened the door an army chaplain came, and thinking that he was a client of the bank, I smiled and said 'Good morning' to him. The chaplain remained silent and did not utter a word. I asked him whether I could do anything for him, and he did not even smile.

"Shortly afterwards he asked me if I was Mrs. Takata. I said 'Yes.' 'Where is your husband now?' he inquired again. To which I replied, 'In North Africa.'

"The chaplain then said kindly that he would do anything for me and not to hesitate to tell him. As I began to feel uneasy I asked him if anything had happened to my husband, and requested that he tell me everything. At this point the chaplain revealed to me for the first time that War Department's notice concerning my husband's death."[4]

The young widow's Japanese name was Fusae. Her full round face was still that of an innocent young bride. The bad news the chaplain brought seemed to her like something in a bad dream. The number 29 kept whirling around in her head. Both she and her husband had been born on the twenty-ninth day of the month. She recalled how they often told each other that 29 was their lucky number. It was on the twenty-ninth that her husband Joe Takata had died in battle.

On September 29, a week after the unit had landed at Salerno, the 100th fought its first engagement. The troops awakened before sunrise at 4:00 A.M. It had been a hard night. Hardly anyone had been able to sleep in the midst of the rain and mud. Lightning streaked the sky, and thunder split the air. At 5:30 A.M. the unit left Montemarano on schedule, marching through the mud toward Chiusano. The sky was leaden with heavy rain. As the horizon lightened they were moving slowly along a back road winding along a low hill.

Major General Ryder had made a promise to the 100th Battalion officers. "No matter how easy the first battle is," he said, "the morale of the troops will never fail afterwards if you win it. I won't take special care of you otherwise, but I will let you win the first battle." He knew from his own experience that the outcome of their first battle could decide the fate of the unit.

General Ryder certainly kept his promise. The Germans had blown up bridges and roads and planted land mines at key points, but they had completely fallen back. There was not much resistance. The enemy was fighting only to gain time. It was under these circumstances that the 100th had its first taste of combat.

On the right of the 100th column was a gorge filled with trees, and on their left a slope covered with an olive grove. The men had been marching about three miles as rivulets of rain poured down their helmets. At about 10 A.M. the third platoon of Company B, led by Second Lieutenant Paul E. Froning, was in the lead, moving down the hill around an S-shaped curve in the muddy road. Suddenly there was the rattle of enemy machine-gun fire, and 75-millimeter shells began to explode all around. To the right the gorge stretched on, but to the left the Germans sat waiting in a small clearing with their sights zeroed in on the Americans.

In a letter home, one soldier described the battle. "We contacted the enemy for the first time and had the experience of being under an artillery barrage. Believe me, it sure made me dive. I never dreamed I'd have to dig a hole with my hands but I was so taken by surprise that I did.

"Some of the artillery shells whistled high overhead; others hissing in close, tremendous blast, left my joints loose and weak. . . . How I wished that this was only a nightmare, from which I would soon awaken and how I wished I were back home in Hawaii. Nobody said anything, but their wild rolling eyes showed the dreadful fear."[5]

In a moment the grassy field was covered with mud and dirt. First Lieutenant Sam Sakamoto later recalled that he pushed himself into the ground, throwing away the cigarette pack in his breast pocket to get flatter. He saw Captain Jack Mizuha unsheath his knife and desperately try to scrape a hole in the dirt. Takashi Kitaoka, the first sergeant of Company B, dug at the soil with his bare hands.

Lieutenant Young Oak Kim's Second Platoon, in the rear of Company B when the fighting began, was the first platoon to recover from the initial confusion. Kim, together with Masaharu Takeba, his assistant platoon commander, and Kenneth Kaneko, the platoon messenger, carefully made their way to the top of the hill. By then the gunfire had ceased. On the S-curve in the road they saw a rifle stuck in the ground with a helmet on it. The Caucasian commander of the Third Platoon was staring straight ahead motionless. The commander of Company B was on his knees. Doc Kometani had rushed over and was standing with his broad shoulders slumped. A medic's flag with a red cross on it hung limply in the rain. That was why the enemy had ceased firing.

Kaneko, half in a dream, thought to himself how strange war is. Then someone shouted in a stifled voice, "They got Joe Takata." The instant Kaneko heard the name of his buddy, the friend he and Takeba had played with on the Aloha Team, time seemed to stop. He did not even want to look at Takata's body.

Strictly speaking the first Japanese Americans to die in World War II were killed on January 28, 1942, a little less than two months after the Pearl Harbor attack. A small military transport vessel, the *Royal T. Frank,* sank after being torpedoed by a Japanese submarine in the waters between Maui and Hawaii islands. Almost all of the twenty-nine men who died were Japanese American soldiers from the big island returning for defense duty after basic training at Schofield Barracks.

Joe Takata was the first rifle-carrying Japanese American to fall in combat. He was also the first Japanese American to receive the Distinguished Service Cross, the second highest military medal. (Forty-seven other Japanese Americans in the European theater received this medal later on.) His citation read in part as follows:

> With complete disregard for his own personal safety, Sgt. Takata took a position in front of his squad and led it in the flanking movement. He exposed himself in an effort to locate the enemy machinegunner and was mortally wounded by an enemy artillery shell. Although he only lived a few minutes after being struck, Sgt. Takata called for his platoon sergeant in order to give him the situation.

Ever since, Joe Takata, the 100th Battalion's first war hero, has been remembered as the man who told his buddies, "I'm going first."

According to a veteran whose job it was to draft citations, most were written in a kind of boilerplate by clerks far from the scene of battle. It was difficult to find witnesses who calmly watched what their buddies were doing in the turmoil of battle. The few surviving veterans who remember Joe Takata's death speak about it only in a fragmentary way. Perhaps fragments are all they can remember from the confusion, but it is possible to put them together like a picture puzzle.

As the troops moved up the road, Sergeant Sakae Tanigawa was scouting ahead of Takata and the Third Platoon. He suddenly raised his rifle level in the air over his head. It was a signal that he had spotted the enemy.

Another scout, Pfc Toshio ("Lefty") Mizusawa, who had also hurried secretly ahead, was second in line. A friend of Takata since boyhood, when the two of them grew up on the same plantation, Mizusawa was a baseball player and got his nickname because he pitched left-handed. Mizusawa remembers that as he turned to look back at the platoon something grazed his head. Just as he became aware that he was hearing the sound of a machine gun very different from the American-made gun he was used to, a shell exploded. The enemy had hidden a self-propelled gun as well as a machine gun nest in a farmhouse about seven hundred yards ahead.

Isaac Kawasaki, the army doctor, had been warned by the troops that it was dangerous to move too far out in front. Kawasaki was somewhere in the middle of the Company B area, but he ran toward the sound of screaming voices in the midst of the enemy artillery barrage. He saw that Takata had fallen face down. His helmet had flown off. When Kawasaki turned the body face up he saw that Takata had been hit in the head and face. His breathing had stopped.

That morning Kawasaki had passed by Takata. "Hi, Doc," he had said with his usual smile. It was Kawasaki who had stuck Joe's rifle in the ground after he died.

The *Hawaii Times,* a Japanese-language newspaper in Hawaii, ran the headline: FORMER ASAHI TEAM STAR JOE TAKATA DEAD IN BATTLE.[6] The paper reported that Shigeo Takata, the second son of Hiromatsu Takata, had "died honorably on the battlefield." The picture showed Joe wearing not his army uniform but a white baseball uniform and holding a ball in his glove.

Two days after Florence Takata heard the news of her husband's death from the army chaplain, there was a simple Buddhist-style funeral ceremony. The day after the funeral the small package Joe had sent Florence from Camp Shelby before going to Africa finally arrived. Inside was his baseball uniform, already yellowing from wear even in his semi-amateur days. The package also contained letters Florence had written him. The young couple had barely had two months of married life. Joe was already in the service. The ceremony had been at Reverend Okumura's Makiki Church in downtown Honolulu, where Doc Kometani had been married earlier.

Since Joe was already in the service, even after the wedding they spent only weekends together. Soon afterward Joe had to leave the islands, and the only way Florence could communicate with him for the next year and a half was by letters to the far-off mainland. Now her letters crossed the ocean once more . . . to return to their sender. They fill a single scrapbook, pasted in neatly with their envelopes.

The young widow appeared in the news again after the funeral. She and her father-in-law visited the Waialua city office to make a contribution to the Red Cross, the Army Relief Fund, and the Navy Relief Fund. They had decided to use the money received in condolence gifts for charity rather than follow the usual Buddhist custom of holding a memorial service on the forty-ninth day after Joe's death.

As Florence told the *Honolulu Star-Bulletin,* "We know that there will be more casualties and it is our hope that other families may follow the same practice."[7] Afterward many bereaved families contributed their condolence gifts to charity.

The photograph accompanying the article showed Joe Takata's father handing over the contribution to a Caucasian city official. His face, burned dark by long years of hard work on a sugar plantation, bore an expression of unflinching pride. When Joe came back on his last leave, he had lightly tapped his father's narrow shoulders with a pat of encouragement. "Don't worry," he said gently in Japanese. "I will surely come back. You don't need to cry." He spoke in a gentle voice as if to persuade his father.

Even today the name of Joe Takata is well known to the Japanese American community in Hawaii as the first casualty of the 100th Battalion. With his death was born their first war hero. Certainly Joe had all the qualifications to become one. Whether he would have wanted to or not, he rendered a service for the Japanese Americans on the home front. Just as he had excited them on the baseball field, so too with his death in battle he gave cause for pride. "Joe died for his country," his young widow told the newspaper. She too, and Joe's father as he handed his contribution to the Red Cross, helped to brace the morale of the Hawaiian Japanese Americans, if not all Hawaii.

No matter what the citation said, some military experts say, the army would not ordinarily have awarded Joe Takata a Distinguished Service Cross given the circumstances of his death. Was Joe Takata simply convenient for the army to pick as the first Japanese American hero? If we recall that some high officials thought the organization of the 442nd was a good way to counter Japanese propaganda, quite possibly that was the case.

About an hour after Joe Takata's death another soldier in Company B was killed. When Lieutenant Kim realized that the company commander, shaken by Joe Takata's death, was unable to give orders, he rallied the Second Platoon and began to advance again with the rest of Company B following behind. Enemy machine guns continued to fire on them. Kim signaled his men to get off the road. It was too dangerous to follow the enemy straight on. Soldiers would be lost. The enemy troops were in retreat. Under the circumstances it was best to disperse and advance while keeping an eye on the enemy. The company commander, recovering from his shock, finally came forward. He ordered Kim to advance directly on the road. Without a moment's hesitation, Kim said no. The commander gave the order once more, and again, but Kim did not move his men. The company commander departed, his face red with anger. Lieutenant Colonel Turner arrived a moment later with Major Lovell and several other headquarters officers. The look on his face was severe. He told Kim to obey the company commander.

"This is an order, Kim," said Lovell, as if to intercede. Kim refused. Attacking that way was bound to sacrifice men and wasn't worthy of the name tactics, he said.

"If you don't follow the order, it will mean a court martial," said Turner.

"That's fine," said Kim evenly and turned away. Doc Kometani came running after him. Breathing hard, he looked at Kim with desperation in his eyes.

"You may be right," he said, speaking rapidly. "But this is an important time for the 100th Battalion. It's the first day at the front. We don't want to have anything dishonorable like a court martial. Be patient—just for today. Please, I'm asking you, Kim."

Kometani had just seen Joe Takata, one of his beloved baseball players, die. Kim might have refused the request from anyone else, but he did not feel that he could argue with Doc.

"Tell the battalion commander that if anyone is killed, it will be on his conscience," he told Kometani. Kim exchanged a quick glance with his assistant platoon commander, Takeba, who had been standing behind him with a worried look on his face. Then he took command of the platoon again. As they came to another curve in the road a rumbling noise shook the ground. Kim heard a sound that cut through the air beside his ear. Enemy tanks had opened fire.

Looking in their direction Kim at once noticed a grove of chestnut trees standing at an advantageous point in the terrain difficult for the enemy to fire on. After calculating when the next enemy round would hit, Kim waved to his men and began running in the direction of the enemy. This was an automatic reaction he had drilled into his men persistently during training even though the men disliked him for it. It was a way of giving the soldiers self-confidence from the first day.

Without a second thought, Kim's men ran frantically after him. Racing to stay alive, Takeba and Kaneko moved faster than they ever had run toward first base. Their feet flew across the ground, kicking up dirt as they went. Just as they reached the chestnut trees and fell to the ground gasping for breath, fire flashed from the muzzles of the enemy tank guns.

As the men in the platoon turned back to where they had come from, they saw several of their buddies being mowed down by enemy fire. Only the last squad had not followed after Kim. They had jumped into a shallow ditch. That had been a decision of the corporal commanding the squad, who had been afraid to run in the direction of the enemy. Seven men were wounded and one died.

The soldier who died was Keichi Tanaka. In contrast to Joe Takata his name is remembered by almost no one, even among the 100th Battalion veterans. Tanaka, whose birthday was only two months different from Joe Takata's, was also twenty-four years old. Raised at Waimanalo on the eastern coast of Oahu, he had gone to McKinley High School. But Tanaka had not made a name for himself in sports. He was an ordinary young man, soft-spoken and clear-eyed, who got a job after graduation as an office worker for an automobile company. He was drafted about the same time as Takata, a month before the Pearl Harbor attack, and he had received his basic training with Joe at Schofield Barracks.

Tanaka seems to have had clear premonitions of his death. The evening before he was killed, he went out of his way to pay a visit to his old friend Francis Shinohara in the Fourth Platoon. "I think I'm going to die," he murmured. In his usual quiet way he asked Shinohara to visit his father and mother after he got back to Hawaii.

On the morning of his death he also said good-bye to Keijiro Umebayashi, a friend in a different squad. "So long, Ume," he said. "I guess I won't see you again." Umebayashi, startled, took the remark as a joke since Tanaka had said it so casually. Tanaka gave his cigarette box to Pfc Jesse Hirata, one of his fellow squad members, and his lighter to Charles Tanaka. Pfc Hirata was moving forward in front of Tanaka when the enemy shell explosion knocked him down. In the next moment he saw Keichi Tanaka's head blown away.

Keichi always spoke to his mother, a picture bride from Hiroshima, in Japanese. She sent him letters repeating over and over, "Please come back alive. Even if you don't win any medals, just live a long life." Keichi's friends remember how he worried about his mother. All that she had after his death was a Purple Heart, given to any soldier injured on the battlefield.

At the beginning of October, just after they had left a rest area, the 100th Battalion troops first heard the sound of enemy rockets they called the "Screaming Meemies." The chilling roar ran through the body like a jolt of electricity. Jim Lovell got hit in the right leg by one of them. He was sent back by jeep to a hospital in the rear area. After lying in the corridor for two hours awaiting his turn, he was finally taken to the operating room. Several days later Lieutenant Colonel Turner came to visit him.

"To tell the truth I've come to say good-bye," he said quietly.

The enemy had mounted a strong counterattack at Dragoni, and again at Alife to the north of San Angelo. Taking advantage of the terrain, they attacked the Allied advance as it moved along the ridges of the countless small valleys in the area. Machine guns hidden in stone farmhouses or hillside vineyards took a heavy toll. In the space of three days the 133rd Regiment lost 59 men killed and 148 men wounded. Among them were 21 dead and 67 wounded from the 100th Battalion.

Right after that, regimental headquarters had ordered Turner to send out a platoon-sized patrol. The Caucasian second lieutenant who led the patrol reported back that there was no sign of the enemy. Another unit moving forward on the basis of the report found the enemy waiting for them. Turner was immediately ordered to the rear on the ground that he needed a rest. It was he who had to take responsibility for this false report.

As he himself probably realized, it was about time for Turner to go. He was too old to serve as a battalion commander. While at Camp McCoy there was already some concern about his blood pressure, and there were those in Washington with reservations about him.

Even now Lovell says that he cannot forget Turner the night Joe Takata was killed. As he sat by the campfire his face suddenly seemed old. He had hardly slept since the day before, and his face was dark with fatigue. The first of his men had died. Turner seemed to have been beaten down by a reality over which he had no control. Lovell told Turner it might be best for him to go to the rear with the company that was going into reserve the next day. He would take care of everything. "Would you do that?" asked Turner.

Then more of Turner's men were wounded, and more of them were killed. The cloud never left his face. The problem was not simply that

Turner was forty-nine years old. He was not a suitable front-line commander. Just before the unit had departed for overseas he had suddenly changed all the company officer assignments. And he often had made questionable personnel changes. But more than anything else Turner was too emotional about the life and death of his men. The battalion had already begun to slip out of Turner's hands, everyone going his own direction. What the 100th Battalion needed at this point was a professional commander who gave firm orders on the battlefield, who knew about tactics, and who was physically strong.

Turner probably had done all he could for the 100th Battalion. He had not given an inch on the honor and rights of the Japanese American unit, and he had opened the way for them to go to the front lines. When the battalion needed a spokesman, he had been a splendid one.

But Turner, a member of the haole elite in Hawaii, did not meet his men on their own terms or try to think the way they did, a knack that Jim Lovell seemed to have. To the soldiers Turner was of the elite. Even so he had high regard for the ability and spirit of the Japanese American troops and had wanted to be their battalion commander. In his own way he loved the Japanese American soldiers. The troops could barely control their emotions as they bid farewell to the "Old Man." His hair was noticeably whiter than it had been when the battalion was just getting started.

One Japanese American soldier wrote home about the war:

> When you read that a town was taken, or a certain hill was taken, remember that in the process of that accomplishment lives of fine fellows were lost, and also, that during this accomplishment for the participants, life was a horrifying massacre. You lose your buddies—fellows with whom you laughed, ate, slept, sweated. They grow to be more than mere buddies. They become blood relations to you and they die before your eyes—not a pleasant, natural death, but an unimaginable kind of mutilation mixed with groans and prayers ending with a gurgling last breath. Only five minutes ago you might have been laughing with that buddy of yours.[8]

The Volturno River flows from northeast to southwest across the Italian peninsula and runs into the sea south of Naples. It was the first position prepared by the German army to repel the Allied forces pursuing them.

On the afternoon of November 3, 1943, the same day American forces began their landings at Bougainville and on the Gilbert Islands in the Pacific theater, Colonel Carley L. Marshall, commander of the 133rd Regiment, assembled his battalion commanders to explain the plan for a river crossing that night. The Third Battalion was to move across first and then enter the town of Santa Maria Olivetto. The First Battalion was to follow and take Hill 550 northwest of the town. The 100th Battalion —really serving as the Second Battalion of the 133rd—was to cross the river a little downstream and then protect the left rear of the First Battalion. The 100th would be on the division's extreme left flank.

The whole area was covered with olive groves. The enemy was skillfully concealed everywhere, using tanks and self-propelled guns to defend the valleys. The Germans were trying to buy as much time as possible holding the line at the Volturno while consolidating the Gustav Line, a long-term defensive position fifteen miles to the north.

The Fifth Army had launched an earlier attack on the German position along the Volturno but had been checked. A renewed attack was delayed by bad weather, heavy rain, and the destruction of roads and bridges. This time an entire army corps was to launch a simultaneous assault along the front. The attack was to begin with a steady artillery bombardment across the river between 11:00 and 11:30 P.M. At precisely midnight the whole Thirty-fourth Division began its advance. The 100th Battalion jumped off through a muddy delta where the Sava River joined the Volturno. Company E and Company B were the first to ford the river. They made their way across in total darkness, at some places hanging onto ropes stretched across the river, at other places with no help at all. The river was somewhere between chest-deep and waist-deep. The water was freezing cold and the current was swift. According to reconnaissance reports, the northwest bank of the river was covered with minefields.

Suddenly the area was lit by the flash of exploding shells. As water and mud showered down on them the troops clung to the ropes in desperation. Friendly artillery, misjudging the distance, had fired a barrage into the river just in front of them. Enemy self-propelled guns returned the fire. The casualties mounted.

When they reached the other side of the river the troops ran into minefields among the olive groves and vineyards. There were about thirty more casualties. Company B was in the lead, with Kim's Second Platoon the forwardmost unit. The company was advancing as fast as it could toward Route 85, thought to be three or four miles from the river. They followed a small path turned muddy by the rain. After advancing fifty to a hundred yards, orders to stop came from the company commander in the rear. A few minutes later he came up to talk with Kim.

"Aren't you going in the wrong direction?" he said.

"No, it's not the wrong direction," replied Kim.

"It's not this way on the map."

"According to the map it's this direction."

That evening before the jump-off the company commander had gone with Kim to battalion headquarters to look at the only terrain map in the battalion's possession. The company commander, an ROTC man from the University of Hawaii, was the oldest of the nisei officers. Even though he had spent a long time in supply and was not familiar with infantry tactics, he had been assigned as commander of Company B just before the 100th left for overseas. He did not have much time to get to know his subordinate officers, and that probably made things difficult for him. (Incidentally the only two officers who stayed with Company B when Turner made these personnel changes were Kim and First Lieutenant Ernest Tanaka, the veteran of the combat dog training project.)

The company commander had already had a fracas with Kim over tactics on the first day of battle when Joe Takata had been killed, but he seems to have appreciated Kim's ability to read a map. Kim had only a few minutes to look at the map at battalion headquarters, but even so its image remained in his head as clear as a photograph.

The dark was so thick it was hard to see faces distinctly. Kim refused to concede that he was wrong. The company commander's voice was rough.

"I'm not going to let you lead the way," he told Kim.

Another platoon was assigned the point position. It moved off in the direction opposite from where Kim had been headed. Having no other choice, Kim's platoon followed at the tail end of the company. Suddenly the sound of mines exploding rent the misty night air. The lead platoon had run into the middle of a minefield. There were seven casualties. The company commander ordered all officers to advance to his position. They moved forward slowly using mine detectors to feel their way forward. One misstep might mean a life blown away.

The wounded troops in the point platoon lay where they had fallen. The company commander, kneeling on the ground, raised his head and asked, "Is there anyone who knows the way?"

None of the other officers had seen the terrain map. Kim said nothing. Finally the company commander called out to him. If Kim agreed to take the point position again, the company commander promised, he would not overrule him again. Just to be on the safe side, Kim turned to First Lieutenant Tanaka and the others. "You are witnesses," he said. Kim ordered his men to go back the way they had come, looking only at the footprints of the soldier ahead. They reached the original path they had been following earlier. After moving forward for a while they could see a narrow road. But once again orders to stop came from the rear. It was the company commander again.

"That is our objective. Go to the left," he said.

"No, that is not the road," replied Kim. "It's one more ahead. There should be an olive orchard in between." He reminded the company commander he had broken his promise not to interfere.

Kim went out to look at the road in front of them. There was an embankment made of piled-up stones on the opposite side, about seven feet high and separated from the road by a hedge. He climbed up a narrow path only wide enough to accommodate one person at a time.

Standing on top of the embankment, Kim pointed ahead with his finger, "It's there." Just as the company commander raised his head behind him, a bullet grazed Kim's arm. There was an enemy position not more than ten feet away. Kim immediately leaped into a shallow ditch that lay between the hedge and the embankment. The company commander rolled back down to the road. Suddenly someone shouted an order in the dark.

"Open fire!"

The soldiers waiting to advance along the road could not see the hedge in the dark, but they started firing in its direction. The only person they had any chance of hitting was Kim. He desperately pressed himself flat against the ground until his lungs creaked. At the same time he could not help feeling how senselessly funny it was. The firing ceased. Then he heard a shout, "Fix bayonets! Charge!" In the next moment a battle cry resounded in Kim's ears. Suddenly he heard the trampling feet of soldiers rushing forward.

Kenneth Kaneko fumbled as he fixed the bayonet on the end of his rifle. Hardly conscious it was his own voice, Kaneko let out a yell and charged ahead. When he heard the sound of the voices suddenly in the dark, someone in another company at a distance from Company B said, "It's a banzai charge." American soldiers in the Pacific had given that name to the near fanatical attacks of Japanese troops.

The first thing the charging troops encountered was the hedge. Kaneko, confused and upset by the darkness, could not figure out what was going on. His bayonet was caught in the thicket. He managed to pull it loose and plunged on, sticking it into the stone embankment.

The order to charge had been given by a flustered sergeant in Kim's platoon who thought Kim might have been killed. When the fixed-bayonet charge began someone had given an order to fire. It was a miracle that none of the advancing soldiers had been wounded, let alone killed. Reports of the engagement later were greatly exaggerated in the press. Many national publications ran articles on the 100th Battalion's "banzai charge," and the Japanese American community in Hawaii stirred with excitement. Like all soldiers in all wars, veterans who knew what really went on recall the battle with sarcastic grins.

In the midst of the confusion Kim finally figured out where the enemy was and tossed a grenade in their direction. Takeba, the assistant platoon commander, and Kaneko, the platoon messenger, came running up to find out if everything was all right. Kim answered, "It's okay." Peering into the dark, he realized they were in the midst of an olive grove. At the spot where he thought the grenade had landed a huge broken branch was hanging down. Kim felt uneasy about it.

As he looked closer he saw the soles of some boots. He gave them a kick. A German soldier suddenly jumped up with both hands held high. So did two other enemy soldiers nearby. They were the first prisoners that the 100th Battalion captured at the front by themselves.

The company commander insisted on going in the direction he thought correct. But Kim was stubborn. Hadn't the company commander made a promise? Finally he yielded and told Kim to lead the way.

Advancing through the olive groves, Kim's platoon finally reached their objective, the road junction. They waited for the rest of the company, but no one arrived. The company commander had led them off in a different direction.

Kim asked Kaneko, "Can you go find the company commander and come back?"

"Okay," answered Kaneko casually. He had come by the route only once in the dark. Retracing their steps was not easy, but Kaneko returned with the company commander and the rest of the troops in tow.

Since he was little Kaneko had played Hawaiian-style "barefoot football." If a player did not move forward, he could be tackled from the side, or he could fall back a little. In a split second he had to decide whether to throw the ball or run with it. For the first time Kaneko began to realize that war was a kind of football game too except that one's life depended on it.

The Fifth Army's overall attack on the German position at the Volturno River line began the next morning. The 100th Battalion found themselves in front of Hill 550, the objective of the assault. There were ditches where the advancing troops could conceal themselves, but it would take too much time to move in daylight while trying to avoid enemy observation. The only choice was to circle to the left, move alongside the hill, and attack from the flank.

As Company E was moving to the left through a dry creek bed, they saw a figure approaching from the other direction. Just as they were about to fire on him, they saw he was an American. His name was Thompson, he said, and he was a paratrooper. He had left his unit in Naples to look for a little excitement. He had come from the direction of Pozzilli, where the 100th Battalion was headed, and reported that the town was deserted but heavily mined. He said he knew a way of getting to the high ground without going through the town.

With this strange Caucasian soldier as their guide, the 100th Battalion made their way forward slowly, keeping their heads down. The battalion had been ordered by Colonel Marshall, commander of the 133rd, to take

Hills 590, 600, and 610 to the left of the First Battalion, whose attack on Hill 550 had been repulsed. When they had reached a spot about half a mile from the base of the hills, a jeep carrying an American armored division major came speeding up a nearby road, approaching the 100th's column.

It was an inopportune moment. Enemy shells began to rain down in the direction of the jeep. Two German planes suddenly appeared in the sky and swooped down to strafe the area. There were twenty casualties in the ranks of the 100th, but the armored division major escaped without a scratch.

When the lead unit finally reached the base of the hills they were assigned to take, they discovered the olive groves were filled with minefields. Booby traps with trip wires were set everywhere. It was about 4 P.M. so there was still enough light to see. Hoping to get the entire unit across the mined area before dark, Mits Fukuda's platoon, which had been on point, moved forward quickly looking for mines. After they had advanced some distance, the sound of a mine explosion rent the air, followed by several more.

Captain John Johnson, who had succeeded Lovell as battalion executive officer, was hit in the leg. On his good leg he hopped back to the aid station, but the wound did not prove to be serious. The commander of Company B, badly hurt, sat squatting on the ground with blood pouring from his arm. He was an older nisei whose upbringing had been more Japanese than most. He depended on Kim a good deal, but he found it hard to put up with the impertinent young lieutenant who did not seem to care much about rank. Both were stubborn men, always at loggerheads, but they parted company with dignity. Before he went to the rear on his own legs, the company commander handed Kim his .45 caliber pistol. A champion marksman during his ROTC days, he always carried it as a good luck amulet.

Several hours later a radio message came to Fukuda that Company D, bringing up the rear of the column, could not move through the minefields. Thompson, the AWOL paratrooper who had been guiding the column, offered to go back to the minefield again. Minutes later he stepped on a mine and was blown to pieces. Not even his dog tags could be found. In fact, according to Fukuda, no one was really sure if his name was Thompson. Afterward a story circulated that he had been a German spy disguised as an American soldier. When inquiries were made to the paratroop unit, it is said that no one by that name was in the unit.

That evening Kim's platoon reached the high ground, bringing up the rear of Company B. It was already hard to see the outline of the hills. As soon as the company was in combat position, Major James Gillespie, who had replaced Turner as battalion commander, ordered Kim to come over. There was an enemy machine gun on the left where friendly forces were supposed to be. He ordered Kim out on patrol. Only two squads were left in Kim's platoon. The new company commander had borrowed one of Kim's squads to secure his own position.

Kim set off from the battalion with his two squads. Stealthily they crossed over the next ridge and moved toward Hill 610, one of the battalion objectives. Kaneko moved tightly with Takeba, and the rest of the men with them.

It was a strange night. The wind blew steadily, and the moon darted in and out behind low-lying clouds that scudded across the sky. Tree branches and underbrush whistled eerily as they bent before the wind. Their ghostly silhouettes stood out against the moon as Kim and his men moved swiftly through them.

There were voices at the top of the rise, perhaps those of seven or eight men. Kim's men hurled six or seven grenades in their direction. They heard stomach-churning screams after the explosions as they raced to the next ridge. Takeba usually followed behind Kim. Since Takeba had practiced judo since he was little, he had exceptional reflexes. Like Kim, he moved at the blink of an eye. He was also calm when making judgments.

As he was making his way through the brush, Kim suddenly saw ahead of him a German soldier with a machine gun belt in his hands. The German dropped the belt and began to reach for the rifle on his back. Kim pulled the trigger on the "good luck" pistol the company commander had given him but the gun jammed. Sensing this with his fingertip, Kim somersaulted to his left. Takeba fired over Kim's shoulder. It was perfect timing, almost instinctive. The bullet missed, but the enemy soldier quickly disappeared.

The platoon could find no place to conceal themselves near the top of the hill, but Kim kept moving forward. When they were near the top, Kim signaled Takeba to stop. "There must be a machine gun nest somewhere around here," he whispered. If the Germans were following their usual pattern, and they seemed to follow rigid rules and discipline in everything they did, Kim's sixth sense told him that there was likely to be a concealed machine gun emplacement nearby.

The platoon was split in two. One group led by Kaneko circled behind the spot where Kim thought the machine gun nest was. The other led by Kim and Takeba moved straight ahead toward it. Kim parted a tall bush and found himself almost nose-to-nose with a German soldier, just as he had thought. Even for Kim it was a shock to stumble right on top of the enemy. The German soldier must have been even more startled. His mouth dropped as he saw an Oriental face appear suddenly before his eyes. In a choked voice, he said two German words that seemed to be the evening password.

Remembering that his "good luck" pistol was jammed, Kim immediately twisted his body to one side. Takeba again fired from behind. Just as one German soldier reached toward the machine gun, Kaneko and his men, who had circled around from behind, leaped into the enemy dugout. They took seven prisoners.

When Kim and his men finally got to the top of the hill, they heard a rattling sound of something moving. The fracas at the machine gun nest had alerted the enemy that the Americans were getting close. They were rushing to pull out. Kim ordered two of his men to take the seven captured prisoners to the rear. That left him with only fifteen men. Telling them not to make the slightest movement, he had the platoon hide alongside a narrow mountain path. About thirty-five German soldiers, drawn up in an orderly column, came marching by, but Kim let them pass. His orders had been to clear out the machine gun nest, and he did not run any risks where he knew there might be casualties.

Kim's relationship with the troops had changed since the first battle. When no one else was able to make a decision in the midst of the panic, Lieutenant Kim remained calm and led his soldiers quietly. He read a situation quickly and gave orders without raising his voice. He did not risk his soldiers' lives for his own glory. He seemed to worry about the safety of his men, and for that reason he often did not make concessions to orders from his superiors. The soldiers, risking their lives on the battlefield, realized that. When the pressures were extreme, and all pretense was quickly exposed, the troops saw Kim's true character come to the fore.

It was clear that some 100th officers were not willing to risk their lives for the Japanese Americans. They never put themselves in an exposed position out front even though in training they spoke with more bravado than anyone else. The Hawaiian soldiers were direct, often to the point of crudeness. To these officers they would say in pidgin, "You go, me go," and then refuse to budge. On the other hand, when they did trust an officer, they trusted him completely.

After the battalion reached the battlefront, the officers were with their troops twenty-four hours a day, eating and sleeping with them for the first time. They ate the same rations, and they slept in the same mud. Some officers tried to use their privileges of rank to look out for their own interests, but Kim was not one of them.

"GI Kim," disliked by the troops for his rigorous training methods, had now become "Samurai Kim." Together with Lieutenant Sakae Takahashi, who also showed exceptional leadership ability, he was one of the most respected officers in the battalion. Kim's attitude had changed too. Here on the battlefield, where everyone wore the same sweaty muddy uniform day after day, he understood how useless the spit-and-polish discipline was. What difference did it make to the battlefield soldier how shiny his shoes were or how long his hair was? Kim came to ignore that sort of thing.

This was not the first time that Kim had been ordered out on night patrol. Jim Lovell noticed from the first that Kim had some special knack for them. Most men hated to go on night patrol, but Kim never hesitated. He would disappear into enemy territory like a wisp of smoke. Choosing his words carefully, Lovell recalled that Kim was "an unusual fellow, somehow different from both the Caucasians and the Japanese American soldiers, almost as though he had nine lives."

One of Lovell's company commanders had no sense of direction at all and always ended up going the wrong way. Kim was just the opposite. When he looked at a scale map, he seemed to be able to visualize the terrain as it really was. Perhaps it had something to do with his sixth sense. Even today Lovell does not understand exactly how Kim did it.

Takashi "Kit" Kitaoka, the first sergeant of Company B and today a retired Honolulu judge, was the only noncom on friendly speaking terms with Kim during the training at Camp Shelby. Before the war he had gotten his law degree at the University of Texas. When drafted, he was thirty-one, older than most of the soldiers, but a gregarious and open person.

Although Kitaoka had to stand between Kim and the troops, who did not like him, he admired Kim's personality. But he felt there was something strange, beyond understanding, in Kim's actions on the battlefield. Kim seemed to know no fear. From the beginning Kim never wore a helmet. When Takahashi and others warned him about it, Kim brushed them off saying that he could not think straight with anything heavy on his head, and besides he did not like wearing a helmet since it attracted the enemy's attention on patrols. Instead he wore a dark brown government-issued knit cap pulled down over his head. It was never hard to spot that knit cap among a group of helmeted soldiers.

When the Japanese American soldiers had left Camp Shelby, many carried amulets called *senninbari* that their mothers or wives had given them. These were cloth towels into which a thousand women had stitched little round balls of red thread. In one corner a nickel was sewn into the folded cloth. Japanese soldiers who went to the front in the Pacific also carried these good luck towels. Instead of a nickel a five sen piece with a hole in the middle was sewn into the cloth. There was a kind of magical pun involved: *"Shisen o koete, gosen ni naru."* Depending on which characters were used to write it, *shisen* could mean either "four sen" or "the death line." The idea was that if you went beyond "four sen" ("the death line") you got "five sen." Hence the five sen piece was sewn into the cloth. How many Japanese Americans could have understood this magical pun, though?

When a soldier got a *senninbari* he usually stuffed it into the bottom of his knapsack with a sheepish smile. But when he got to the battlefront, sooner or later he tied it around his waist. Even the soldiers who did not have *senninbari* often carried protective amulets their families had sent them from the Honganji Buddhist Temple in Hawaii.

Mits Fukuda and Sakae Takahashi are among the very few who say they carried neither a protective amulet nor a *senninbari*. But even Fukuda, who did not smoke, always carried in his left breast pocket a pipe given him by a friend before going overseas, and Takahashi always kept an army-issued Bible.

Kim never carried anything. Perhaps the knit cap was his good luck piece. According to army regulations, a soldier was to be fined fifty dollars for not wearing his helmet. Turner, who was usually sticky on the matter, made an exception of Kim and ignored his cap.

Some soldiers said with bravado, "When I'm going to die, I'm going to die. If the bullet's got my name written on it, there's nothing I can do. No need to get upset about it." But when the going got rough they pulled their helmets down and hugged the ground. They dug their foxholes deep and did whatever else they could to protect themselves. All the soldiers, whether they had signed up to show their true loyalty to the United States or had been drafted with no choice but to go into the service, had but one thought. They did not want to die.

Kim never dug a foxhole, even when he went to sleep. He had dug a hole two or three times, but after that he simply stretched himself out on the ground. Since Takeba and the other platoon members worried about his safety, they often dug a foxhole for him, but Kim rarely used it.

Kim was really expressing in deed, not in word, the idea that "if you're going to die, you're going to die." In the eyes of Reverend Yost, the battalion chaplain, it seemed a saucy kind of bravado that defied understanding.

If Kim had had any anxieties at all, it was before the first engagement. He feared what his own reaction would be on the battlefield. Would he get cold feet? Would he panic? He could not guess. He only wanted to do nothing that would shame him for the rest of his life. Perhaps he was conscious of his position as the only Korean American in the midst of a Japanese American unit. Or to put it a little differently, until the first battle he was made conscious of that position by some of the Japanese American soldiers. But in the first engagement he learned how to master his own nerves. In the midst of the total confusion, as though hell had exploded on earth, he behaved with his emotions under control. It was as though another human being, emerging out of his body and completely cut off from his emotions, was gazing steadily at his actions. Kim felt he was judging what was happening from afar.

Perhaps Kim broke out of his shell at that moment. In the midst of enemy fire, there was neither white nor black nor yellow. For the first time since his birth he was released from the skin color which had bound him so tightly. For the first time he walked freely as an independent human being. He must have felt that even more strongly for having been raised on the American mainland.

Kim was not the only one to have that experience. There were others, like Richard Oda, a sergeant in the 442nd, who said, "On the battlefield I recovered my manhood." Though they did not realize it, prejudice had stunted their feelings for a long time. Now they learned that skin color had nothing to do with a man's humanity or masculinity.

That night Kim's platoon returned to a point just in front of the battalion's position on Hill 600. Kim went to report to the battalion commander, Major Gillespie, who had been with the 100th since its days at Camp McCoy. Gillespie had long suffered from ulcers, and after he took command of the battalion his stomach had gotten worse. When Kim reported about his patrol, Gillespie was bent in pain, just getting over an attack. Kim said he thought his unit ought to stay and occupy the high ground where the German machine gun nest had been. The battalion commander nodded his head with approval as he listened to Kim's report, then groaned. He issued no order. Kim returned to his men who were waiting on the edge of a ridge with no place to take cover. If the platoon did not move before light, they would be in danger.

Takeba suggested digging stones out of the middle of piles left by farmers after clearing their fields. The stones were rather large, but by sharing the work the platoon pulled them free. Some men climbed into the holes that were left. Others hid themselves in the low-lying brush, waiting silently for dawn to come. The night was cold and frost began to settle on the ground.

As Kim had warned, the Germans attacked as the sky began to lighten. The battalion moved out to counterattack, but after an hour visibility disappeared when the enemy laid down a smoke screen. The men readied their rifles, waiting for the enemy soldiers to appear suddenly. The Germans had already infiltrated the area between the 100th Battalion and the First Battalion. At about 9:00 A.M. enemy soldiers emerged out of the smoke screen on a ridge to the south of the 100th's position and on its right flank. It was the high ground Kim and his platoon were supposed to have occupied. A party of about seventy German soldiers was moving carefully down the hill.

What were Kim and his men doing? Why weren't they fighting back? Were they still asleep after getting back so late the previous night? . . . In the forwardmost position Takahashi and the men of Company F were jittery. Battalion headquarters on the opposite slope gave no orders since they did not know what Kim was doing.

Kim and his men had already moved to the top of the ridge, behind the Germans who were marching down it. "Open fire!" shouted Kim. Struck from behind, the enemy troops tumbled to the ground. Those trying to escape into the valley were captured by the main force of the 100th waiting there. As Kim walked down the slope to look at the writhing enemy wounded, a German soldier who had been lying immobile on the ground suddenly sprang up, his back drenched with blood. He began to run. After two or three steps he fell backward, both hands spread out. The light machine gun he had been carrying started to fire when it struck the ground. A stray bullet hit Kim, who felt as though someone had swung a baseball bat at his thigh. He stumbled to the ground. Acting as though nothing were wrong, he stood up and started moving down the hill giving orders to his men and rounding up the Germans who stood up with their hands raised. One of his men, noticing the blood on Kim's thigh, quickly put a tourniquet on it, but Kim felt no pain at all.

The wounded Germans were brought to a flat place and laid out on the ground. One kept sobbing. Takeba and several other men gathered around. They took off his helmet and brushed back the blond hair from his forehead. A few minutes before the soldier had fallen under their fire, and now they were trying their best to help him. Blood was spurting from his chest and stomach. The blanket they spread over him was immediately soaked red. There was no way to save him.

The German's body was husky, but his face was that of a child. He kept looking up as if to ask for something. His lips moved as he tried to say something in a barely audible voice. His hands moving weakly seemed to point to his chest. Kim pulled a leather wallet from the soldier's chest pocket. Inside was a photograph of the soldier's smiling mother and father. He held it in front of the soldier's blue eyes, but they could no longer see anything. The American soldiers stood stock-still. A silence enveloped them, engraving the moment in their memories.

The troops rarely saw the faces of their German adversaries on the battlefield. All they usually saw was figures moving in the distance. And often the enemy was one they could not see at all, firing shells from far off. The Japanese American soldiers tried to ignore the fact that the enemy soldiers were human beings like themselves, with faces and eyes, with flesh and blood, with feelings and families. It was better not to know that they too were suffering the same inhumane conditions, that they too were forced to the same limits of endurance. On the battlefield it was better to point a gun at an enemy without a face. This was the first and last time that Kim saw the face of his enemy.

Lieutenant Ernest Tanaka, also in Company B, came forward to replace Kim. When he saw the accumulated blood dribbling out of Kim's shoe, he called for a stretcher. Kim ignored it. Without uttering a word he walked by himself back toward the aid station. Silently Takeba and

Kaneko watched his figure recede in the distance. The next morning Kim was sent to a hospital in Naples.

Kenneth Kaneko was wounded in the chest several hours after he saw off the wounded Kim. Shrapnel from a German shell hit him as he was napping in the shade of a tree, and also got his best friend, Yozo Yamamoto, a baseball player from Company E, in the leg. Many other members of the Aloha Team had also become casualties. As Doc Kometani wrote to Joe Takata's young widow, "You will be consoled also to the fact that Joe has not gone alone. There were many of his friends together with him and there are some ballplayers there too."[9]

Sergeant Masayoshi Miyagi, the best hitter on the Aloha Team, was in the same platoon as Yozo Yamamoto. He was lost as the platoon was crossing the Volturno River in the dim early morning under enemy shelling. His body had been swept away by the swift current and could not be found. He left behind a bride he had married just before leaving from Honolulu. Handsome Pfc Shigeo Igarashi, another Aloha player, later buried by his widowed mother at the Taiyoji Buddhist Temple at Waipahu on the island of Oahu. Sergeant Daniel Wada, an Aloha Team member who had not gotten to play much, sent his two-year-old son a fifty-dollar war bond that arrived a few days after his wife received official notice of his death in battle.

Pfc Turtle Omiya, a member of Second Platoon, Company D, who had starred in the North Africa series, later reproached God over and over again that he had not died when a German mine called a "Bouncing Betty" went off nearby. The mine shot up in the air, exploded, and rained a hot spray of shrapnel in every direction. The radioman in Turtle's platoon was killed instantly, but the startled soldier who stepped on the mine, safe under the umbrella pattern of spray, received only a grazing wound. Just behind him Lieutenant "Spark" Matsunaga, the platoon leader, was immobilized by a serious wound in the leg.

When the mine exploded, Turtle was carrying a machine gun tripod, he says. He thought he saw the soldier in front of him stop suddenly. The moment he looked up, his brows knitted as usual, he saw a blue flash. A tiny piece of shrapnel hit him. Ordinarily it would have caused only a slight wound, but it grazed his eyebrow and struck his right eye directly. Turtle covered his face with both hands. The shock affected his left eye, too, and eventually he lost all sight.

On October 21, 1943, just before the Volturno River crossing, Secretary of War Stimson announced that the 100th Battalion had fought its first engagement. The newspapers carrying the news quoted the words of General Mark Clark, commander of the Fifth Army. As an AP dispatch put it, "This Army rang with praises today for the 'guinea pigs from Pearl Harbor'—a unit of American infantry composed almost entirely of men of Japanese descent. . . . Officers who witnessed the action were unrestrained in their admiration. They declared they never saw any troops handle themselves better in their first trial under fire."[10] The dispatch reported that the 100th Battalion passed the test of Japanese American loyalty.

The 100th had passed that test with high marks. The Japanese American soldiers from Hawaii had volunteered to go to the front instead of remaining behind the lines as a labor battalion. They never once retreated on the battlefield. They took every objective. And their adeptness at learning and their morale were outstanding. For the first time the 100th troops were permitted to wear the "Red Bull" insignia of the Thirty-fourth Infantry Division.

But the 100th still remained an orphan battalion. It had an organizational structure that allowed it to perform the functions of a regiment. This meant that the battalion had to provide all its own supplies—from weapons and uniforms through rations and medicine. Shortly after the unit arrived at Camp McCoy, Jim Lovell, the executive officer, had been called to Washington, where he was ordered to make the unit self-sufficient, the first time that the American army had tried such an experiment. The battalion could now exist by itself, moving fast, without depending on the support of a regimental unit. Without plan or design, the battalion of "guinea pigs from Pearl Harbor" had demonstrated that it was indeed something special on the battlefield.

V

Fanatic Soldiers

"SOME of the senorina are beautiful, but only their dress is bad compared with the girls back home. . . . Men wear shoes but women do not wear any, just going barefoot, even when they go out too." So reported Private Masaru Kadomoto in November 1943.[1]

It was only after they bivouacked in a rest area near Alife that the 100th Battalion began to come into contact with the Italian country people whose lives had been seared by war. The rest period lasted ten days. Every night there were movies. Visits by movie stars like Humphrey Bogart also helped distract them from the tensions of the battlefield.

All the men wanted to take off for Naples, the largest port in southern Italy. The city had been thoroughly ravaged by the war. Its battle scars were still raw, but Naples pulsed with human life. It was a city of slopes. People were everywhere on its meandering stone steps. The narrow streets were filled with a cacophony of smells—unwashed bodies, rotting fish, dogs and cats, urine in the gutter, dust rising from the debris.

Supplies for all the Allied forces came through Naples. The uniforms not only of Americans, but of New Zealanders, Britishers, even Algerians in the French army, were visible everywhere. Jeeps jammed the streets and MPs tried desperately to keep the traffic under control, wildly waving hand signals at intersections. The plaza at the center of the city was lined with tiny shops selling cameos and tortoiseshell. The shopkeepers spread their meager wares on tables scavenged somewhere or other from the shells of bombed-out buildings. The GIs swarmed around to buy souvenirs and gifts to send home. Children stuck out their hands for chocolate and gum. Ragged shoeshine boys wore dirty sweaters that hugged them like skin.

"Black markets flourish everywhere along the narrow Italian streets," another soldier wrote home. "One egg costs two dollars and fifty cents, etc. Poverty reeks and advertises itself on the faces of young and old alike. Youth here mature early. War taught them to learn fast."[2]

Girls, some of them scarcely out of childhood, stood waiting for customers on the street, hoping to make enough money to buy food. One soldier was shocked to discover a pimp was offering his own daughter. The family lived in a narrow room, where the younger brothers and sisters huddled together along with an old woman who seemed to be the grandmother. The daughter sat waiting for customers on a bed separated from the rest of the room only by a thin curtain. She could not have been more than seventeen or eighteen. She looked at the soldier with no emotion. Flustered, he thrust into her hand the money he had pulled from his pocket and ran out of the room as fast as he could.

Other soldiers were pursued by little boys offering their sisters for sale in broken English. This city of smells was a city of people gasping for air in the midst of utter poverty.

There was only one place to stay in Naples, the Volturno Enlisted Men's Hotel at 71 Via Roma. The charge was fifteen lire a night. The 100th soldiers vied to get passes to Naples, even though most found it a depressing place when they got there. The competition was stiff, and it was not all that easy to get a pass.

The only Italian phrase that Kenneth Kaneko still remembers is *"No capice,"* but he remembers his holiday in Naples well. After his chest healed he reported back to his unit and shortly afterward got the pass he had been waiting for. It just so happened that Takashi Kitaoka, the first sergeant of Company B, got a pass the same day. Kaneko found himself going to Naples with Kitaoka.

Even though in the same company, the two men were not particularly close friends. "Kit" Kitaoka had opened a legal practice in Honolulu after he graduated from a mainland university. He was married and had children. He had always admired Italian art and he wanted to see a real Italian opera. Despite the war damage there was a performance every day. "Kane" Kaneko, on the other hand, was a carefree bachelor. He only wanted to spend his day sitting in a bar feasting his eyes on the smiles of the signorinas. It would have made better sense to spend the day separately, but each was a little timid about going into the city alone so they decided to stay together. During the day they went sightseeing, and then in the evening they went to the opera. As Kit sat watching *Tosca* and *La Boheme,* his heart racing with excitement, Kane was snoozing in the seat beside him. At the bar they visited afterward Kane's eyes were sparkling again, but it was Kit's turn to nod off. "We were a strange combination," recalled Kaneko with a nostalgic smile.

There were few special facilities for officers. The Vittoria Hotel was the only one with a whole view of the Bay of Naples. The hotel also had a pool and a tennis court. Mits Fukuda was one of the lucky ones who got to go there. The wedding pictures of his younger sister arrived while he was staying at this oasis so far removed from the realities of the battle-front. He wrote her a letter saying that he was relieved to see that the face of their mother, also in the pictures, had not changed all that much. His wife, Toshiko, staying in Milwaukee with a Caucasian family, was expecting a baby in three months. He wrote her too, telling of the emotions that had been building up in him. While in Naples Fukuda was promoted to captain. To celebrate Christmas one hundred officers from the Fifth Army were decorated, and Fukuda was one of them.

EISENHOWER NAMED COMMANDER FOR INVASION—3000 PLANES SMASH FRENCH COAST—BERLIN HIT—ROOSEVELT PROMISES NATION A DURABLE PEACE.

Those were the headlines in the *New York Times* on Christmas Day 1943. Roosevelt and Churchill had met with Chiang Kai-shek at Cairo in November, and later at Teheran the Anglo-American leaders agreed with Stalin to attack German-occupied Europe on two fronts, with landings both at Normandy and in the south of France. In the Pacific the American army was about to begin bombing the Japanese army's southernmost outpost on Rabaul in preparation for landings in New Britain. The pope appealed to the people of the world to pray for peace.

For the men of the 100th Battalion it was their second Christmas away from Hawaii. Doc Kometani wrote his wife, "Wherever we may be, and with the approach of the day, I am thinking of you and Frankie and Jimmie and Carol."[3] The year before at Camp McCoy the soldiers made snowmen for the first time in their lives and decorated them with leis of charcoal. In the snow they had stamped out "Mele Kalikimaka" (Hawaiian for "Merry Christmas"). Now many of those soldiers were gone.

Christmas was the only day when fighting ceased. Not even the sound of enemy artillery rumbling in the distance could be heard. The 100th Battalion troops decorated two huge Christmas trees, trying to forget for a day the grim reality they had lived with since their landing at Salerno. Christmas Day was cold but beautifully clear. That night Sergeant Masaharu Takeba, warming his hands at the campfire, wrote to his sister Doris:

> X'mas wasn't anything in the past, but it was far from being unpleasant, no sir! The Yuletide spirit was much in evidence. The quiet and peace we enjoyed was much to be thankful for, and supporting it we had a real X'mas dinner of turkey, mince pie, fried rice and nuts, candies and fruits, and a whole day of free time. In the evening the men gathered in several different

groups and harmonized through all the carols and several encores. We feel we're pretty lucky to have had as much. Only complaints, no beer.

For his mother, who could read no English, he added in Japanese that he was fine and healthy.

On the morning of December 31 the 100th Battalion left its bivouac area headed for Cassino. The Fifth Army, with manpower equal to ten divisions, was attempting to smash the Gustav Line (also called the Winter Line). The German defenses began at the mouth of the Garigliano River and stretched through rugged mountainous terrain along the upper reaches of the river and its tributary, the Rapido River, to the Liri Valley. Cassino was the key to the Liri Valley.

To reach Cassino the troops had to cross steep mountains. The difficult terrain and bad weather slowed the Allied forces down. They marched through snowstorms, hardly able to see the road ahead. Day after day valuable time was wasted when they lost their way. It was not only the terrain and the weather that gave the Allied forces so much trouble. The Allied commanders were extremely cautious, consolidating their every position as they advanced, and paying too much attention to troop strength and supplies. As a result they allowed the enemy to gain time.

Cassino lay beyond Monte Majo. It was here that Sergeant Masaharu Takeba, who had been with Kim since the first engagement, lost his life. It happened as Company B was pinned down by an enemy machine gun in the saddle between two mountain passes. Kim, who had returned from the hospital a month before, was lying on his stomach with Takeba, planning what to do next. The new battalion commander, Major Caspar Clough, who had replaced Gillespie when his ulcers finally forced him to be hospitalized, had appointed Kim as battalion intelligence officer (S-2). Takeba was made platoon leader in place of Kim. It was only a matter of time before he would be promoted to officer.

The sky was already darkening, and the snow had stopped. Kim and Takeba were in a long, narrow, shallow trench, lying so close to one another that even in the cold and mud they could feel each other's body heat. Without any warning Takeba's head suddenly slumped. The full bulk of his strong body, tempered by judo and football since his childhood, suddenly weighed down on Kim, as though he were trying to snuggle against Kim for comfort. A bullet had hit him between the eyes. Beneath his heavy brows, his lids were closed and there was hardly a sign of blood. His face looked like that of a sleeping child.

Kim has no hesitation in calling Takeba his best soldier. There may have been other soldiers in the 100th Battalion who were physically or psychologically more impressive when it came to valor, but Takeba never showed any fear. He was able to bring his emotions under control instantaneously, and after a cool assessment of his situation, he would quickly take appropriate action. According to Kim, few soldiers could act so quickly even if they knew what to do next.

The final moments of Kim's "best soldier" were sudden and quiet. He did not die a heroic death, protecting his buddies or charging at the enemy with a shout on his lips. His quiet passing was a picture forever frozen in Kim's mind's eye. Masaharu Takeba was twenty-five years old.

From neighboring foxholes the other men looked at Kim. His face was masked by an empty expression that was hard to interpret. It lasted only a few seconds. Then, as if heedless of enemy fire, he stood up and walked over to a nearby foxhole. He began giving orders in his usual composed voice.

Cassino was a mountain town located between Rome and Salerno, about ninety miles to the south of the Italian capital. To the east of the town was Monte Cassino, a low hill, with an elevation of 1,500 feet. Even from some distance you could see the outline of the magnificent medieval abbey on its summit. Originally founded in 529 by Saint Benedict, the abbey was one of the most important monuments of the Roman Catholic church, but the dazzling gilt mosaics one sees today in the main basilica, and the magnificent paintings in the dome, were all done after the war. The town of Cassino below the monastery has a quite modern look too. It was rebuilt from heaps of rubble and ashes. Eleven hundred Polish soldiers rest in a cemetery on the road up to the monastery. It is the only sight to remind the visitor of the fierce battle once fought there.

In his memoir *Calculated Risk,* General Mark Clark, commander of the Fifth Army, recollected, "The battle of Cassino was the most grueling, the most harrowing, and in one aspect the most tragic, of any phase of the war in Italy." For the men of the 100th the battle of Cassino, fought in cold snow and rain that chilled to the very marrow, was a cruel experience. Indeed for all the Fifth Army troops it was, as one Thirty-fourth Division sergeant later said, "just plain hell—the roughest thing we ever ran into."[4]

Cassino was a strongpoint on the defense line the Germans had built to prevent an Allied invasion of Rome. The German commanders were determined to defend their position with desperation, and they had picked special troops for the job. To take the German position the Allied forces had to launch four assaults on Cassino. The 100th Battalion went into battle during the first and second waves.

When the 100th landed at Salerno about 1,300 men were in the battalion. According to a report on January 20, 1944, on the eve of the battle of Cassino, their number had shrunk to 832 men, including officers, and three weeks later there were not even 500. When the fighting at Cassino began, Company A, commanded by Mits Fukuda, had more than 170 men; at its end only 23 remained.

On January 24, 1944, the 100th Battalion was ordered to move into the attack under the command of the 133rd Infantry, Thirty-fourth Division. This was their first challenge to the German forces at Cassino. The orders to move came after the two regiments of the Thirty-sixth Division, a former Texas National Guard division, were nearly annihilated while trying to cross the Rapido River, which ran along the town of Cassino. In 1946 the state of Texas made public its anger by calling the battle at Cassino "one of the most colossal blunders of the war" and asking for a congressional investigation of General Mark Clark, the Fifth Army commander. The 100th Battalion's objective was to make a direct attack across the Rapido and take the town of Cassino, following a route not far from where one of the Thirty-sixth Division regiments had been completely smashed. The battalion began deployment at San Micheli, several miles from where the attack was to begin.

The Germans were positioned high on the ridges overlooking the attacking Allied forces. They had carefully concealed long-range heavy artillery, mortars, and machine guns on their mountainous defense line. All the trees obstructing their view of the slope that stretched from the summit of Monte Cassino to the surrounding farmland had been cut down. Farmhouses where an attacking force might hide were blown up. A stray dog or cat could hardly have approached the German positions without being seen. The Germans also had flooded the surrounding farmlands by blowing up the dam on the Rapido River. The terrain was a knee-deep sea of mud. In the morass stretching between the 100th Battalion's jump-off point and the Rapido, the Germans had planted a new type of mine difficult to discover with mine detectors.

The American attack began at midnight with a rolling artillery barrage of the kind used during World War I trench warfare. The barrage moved across the muddy flatlands, across the Rapido River, and then up and over the first hills while the 100th was moving forward. It only served to alert the Germans.

Under the cover of darkness Company A and Company C started across the flatland. As he was feeling for mines in the mud with his bare hands Captain Richard Mizuta, the commander of Company C, was wounded so severely he almost lost his right arm and leg.[5]

The stone dike toward which Company A and Company C headed was seven to twelve feet high. The top was strung with barbed wire. Behind it flowed the swift current of the Rapido River. The midwinter water was cold enough to numb the body instantly. On the opposite side of the river, beyond the dike on the western bank, was a road paralleling the river that veered off to the left into the town. The ground rose sharply beyond the road. Hidden among the rocks and trees on the slope the Germans had built pillboxes, dug out of solid rock with airhammers and strong enough to withstand heavy shellfire. As the Allied forces discovered later, the pillboxes were connected by a corridor of tunnels in which even tanks were concealed. A few months later Major Kermit Hansen of the Thirty-fourth Division told a reporter from a St. Paul newspaper, "The line never could have been broken by infantrymen. Every officer in the Thirty-fourth is convinced of that. It couldn't even have been broken by tanks."[6]

During the night Company A and Company C made their way across the dark sea of mud with many losses. By dawn on January 25 they had reached a position just in front of the dike on the east side of the river. Among those who made it was Mits Fukuda, the Company A commander.

When Colonel Marshall, the regimental commander, ordered Company B to advance to the river dike, Major Clough, the 100th Battalion commander, made no reply. If Sakae Takahashi and his men were to advance in broad daylight, all of them would be killed. After another radio message came from Colonel Marshall, Major Clough refused again to order Company B forward. Regimental headquarters kept urging them to attack. It was clear that the regimental commander was furious. Clough still did not reply. A final message relieved Clough of his command.

Caspar Clough, a native of New York, was a West Point graduate, a professional officer with a promising future. He was a fearless and experienced officer who had commanded a battalion in North Africa. Refusing to follow a superior's order on the battlefield was sure to impair a bright professional future for him, but Clough was determined not to give in. Kim saw Clough's lips tremble when he was relieved of his command. In the official journal of the 100th Battalion, however, it is only recorded that Clough was "wounded" and sent to the rear.

That evening Major George Dewey, executive officer of the 133rd, was sent to take over command of the battalion from Clough. After he was briefed on the details of the situation Dewey immediately called back to regimental headquarters. Clough was right, he reported. But Colonel Marshall, the regimental commander, would not accept the word even of his executive officer.

His brows deeply furrowed, Dewey said in a low voice, "I can't order the men of Company B forward unless I personally make sure what conditions on the ground are like." He wanted to go up to Fukuda's position beside the dike that evening, and would send his orders back from there the following morning. The battalion executive officer, John "Jack"

Johnson, strongly opposed the idea. It was too dangerous, he said. But Dewey would not change his plan to make his way across the sea of mud that evening. Johnson sent a message to Fukuda asking him to come back to explain the situation and guide them across.

Accompanied by a messenger, Fukuda made his way carefully back through the minefield following a path marked by little bits of toilet paper left as markers the night before. By the time he was on his way back to the dike with Dewey and Johnson in tow it was already after 10:00 P.M. With them were two wiremen carrying radio equipment and a cook who had been sent to replace Johnson's aide, killed the day before.

The darkness deepened. Fukuda nevertheless had managed to make his way along the path he had already traveled twice. He, his messenger, and the two wiremen had nearly made their way through the minefield. Johnson and Dewey were far behind. The enemy machine guns kept rattling away. The fire was not heavy. The enemy aimed their machine guns at the toilet paper trail in daytime and were just firing randomly to prevent a night attack. At least that was the only reason Fukuda could think of.

Suddenly a mine exploded. Fukuda heard a scream behind him in the darkness. Then came a series of mine explosions. It was impossible to move even one step to help out. In the dark Fukuda heard Johnson calling out, his voice rasping with pain. When a report came that the cook had been killed instantly and Dewey and Johnson were wounded, battalion headquarters sent two medics with a stretcher to bring them in. Because of the danger it was impossible to send out more, and there were few to send in any case. The medics were ordered to "save Jack first."

Like Jack Johnson, Major Dewey had a sturdy muscular build. He had fallen in the mud covered with blood. The medics picked up a man they thought was Johnson. In the midst of the minefield, it was hard to be sure. Since both medics later died in action, today it is hard to know exactly what happened. People like Reverend Yost, who knew Johnson well, think that Johnson himself ordered the medics to take Dewey out first. Dewey, after all, was older, and he was the new battalion commander. It was only proper military procedure to rescue him first. That would have been Johnson's way of doing things.

Dewey was near death when he was brought in, but they got him to the operating room with a speed that saved his life. Everyone was quite surprised to see that the wounded man was not Jack. The two medics were ordered to go out again to bring him in right away. It was already 3:00 A.M.

Johnson had not been wounded as badly as Dewey, but he had lain hemorrhaging in the mud for several hours. By the time the medics brought him in he was barely breathing. Kometani and Yost, who had been waiting anxiously, decided that there was no time to lose. They were impatient to get him to the main aid station right away. On the way there Yost, who accompanied the stretcher, ran into the regimental head-quarters, pleading that an ambulance be sent right away. It was still the middle of the night and no one paid any attention to him.

Yost says that even today he is overwhelmed with anger whenever he thinks about how resentful he felt at the time. His judgment is harsh. The Allied army had no strategy at all, he thinks. There was only a wasteful loss of life.

As Johnson breathed his last against Yost's chest, the chaplain thought about the time Jack had told him after a burial ceremony, "You do a nice job. But don't bother to take much time when my turn comes." He was thirty-one years old.

The recollections of surviving 100th veterans about the battle at Cassino all seem to come back to the death of Jack Johnson. Their eyes cloud with a distant look as they speak of the battle. "There wasn't another white officer in the 100th Battalion who was liked as much as Jack Johnson," they all say.

Johnson's father was a talented agronomist who specialized in cross-breeding plants. As Johnson was growing up, there were always Japanese around the house helping his father with his work. Johnson was without prejudice. He was friendly toward the Japanese American soldiers in a natural way. Before the war it was normal for haole children brought up in the islands to go to college on the mainland, but Johnson, following his father's educational goals, went to study at the University of Hawaii, where over half the students were Japanese American. As star player and captain of the football team, he was well known in the islands during his student days. James Lovell had been his coach. After graduation Johnson returned to his home island of Kauai to become an agronomist like his father. He was drafted. When the war broke out he was one of the offi-cers in the National Guard involved in the Niihau incident. His wife came from a distinguished haole family related to the Robinsons, the owners of Niihau.

When news about the wounding of Dewey and the death of Johnson reached regimental headquarters, Major Clough was ordered once again to assume command of the 100th, but the order to commit Company B to battle remained unchanged. On the morning of January 26, Company B had to move forward in broad daylight toward the position occupied by Company A and Company C by the river dike. When wind blew away the smoke screen covering their advance they were hit by a heavy enemy artillery barrage. Mines began exploding like a string of deadly firecrack-ers. Lieutenant Ernest "Candy" Tanaka fell with a wound that paralyzed him from the waist down for several months. Only eleven men, including Sakae Takahashi, reached the dike.

As night fell soldiers from the company began straggling in to the dike. They had played possum in the mud, waiting for the dark. That was the only way that Company B managed to escape complete annihilation.

No sooner had Takahashi and the other men reached the river dike than orders came from regimental headquarters to withdraw immediately. The other two battalions of the 133rd who were assigned to cross the river had gotten as far as the Rapido, but they too had failed to get across. Their advance was completely repulsed by the enemy. The first assault on Cassino had ended in a cruel defeat, and the 100th went into reserve a few miles to the south.

On February 8 the 100th Battalion once again joined in the assault on the German citadel. Jim Lovell, who had just returned from the hospital in North Africa, was in command. The battalion went into action on a low hill near Rocca Vanula called Castle Hill, which controlled the only paved road leading to the abbey. Above and to the right towered the abbey itself. During Roman days the hill had been an important stronghold, and the remains of Roman fortifications could still be seen. Allied soldiers called it "Hangman's Hill." The only cover was low rock outcroppings. The hill was in the palm of the enemy's hand. It was here that Gurkha troops later were to fight to their death in a bitter engagement. The Germans fired whenever one of the attacking soldiers so much as moved an arm or a leg. The troops could not even take care of calls of nature. But the 100th Battalion remained on the hill for four days and three nights fighting desperately to break through. Two more members of the Aloha Team died here—twenty-four-year-old Corporal Henry Shiyama, who played right field, and twenty-nine-year-old Pfc Stanley Funai, like Joe Takata, from Waialua. Jim Lovell, the battalion commander, was wounded again, this time a hit that crushed his calf bone. He was not to return to the battleground again.

The 168th Regiment of the Thirty-fourth Division attacked the abbey from the north, and New Zealand forces were supposed to take the town, but neither was able to achieve its objectives. The 100th was ordered to pull back once more.

Three days later, on February 15, a force of 255 Allied planes bombed the town of Cassino and the abbey. It was the first time in the history of the war that more than 2,500 tons of bombs had been dropped in a concentrated attack. Despite appeals from the pope, the venerable abbey was reduced to ashes along with the priceless collection of miniature manuscripts, frescoes, and mosaics that had such great impact on medieval European art and the library collection that the Benedictine Order had preserved since the Middle Ages. The 100th Battalion troops watched the frightful destruction from afar. They later recalled the ear-shattering roar and breathtaking flashes of deadly fireworks.

When the air attack ended, a concentrated assault on Monte Cassino abbey was launched by Gurkha troops, and a New Zealand division famed for its valor on the North African front assaulted the tower. After three days they too had to withdraw. The Allied air attack on the abbey had made the rubble an even more formidable defensive position.

Another air attack on the monastery was mounted a month later on March 15. It was on an even larger scale than the first attack. One war correspondent cabled home: "Cassino is dead." But the German troops, who survived in the midst of the rubble as if impervious to death, still fought back. It was already May by the time the Allied forces made their fourth assault. On May 17, British forces, including a Canadian division, took the town of Cassino. Polish troops, undaunted by heavy casualties, mounted an intense attack, and the next day they finally reached the monastery on the summit.

Since landing at Salerno the 100th Battalion had taken several hundred prisoners of war. The number grew steadily. Only a very few Japanese American soldiers were captured by the Germans. The first Japanese American officer to become a POW was taken during the battle at Cassino.

Thirty-one-year-old Second Lieutenant Hisae Shimatsu, a member of the Aloha Team, was captured by the Germans while on patrol the day before the first assault. Before the war Shimatsu had been an irrigation construction supervisor working for the Kekaha Sugar Company on Kauai, and captain of the local baseball team, until he was drafted. His wife, Tomoe, had to wait anxiously on Kauai with her two-and-a-half-year-old daughter until the end of the war to find out what had happened to her husband. Shimatsu's younger brother was a sergeant in the 100th Battalion.

Immediately after his capture Shimatsu was sent to Berlin, where he says he was questioned not only by the German military authorities but also by members of the Japanese embassy in Berlin. Many 100th veterans insist that about this time the infamous "Axis Sally" began asking in her radio broadcasts whether "the little brown soldiers" were not fighting on the wrong side.

Thirty-year-old First Lieutenant Sam Sakamoto lost his left little finger at "Hangman's Hill." A machine gun bullet took it off as he put his hand on the rock he was hiding behind. Sakamoto was not taken prisoner until eight months later during the fighting in mountains of France when he was wounded in the back. The Germans who captured him immediately sent him back to a hospital near the German border to be operated on. After the wound had healed somewhat, he was sent to a larger hospital in Frankfurt. There too he was very well treated.

While hospitalized in Frankfurt, Sakamoto was interrogated several times. The Germans apparently already had a good deal of intelligence about the Japanese American unit. But every time a new interrogation officer appeared, he would ask Sakamoto, "Why are you fighting for America?" Sakamoto got thoroughly sick of hearing it over and over again.

Masao Yamada, chaplain of the 442nd, had a similar experience when he went behind enemy lines near Florence to retrieve an injured soldier. The German officer who came to meet him offered a cigarette and began to talk to him in Italian.

"What country are you really from?" he asked.

"America," replied Yamada. "I am a Japanese American."

"But why are you fighting on America's side?"

"Because I am an American," said Yamada. The German officer asked no more, but he simply stared at Yamada's slanted eyes with a sarcastic smile.

After Frankfurt, Sam Sakamoto was sent to a prisoner of war camp near the Polish border. There was one other Japanese American officer there, a second lieutenant who greeted him with eyes brimming with tears. Sakamoto says that for a moment he did not recognize the hollow sunken face, but then he realized that it was Shimatsu, who had been taken prisoner at Cassino.

It was at this camp that Sakamoto tasted the life of a POW for the first time. He found himself constantly thinking about food, constantly carrying on a struggle with hunger. He clutched to his chest the tiny loaf of bread rationed every week for fear that even a crumb might be stolen. Everyone in the camp was willing to kill to defend his rations.

The five-foot-two-inch Sam Sakamoto was said to be the shortest officer in the 100th Battalion, perhaps in the whole American army. But the big eyes under his flat brows were full of stubborn spirit. It was well known that when he had a few drinks, those eyes would flash. Sakamoto had an extreme dislike for those Caucasian officers who were always looking out for their interests. He was never afraid to challenge even husky types a head taller than he.

Sakamoto's father, a native of Kumamoto, had migrated to Oahu after serving in the Russo-Japanese War. (During the two years after the Russo-Japanese War the number of Japanese going to Hawaii quadrupled, and the majority were unmarried war veterans.) He raised pineapples for a while, but spent most of his life as a reporter for a Japanese-language newspaper in Hawaii. When the Japanese attacked Pearl Harbor,

Sakamoto's father was one of the issei rounded up by the FBI on suspicion of being pro-Japanese.

Sakamoto was the second of five brothers. His older brother had died of tuberculosis while attending Osaka Imperial University. His next younger brother, a graduate of Meiji University in Tokyo, joined the Japanese army and later became a POW of the Americans in the Philippines. His youngest brother, after graduating from the Military Intelligence School at Camp Savage, was assigned to the South Pacific as an interpreter for army intelligence. The Sakamotos were not the only family whose sons, in spite of themselves, were forced to fight on both sides in the war between Japan and the United States. In the 100th Battalion there were many similar stories. Sakamoto did not talk about his family's situation even to Kim, a drinking buddy and a close friend, nor did he ever mention what was troubling him inside. But when he started to drink, there was something frightening about the look in his eyes.

After the war Sakamoto stayed in the army, and today he lives as a retired officer in Honolulu. He does not talk about how it felt to become a POW. Indeed, a number of veterans refused to talk with me about their experiences as POWs. It was Stanley Akita, now a Hawaii state highway official, who helped me understand how the Japanese American felt about being captured.

Akita was a sansei from Hilo. He was sent from the 442nd as the first replacement to the 100th Battalion after the battle of Cassino. A member of Company C, he was captured in the mountains of France at the same time that Sakamoto was.

"My grandfather was a Russo-Japanese War veteran," he said. "I heard over and over again stories about Japanese soldiers so proud that they chose death rather than be captured. And, of course, I knew about the 'three human bullets.'" These were three Japanese soldiers who carried out a suicide mission during the Shanghai Incident in 1932, carrying a torpedo to blow up a Chinese position. "When I was captured and had to throw down my rifle, I was almost in tears. I was in Stuttgart at the end of the war, and it was awkward to go back home as a former POW. I didn't even talk about the war with my family. I was always followed by a feeling of guilt. Then the Americans at the Teheran embassy were taken hostage, but they were treated as heroes when they returned home a year later. That was the first time I realized that in America it is not all that shameful to be taken as a POW."

Etsuo Kohashi, a sergeant in Company K of the 442nd, was known for his bravery. He never became a POW but he told me how afraid he had been that he might be captured at the front. He was afraid that he would be sent to Japan, tortured as a traitor by the Japanese army, then finally beheaded. That would cause trouble for his relatives too. Even death would be better than that, he thought to himself. Many of his friends had the same feelings. He would never forget the words that his uncle, a Russo-Japanese War veteran, had said to him when he left Hilo. "Come back dead," his uncle had said. That is how young Japanese were sent to war to encourage them to do their best on the battlefield without worrying about home.

The first reports of shell shock among the 100th soldiers came during the battle of Cassino. In contrast to other units, there were very few cases among the Japanese Americans. If asked why, many veterans, even sansei, reply that it was *"Yamato damashii"* (Japanese spirit). But was that what kept the Japanese Americans from breaking down on the battlefield, or was it something else?

Living in a foreign country, the issei inculcated their sons and grandsons with the ethical values they had learned growing up in Japan. As one soldier wrote home, "Dad, all your lecturing while I was small hasn't been in vain—I still remember your telling me to work hard at whatever job I may have and sooner or later I would get ahead."[7] The issei taught the young Japanese Americans not only the value of hard work but also the ethic of shame and the value of the family name.

Soldiers in most army units came from different places in the United States. Once the war ended they would part with their buddies, perhaps never to see them again. But the Japanese Americans, especially those from Hawaii, came from the same tight little island, the same towns, and the same plantations along with their brothers and cousins and friends. "Shame" on the battlefield meant "shame" for their families. It would follow them the rest of their life.

A sense of shame is not the only explanation for the low rate of psychological breakdowns on the battlefield. The Japanese Americans may have had a stronger sense of purpose than the ordinary American GIs. They were fighting not simply to defend their country but to prove to their fellow countrymen that they too were loyal and patriotic Americans. This strong sense of purpose was armor against the tensions and fears of the battlefield.

The Japanese Americans' sense of comradeship was also strong. The solidarity of these young men, risking their lives to establish their Americanism, was incomparably tighter than other units. Almost no Japanese Americans were ever court-martialed. Insubordination toward officers or other small infractions of the military code were matters of concern only to themselves. Neither would the Japanese Americans ever desert their buddies even in death. Only at the battle of Cassino, when there was no other choice, did they abandon their dead on the battlefield.

Press reports about the Japanese Americans were glowing. In July

1944, *Time* reported that the War Department had put its stamp of approval on the 100th. "From a cautious experiment the Army has received an unexpectedly rich reward," reported the magazine. "A group of sinewy oriental soldiers only one generation removed from a nation that was fighting fanatically against the U.S. was fighting just as fanatically for it."[8] Some correspondents were surprised to find that the nisei troops were not all that different from other Americans. One wrote back from Italy, "I visited with the unit at a forward command post today and found they had none of the impassivity and stoicism I associated with the Japanese I saw in the Far East. They joked and laughed and spoke American slang so glibly it was difficult to distinguish them from other Americans in the dark."[9] And, as an editorial in the *New York Times* put it, "There is nothing in the Japanese blood, or in any racial blood, that makes men ignorant or brutal. Education and environment turn the scales one way or another."[10]

As public attention turned more and more toward the extraordinary performance of the Japanese Americans, however, the 100th Battalion soldiers were often compared with the Japanese Imperial Army. Everyone, including the military authorities, seemed fascinated by that point. It was as though they were trying to understand the enemy soldiers who continued to go down in honorable defeat in the Pacific by looking at the Japanese Americans. When the military authorities first debated whether or not to organize the 442nd, they had tried to do the reverse. Some argued that since the American army was less concerned with rank than the Japanese army, there was nothing to set the suppressed energies of the Japanese Americans afire. It would be impossible, they said, to expect a fanatical "Japanese spirit" to emerge under a democratic system.[11]

For whatever reasons, both the public and the military authorities remained impressed by the nisei soldiers. A pamphlet published in April 1945 by the Ninety-second Infantry Division to which the Japanese American unit was then attached noted that they "proved from the beginning to be willing, conscientious, loyal and anxious to prove their devotion to country." At the same time the pamphlet pointed out that the Japanese Americans were "shy, self-effacing, extremely polite and personally clean"; that they were "cheerful and anxious to do what is expected of them"; that they "*all* get up and move forward at 'zero hour' "; and that "they will never leave a cut-off individual or unit."[12]

At the time of the first assault on Cassino, the Allies tried to dislodge the German forces south of Rome by opening a new front behind the Gustav Line. Allied troops landed on the coast at Anzio, meeting hardly any resistance. The commander of the Sixth Corps, Major General John P. Lucas, however, was extremely cautious. Instead of moving inland, he concentrated on strengthening his beachhead. Contrary to Allied expectations, the Germans, while continuing to hold the Gustav Line, immediately rushed eight divisions south from Rome to put up a strong defense. The Allied commanders optimistically expected success for their Operation Shingle, which would peel away the enemy resistance like shingles off a roof. However, the Gustav Line, caught between Allied forces on both sides, continued to hold out, and a considerable number of Allied troops were tied down at the Anzio beachhead.

At the end of March the 100th moved through Naples to the Anzio beachhead by sea. It was just before the fall of Cassino. Allied forces occupied part of a semicircular beachhead stretching fifteen miles along the coast following the Mussolini Canal inland for about seven miles. The Allied troops were separated from the enemy by a no-man's-land as flat and easy to see across as a football field. Both sides had a silent gentlemen's agreement not to move during the daylight hours. Through their binoculars American observers could see the German soldiers stripped to the waist trying to get a suntan. And probably the Germans could see the Japanese Americans busy every day trying to gather watercress in the canal. Deprived of sufficient vitamins during the winter months, many had developed heavy cases of jaundice. Indeed, Kenneth Kaneko was saved at Cassino because he had become so sick from jaundice that he had to be hospitalized.

The nisei soldiers got tired of canned rations. They were always on the lookout for fresh food wherever they could find it. Their enthusiasm for food was astonishing. For Rikio Nakagawa, a Pfc in charge of rations in the supply section, the war was a constant search for food. No matter where he was, even in the midst of a minefield when he should have been lying flat with his head pressed to the ground, he was absorbed in picking nuts and berries or anything edible-looking. Danger was of no importance.

"Rinky" was always resourceful. When he heard that a nearby Caucasian unit had some rice, he loaded a donkey with potatoes to barter for it. and set off across some dangerous hills. His most distinguished battlefield service may well have been the time he delivered rice balls *(nigiri-meshi)* to the troops on the front line. That night the password was *"musubi"* (a colloquial expression for rice balls), and the answer was *"meshi,"* the Japanese word for food. Nakagawa also made Japanese pickles in his helmet, filling it with cabbage sprinkled with salt and pressed with a rock. Some impatient troops made off with the cabbage before it was fully pickled. Rinky also found a substitute for soy sauce. He mixed up consommé with water and used it on everything he would put soy sauce on. His favorite dish was "chicken hekka," a sukiyaki-like mixture made from chicken and vegetables he had "silently requisitioned" and seasoned with the consommé mixture.

Whenever he was near the sea or a river Rinky began to crave seafood.

He would throw a grenade in the water and gather the dead fish that came floating up after the explosion, but usually the fish were too shredded to be much good for sashimi. He is certain that he also caught some eel in the Mussolini Canal and grilled them Japanese style.

At Anzio some of the 100th soldiers spent a busy afternoon fishing in the Mussolini Canal using grenades and army-issued mosquito netting. As they turned to go back up the canal bank they saw General Ryder, the Thirty-fourth Division commander, staring down at them. They could not throw away the fish they were carrying, so they just stood there, faces growing paler by the minute. It was, of course, against army regulations to use grenades and mosquito nets for fishing.

With a serious and concerned look on his face, Ryder asked, "What's the matter? Come on up. What's the trouble? Aren't you getting enough to eat?" Whenever he visited the battalion Ryder always asked whether the troops had enough rice. The staff officers in division headquarters had often heard his order, "Make sure that they eat rice." Everyone in the division knew that the Japanese Americans liked rice just like Popeye liked spinach. Even General Mark Clark, the Fifth Army commander, remembered that.

In early April 1944, thirty-eight-year-old Lieutenant Colonel Gordon Singles assumed command of the battalion. He had no combat experience at all, a fact he was well aware of himself, and from the beginning he did not push his own point of view or force others to do what he wanted. When Singles took over the battalion there was not much action on either side of no-man's-land, so he had a chance to take the measure of the personalities and the abilities of the battalion's main officers. A generous and openhearted person, Singles was never a nitpicker in dealings with other people.

Men in the ranks ordinarily do not know much about strategy or the general combat situation. Perhaps for that reason few 100th veterans have any impression of Singles's strong leadership. But Singles was an intelligent, and therefore superior, commanding officer. He listened to the advice of those with more battle experience than he had, but he always used his own judgment to make the final decision. He handled his officers well. He was able to put the right man in the right place. He trusted his subordinates to act according to their best judgment, but always took the final responsibility himself. It was Singles who turned Kim free, and it was Singles who pushed Kim's special talent to the fullest. Kim had become battalion S-2 at Cassino, but Singles began to use him as S-3, the battalion operations officer.

Singles, whom Kim casually called "Gordon," came from Philadelphia. For generations his family had been military men. He spent his childhood in the Philippines where his father was stationed, and eventually he chose to become a soldier himself, graduating from West Point. While on duty in Denver, he had met and married the daughter of a mine owner. They had a ten-year-old son.

Singles was at Camp Shelby, where the 442nd was training, when he received orders to take command of the 100th. "What good luck," he thought at the time. The unit's reputation was already well known among the military in the United States. Becoming the commander of a unit expected to render distinguished service meant distinction for the unit commander too. Singles had no misgivings at all that the 100th was a Japanese American unit.

In the middle of April the 100th was ordered to move on thirty minutes' notice to a position directly next to no-man's-land. The 100th soldiers called their life at the Anzio front from then on their "Dracula days." During the day they slept, and at night they kept watchfully awake. The men passed the daylight hours dreamily watching bright yellow daffodils pushing up and butterflies dancing among them. It all seemed so unconnected with the ravages of combat. When the sun began to fall everything suddenly became active. All their nerves strained to detect signs of enemy movement, and the men were surprised to find how well they could see in the dark once they got used to it. Every night patrols went out. Kim usually wandered off into the dark by himself.

When Cassino finally fell in the middle of May, activity stepped up tremendously at the Anzio beachhead. The moment was ripe to crush the Germans. If the enemy's line of retreat from the Gustav Line were cut off by a sudden push, Rome would almost fall by itself. The opening of an all-out attack was planned for May 23. But there was one problem. The German defenses opposite the Thirty-fourth Division's position were strong. So far not one German POW had been taken there. It was thought that possibly a crack tank division was concealed there, but no one could be sure. The entire Fifth Army was concerned about finding out. General Ryder, under constant pressure from Fifth Army headquarters, was at the end of his tether. Patrols had gone out time and again, but all had ended in failure. An entire company backed by tanks had even been sent out, but they had been forced to withdraw without gaining more information. Naturally the 100th Battalion headquarters was well aware of the problem too.

"If you send me out," said Kim one day, "I'll bring back a POW."

"That's crazy," said Colonel Singles, refusing to take up the offer.

"I'll come back alive," replied Kim.

One reason why the earlier patrols had failed, he thought, was that they had gone out at night when the enemy was most on the alert. The other reason was that too many men were sent out on the patrols. The fewer men there were, the less noticeable they would be. Staff officers at division headquarters argued that a daylight patrol was suicide. They refused to take responsibility, and so did Second Corps. "Somebody says he wants to try it, that's okay," they said. "But the responsibility won't rest here."

Kim immediately began to make plans. He asked division headquarters for aerial photographs. Hiding behind a blanket hung across the second-story window of a farmhouse used as the battalion command post, Kim double-checked the terrain with his fieldglasses, etching all its details into his memory. The section of no-man's-land he proposed to cross was a flat wheat field with no trees. Precisely for that reason, he thought, the enemy would not be expecting anyone to attempt a crossing in broad daylight. With his binoculars he discovered that the enemy soldiers, after working all night, went to sleep right after breakfast.

Kim decided to take only one other soldier with him. Since the mission was extremely dangerous, it had to be a volunteer. The three men who worked under him in the battalion S-2 section—Minami, Akahoshi, and Kubokawa—immediately said that they would go. All were from Honolulu, and originally they had been assigned to an antitank unit. They called themselves the "Three Musketeers." When Kim's platoon needed replacements after the first engagement, all three volunteered to join it. Many troops felt that if they had to fight it was better to serve under Kim. As Masaharu Takeba and other noncoms died at his side one after the other, Kim dejectedly thought to himself, "I'm like the plague." But among the troops there was almost a superstitious awe that if you were with Kim no bullet would ever hit you.

When Kim was wounded at the battle of the Volturno River, the "Three Musketeers" decided the platoon was no longer interesting and volunteered as replacements for the S-2 section. When the S-2 officer left, Jack Johnson, the battalion executive officer, had asked who they thought might replace him. All three at once proposed the name of Kim, who had just returned from the hospital for duty in Company B. Whether for that reason or not, Clough appointed Kim S-2. During the battle of Cassino, the three men were constantly with Kim.

None of them hesitated to volunteer for Kim's special patrol, but Pfc James Kubokawa, who was his parents' only son, changed his mind the next day and decided to drop out. Kim decided to leave Sergeant Yoshio ("Ginger") Minami, a man with a calm set of nerves, back in the S-2 section. Minami, usually quiet and obedient, looked at Kim resentfully when he heard that decision. Instead Kim chose twenty-four-year-old Pfc Irving Akahoshi, the son of an immigrant who had come from Kumamoto to work in the Hawaiian sugarcane fields.

Akahoshi had grown up in Honolulu, the fourth son and the youngest of eight children. His Japanese name was Mitsuo. He was drafted a month before the Pearl Harbor attack. His father, Shotaro, was over-joyed when he saw his son in uniform. The thought crossed his mind, Akahoshi says, that his father might have been even happier had he been wearing a Japanese Imperial Army uniform. His next older brother volunteered for MIS. Kim never saw Akahoshi smoke or drink. Neither did he shoot dice, as the 100th soldiers loved to, or play cards. His poker face hardly ever changed expression. Perhaps because he drew in his chin when he looked at anyone, his puffy eyes always seemed to be peering up from underneath his slanting eyebrows. He was extremely shy. But Kim knew that once Akahoshi had made up his mind he would not budge.

Company B was directly facing no-man's-land. Kim arranged with Sakae Takahashi, the company commander, to take along several of the company's best BAR (Browning automatic rifle) men. At 10:00 P.M. on the night of May 16 Kim and Akahoshi rendezvoused with the BAR men at the farmhouse that represented Company B's command post. They moved quickly across the Allied side of no-man's-land. Company B had already disarmed the mines on the path where they were to cross.

"It was spring, but the nights were still pretty cold," recalled Akahoshi. "Lieutenant Kim and I were wearing heavy underwear inside our jackets. We each carried only a pistol, a submachine gun, and some grenades. That was so we could move a little easier. Lieutenant Kim was wearing his worn knit cap as usual, and I had on a helmet.

"I think it was about 2:00 A.M. by the time we got to the barbed wire on the boundary of the enemy line. A few moments later we heard the rustling of some enemy troops moving back to their lines in the dark ahead of us. Behind us we heard the sounds of Company B soldiers returning to their position too. We cut through the barbed wire just in front of us. The BAR men were to dig foxholes and wait for us there. That itself was a dangerous gamble. I crawled through the cut barbed wire after Lieutenant Kim, and we followed the enemy soldiers back to their line trying to cover our movements with the sound of theirs."

To infiltrate from the barbed wire at the edge of the enemy line to the line of the German outposts required the two men to travel six hundred yards. After they had gone some distance, they finally came to a small ditch Kim had seen in the aerial photographs, where they could hide. Since it had not rained for a while, the ditch was empty of water. The two of them lay down flat.

"The sunrise had gotten earlier," continued Akahoshi. "It was already getting light all around us. We could hear the sound of Germans talking, carried by the wind. The sound of metal clanking was mixed in with it. I guess they were cleaning their weapons and glad that they had made it to daybreak without any trouble. Then when that all quieted down, I remember that we heard the sound of snoring.

"It must have been 9:00 in the morning already. Lieutenant Kim had figured out that their guard was most relaxed just at this hour, when everyone was getting to sleep. And there was no possibility that the guards with binoculars in the forward outposts, who slept through the night and got up in the morning, would be cautious enough to look at the area right in front of their eyes. They were sensitive to movements on enemy ground, but they didn't pay any attention to what was going on right in front of them.

"Lieutenant Kim signaled me with his eyes and we began crawling forward out of the ditch. In parts of the wheat field there was dry stubble about a foot high. The lieutenant and I moved forward slowly on our stomachs with our heads all the way down. We crawled a bit, stopped to see how things were, and then started crawling forward again. I kept thinking to myself, 'We're just like worms.' Somehow it all seemed so funny."

From the Allied side many eyes were fixed on the two men. No one thought it was funny at all. Colonel Singles, scarcely breathing, watched through his fieldglasses from the second floor of the farmhouse. Takahashi felt cold sweat, and something like anger at Kim for being so stupidly brave, not caring about whether he lived or died.

It took Kim and Akahoshi almost two hours to crawl 250 yards in a broad circle to the left and south. Luckily the wind blowing in their direction began to get stronger. The wind concealed the trail of bent grass they left behind as they crawled along. Kim's plan was to take a prisoner near the area he called "Twin Three," where there were two machine gun nests side by side. What he wanted was a soldier from whom they could get detailed intelligence information. Kim had guessed that there was a headquarters in that area. They did not approach head-on, but moved in a circle to go in from the left flank.

"Lieutenant Kim suddenly stopped right in front of me," said Akahoshi. "He was startled by some unexpected movement. Way out in front of our objective was a small dugout with two German soldiers asleep in it. There may have been a whole squad in the outpost we were aiming at. With only the two of us against them the chance of success was much lower. But Lieutenant Kim seems to have had a hunch that we might have a little good luck."

Kim sneaked in a half-circle around the dugout while Akahoshi approached it from the front. The two enemy soldiers, not expecting anything, were sound asleep, breathing deeply, their mouths open. Quietly but quickly, Kim and Akahoshi stuck submachine guns in the mouth of each. When the two German soldiers opened their sleepy eyes, as if they were still half-dreaming, fear spread over their faces.

Kim signaled them to put down their weapons and raise their hands, and they nodded quietly. Trembling, they slid out of their dugout and began crawling in front of Kim and Akahoshi. On the way back, they did not make a flanking movement. They crawled as fast as they could straight toward the ditch where they had hidden that morning. Kim thought there would be less chance of the four of them being spotted that way. From there they headed at full speed toward the boundary of the enemy line. When they finally got through the barbed wire on the friendly side, they pushed the captives down into the foxholes where the BAR men were waiting. They sent Singles a signal saying they had achieved their objective.

As the inky black of night melted over the landscape, the whole party, carefully keeping a low profile, made their way back to Company B. A jeep from division headquarters was already waiting for them. The two German "guests" were a Pfc and a sergeant evidently from their division headquarters. They gave their interrogators all the information they asked for.

For a long time there had been almost no action on the Anzio beachhead. Everyone was bored and tired of waiting. For that reason alone many were excited by the dramatic capture of the prisoners, which, on sober second thought, had been quite rash. The United Press reported the "daring mission" of the two 100th Battalion men.[13] General Ryder was in such high spirits that by the time Kim and Akahoshi had returned safely he had already awarded each the Distinguished Service Cross and had submitted the necessary paperwork.

At the award ceremony a month later General Mark Clark gave a sudden exclamation of surprise as he pinned the medal on Kim's chest. It was the same lieutenant to whom he had given a Silver Medal only a few months before. Clark called over one of his aides, took off his captain's bars, and pinned them on Kim. Even today General Clark remembers the "Japanese American soldier" Kim when he reminisces about the war in Europe. Until I told him he had not realized that Kim was of Korean descent.

It was not until the next day perhaps that Akahoshi realized how bold his special duty had been. As he was answering the questions of war correspondents making a fuss over him, he felt a strange chill go down his spine. As each day went by, indeed as the years passed, Akahoshi says, his feelings of fear—that he should never have returned alive—grew stronger.

Akahoshi was wounded on May 23, a week after he had returned from his special mission with Kim. That day, following a strategy confirmed by the information extracted from the two POWs Kim and Akahoshi had captured, the Fifth Army launched its main attack where the prisoners were captured. Early that morning, when Kim decided he would send two soldiers from S-2 on a patrol into enemy territory, Aka-hoshi replied he would go by himself. He was wounded while trying to make his way back to the unit by following friendly tank tracks through no-man's-land. He knew that friendly mines had been planted in some places. It was careless of him to think that he would be safe on a path a friendly tank had taken.

Strangely enough, he did not get even a nick from the mine explosion, but when the Germans saw the mine go off, they fired mortar shells nearby. As Akahoshi began to run for safety the landscape around him suddenly stood completely still. He noticed that one of the hands he flailed wildly as he ran was drenched with red. He tried to wipe the blood off with his other hand but found no wound. Breathing a sigh of relief, his eyes moved down until he noticed that there was a gaping wound in his thigh that looked like so much hamburger meat. His hands had grazed it as he ran. By the time he finally made it back to the 100th, he had also been hit in the back.

The big push toward Rome began right afterward. The Allied plan was to move inland at a stroke to cut the main highways and block the retreat of the German troops defending the Gustav Line. But the Fifth Army and the British army on its flank were out of step with one another. While the British tried to cut off the retreat of the German troops from the south, the Fifth Army quickly turned its advance in the direction of Rome. Just south of the city it met stiff enemy resistance at the Caesar Line.

In early June the 100th Battalion was made part of a special unit under Colonel Singles's command. Known as "Task Force Singles," it was made up of two artillery battalions, two antitank companies, and a chemical mortar company together with the 100th. Answering General Ryder's request, they opened up a hole in the enemy defenses and moved swiftly up Highway 7, making it possible for the Fifth Army to enter Rome ahead of the British. For the first time among the names of those whose lives were lost were those of eighteen and nineteen-year-old Japanese American volunteers. Replacements sent from the 442nd to fill out the depleted ranks of the 100th had fought for the first time.

On June 5 the 100th troops saw a road sign that said: ROMA—10 KM. It is not difficult to imagine their excitement. Like all the Allied troops and officers they had hoped to be the first unit to enter the city. It lay just ahead under the humid summer sky.

Instead of moving on they were told to halt by General Harmon, commanding general of the First Armored Division, which made the final dash into Rome. The Japanese Americans sat by the roadside, jealously watching the other units go by in a swirling stream of dust. Mits Fukuda, who sat there with the other officers and men of Company A, had a dissatisfied expression on his face as he talked with me about it. He was not the only one. Even today many 100th veterans make no secret of the anger and frustration they still cannot get over.

ROME CAPTURED—THE FIRST OF EUROPE'S WAR CAPITALS TO FALL TO THE ALLIES—AMERICANS IN FIRST

The *New York Times* reported the fall of Rome in huge headlines. The world's attention focused on its liberation. Why weren't the Japanese Americans the first in? From the Japanese Americans' point of view, it was an unparalleled chance to show that the death of their buddies, fighting as Americans in a foreign land, had not been in vain.

Both Singles and Kim say that was an "overreaction." The first units to enter Rome ought to have been the units that landed at Anzio first and had fought for so long. Furthermore, Rome was an "open city," so it was natural that an armored force able to deal with enemy snipers should be the first to go into the city.

The *New York Times* article said only that the 135th Regiment of the Thirty-fourth Division had broken through the road to Rome. There was no mention of the fact that the 100th had been the spearhead of the attack. But it is probably overinterpretation to think that the army had intended this oversight.

General Clark had gotten to Rome ahead of the British commander, General Alexander, with whom he constantly competed. Clark, the triumphant and long-awaited liberator of the city, entered Rome riding casually in the front seat of a jeep. The people of the city followed after him throwing flowers. At 9:00 P.M. that night the 100th troops were loaded into trucks. An hour and a half later they entered the northwestern outskirts of the city. It was exactly two years since they had shipped out of Honolulu on the *Maui*. The troops pondered that thought with complicated feelings.

Allied invasion forces landed at Normandy on June 6, 1944, the day after Rome fell. In the Pacific theater the Americans were moving ever closer to Saipan. About two weeks later the battle for the Marianas began.

VI

The Home Front

AT Christmastime 1943, some 182 men from the 442nd Regiment visited the relocation center at Camp Jerome. The camp USO always kept forty or fifty blankets ready for visiting soldiers, but not all of them were there just for the Christmas holiday.

Even though they were volunteers, the 442nd troops began to have morale problems as they trained day after day in the wet Mississippi winter. Masao Yamada, the chaplain, thought the best medicine for poor morale was to get the soldiers together with young women their own age. He often led excursions to Camp Jerome.

The Camp Jerome USO planned dances and other entertainment, and for sixty cents a day the soldiers could take meals at one of the block mess halls. That gave them a chance to feel as though they were back with their own families, eating with their issei parents and their kid brothers and sisters—even if only for a day. And they could eat Japanese food—rice and bean paste soup and Japanese pickles—instead of army chow. The soldiers enjoyed the food so much that the USO arranged "*chazuke* parties" every Sunday afternoon when the boys were leaving to go back to Camp Shelby.

Of all the girls who helped out at the USO, few were more dedicated or enthusiastic than Mary Yuri Nakahara. Mary had the refined features and delicate skin, but not the coldness, of a Japanese doll. There was a softness in her eyes and she always worked briskly, never complaining. When the Aloha Team had visited Jerome before the 100th left for overseas, Mary had been one of the USO hostesses welcoming them in the middle of the night. The team spent only two days there, but their memories of Camp Jerome were mingled with memories of Mary.

Mary was the central figure in a campaign called "Crusaders" to write letters to Japanese American soldiers at the European front. It had begun when Mary was at the Santa Anita Assembly Center. The inmates were lodged in converted horse stables at the Santa Anita racetrack on the outskirts of Los Angeles. The stench of horse manure permeated the buildings. Mary says that her mother found the smell so overwhelming she was not able to eat for several days.

Mary was twenty years old at the time. Some of the children in the camp seemed depressed and out of sorts. Mary wanted to find something for them to do so they could put up with their adversities without resentment. Together with five junior high school students she began a campaign to write letters of encouragement to Japanese American orphans and to Japanese American tuberculosis sanatorium patients who had been separated from their families. The motto of the campaign was "Think About Other People."

Gradually the campaign grew, spreading to other camps, with high school students and even college students joining in. When her family was sent to Camp Jerome, Mary decided to start writing letters to the Japanese American soldiers. Whenever a busload of 442nd soldiers arrived from Shelby, she moved among them busily jotting down the names of the other men in their platoons and their friends in the 100th Battalion. She soon assembled a list of more than thirteen thousand names for her letter writers. Replies from the soldiers were sent to newspapers in the relocation camps or in Hawaii and were run as "Letters from the Frontline." Mary's group raised the money to pay for stationery and postage by themselves. Mary herself worked as a waitress in the camp mess hall to help pay the costs.

Mary Tsukamoto, who now lives in Sacramento, was the first director of the Jerome USO. She remembered Mary Nakahara's dedication. "It was because she was young, I guess. She had a fearless strength." But, she added, there were some in the camps, especially among the issei, who called Mary an "idealist who doesn't understand anything."

Mary's strength came from her upbringing. She was born the only daughter of a well-to-do Los Angeles shopkeeper. Her father, the son of an educator from Iwate, had graduated from a Japanese university and emigrated to the United States. He went into business selling provisions to Japanese ships putting into the port of San Pedro, south of Los Angeles. Most Japanese American families were not well off economically, but Mary grew up in comfortable circumstances. That always troubled her. Sumi Seki, the wife of a Company L veteran, grew up in the same neighborhood. Even then, she says, Mary was well known for her efforts to help others. Mary had an inner spiritual strength. Her outlook on life clashed head-on with the values of her father, who put all his energies into his business, and those of her mother, who had graduated from a Japanese women's college before coming to the United States.

On the day of the Pearl Harbor attack, Mary's fifty-four-year-old father was arrested. He had just gotten out of the hospital after an operation for the ulcers that had been troubling him for some time. Mary, who had come home from teaching Sunday School, answered the doorbell. Two FBI agents asked to see her father. He got out of bed and came to the door in his bathrobe. The FBI men led him off. Mary's mother was not at home at the time. Neither she nor Mary found out where he had been taken until ten days later.

A month after his detainment Mary's father was suddenly brought home by ambulance. His eyes were dark and hollow. He no longer even recognized his daughter's face. Mary's twin brother, who had been drafted while a student at the University of California, was in the middle of military training. (He later was sent to the MIS Japanese-language school.) When he came home on pass in uniform, his father, mistaking him for an army investigator, deliriously tried to answer his questions.

The next morning Mary's father died in his bed. According to her mother, who had visited him in jail, he had told her that during his interrogation the FBI had confronted him with photographs taken secretly over the years when he had gone golfing with Japanese sea captains or attended banquets with them. Mary's mother afterward often wondered aloud who could have taken such photographs. There were only Japanese at these social gatherings.

Mary never talked with the soldiers about her father's death. The 100th and 442nd veterans remember only her constant and carefree cheer. Reverend Yamada, who got to know her when he brought soldiers to Jerome, remembered that cheerfulness too, and he also lent a friendly ear as she struggled with the heartaches of love.

On a weekend just before Christmas 1943 Mary met the young man who was to marry her after the war and father her six children. Ever since the Aloha Team's first visit, the rented bus carrying the soldiers from Shelby to Jerome usually arrived in the middle of the night. Mary, always with a warm welcoming smile on her face, had the job of asking the soldiers their names so they could be assigned beds for the night. The GIs were billeted in different blocks where there were empty units. To find out whether they were Hawaiians or mainlanders she would ask where they came from. That particular evening one soldier, a cigarette dangling from his mouth and a mischievous expression on his face, answered, "Manhattan Island." Mary, busy with so many things, simply jotted it down and pushed her way on through the crowd. The soldier looked after her, amazed at her lack of reaction.

About twenty minutes later she came back looking for him.

"Which island did you say you were from?" she asked politely.

"Man-hat-tan," he replied.

"Is that one of the Hawaiian Islands?" she said, bursting into a giggle even before she had finished the sentence. The soldier looked back at her with an irresistible smile.

At the dance that evening the soldier turned out to be a splendid dancer too. Nisei from the East Coast were unusual. The USO hostesses were all aflutter at the sight of this dashing and refined New Yorker. Mary was one of them. To the disappointment of the Hawaiians the soldier from New York quickly swept her off her feet. It did not take long for word to get around that he had become "Mary's Bill."

Private Bill Kochiyama was twenty-two years old. His mother had died right after he was born. His widowed father could not take care of his only son himself, so Bill grew up in a Christian children's institution until he graduated from high school. As the only Japanese American in the midst of Caucasians, he was much fussed over.

After high school he set off for the West Coast with money that his father had saved to send him to the University of California. With him was a Caucasian friend he had grown up with who was like a brother to him. Soon after they arrived in California, war broke out. Since Bill's father lived in New York he did not have to go to a relocation camp, but Bill, who had just come to California, was sent to the camp at Topaz, Utah. While there he volunteered for the 442nd. Bill had grown up completely unconscious of whether he was a Japanese or even a Japanese American. He often got letters from friends in New York. One after another they went off into the service, so Bill was proud to have the chance to fight as an American too.

While he was growing up his father had come to visit him every Sunday. Invariably he took Bill to a Japanese restaurant called the Miyako. Even though Bill had no sense that Japanese blood ran in his veins, his favorite foods were bean paste soup and noodles. That seemed strange even to him.

The Miyako became a gathering place for Japanese American soldiers visiting New York on leave. They went to wolf down their favorite Japanese food. Kelly Kuwayama, oldest son of the family who ran the restaurant, had known Bill since he was little. The two of them were reunited at Shelby. Kuwayama, who was four years older than Bill, had been drafted before the war. Even though he had graduated with a degree in economics from Princeton—an unusual achievement for a Japanese American of his generation—he was assigned to the 442nd as a medic. Perhaps there was some question about his "loyalty."

Before being drafted Kuwayama had worked for the Japanese Chamber of Commerce in New York. Even a Japanese American with a degree from an elite university could not find a job with an ordinary American firm. The few Japanese immigrants who made their way to the East Coast believed there would be no racial discrimination against them since they posed no economic threat to anyone, but most had only been able to get jobs as live-in houseboys or domestic servants since they did not speak English well enough to do anything else. Their nisei children met with the same obstacles even though they had no language problem.

Because so few Japanese immigrants lived on the East Coast it was only natural that there were only a few nisei Easterners like Kuwayama and Bill Kochiyama in the ranks of the 442nd. A surprising number were the children of mixed marriages. Some Japanese immigrants employed as domestic servants ended up marrying the Irish maids they worked with. Some soldiers in the 442nd had taken their mother's surname after the war broke out, and some had volunteered against their parents' wishes even though they had not been sent to relocation camps. Some of these young men died in battle. And there is one veteran living in Staten Island today whose mother was an Apache Indian.

After he returned to Camp Shelby, Bill Kochiyama began getting letters nearly every day from "your Mary." The letters to Mary from Bill began piling up too. The long bus ride between Shelby and Jerome did not hamper the romance between the two young sweethearts. Neither had much money, so they could not ride the bus all that often. After New Year they talked about getting married. Their parents were opposed to the idea. The troubled Mary turned to Reverend Yamada for help. Not long afterward she got an invitation to come help out at the Aloha USO in Hattiesburg.

The attitude of Hattiesburg citizens toward the Japanese Americans, unlike the attitude of those who lived around Camp McCoy, remained the same no matter how much time passed. Bothered by this, Japanese American community leaders in Hawaii had raised money to set up an Aloha USO in Hattiesburg to cater only to Japanese American soldiers. The wife of a sergeant in Company L, Tak Iijima, helped Mel Hunter, a missionary who had spent some time in Hawaii, to get the project under way. The USO arranged programs for the soldiers, and it also hunted housing for wives and children who had left the relocation camps to be near their soldier husbands. That was Mary's main job.

Since the families of the several thousands of other troops at Shelby also wanted places to stay, it was hard to find any place unoccupied. But word got around that the wives of the Japanese American soldiers were quiet, tidy, and always paid their rent on time, so there was surprisingly little trouble about people refusing to rent to Japanese American tenants. Even so they were not welcomed with open arms.

On the other hand, there was William Oda's memory of Hattiesburg. Oda, a sergeant in Company G from Portland, Oregon, had been sent to Camp Shelby early to make preparations for the arrival of the volunteers from Hawaii. Immediately after his arrival he requested that he be allowed to get married in the camp chapel. The Caucasian chaplain refused. "I don't think so," he said simply.

Oda's fiancée, Esther, had already completed the process for leaving her relocation camp, Camp Minidoka in Utah. In photographs taken at the time Esther looks like a cute little girl, but she was neither shy nor timid. Since she had been a member of the YWCA in Seattle, where she had grown up, Esther decided to go to the Hattiesburg YWCA for help. She asked the middle-aged Caucasian woman at the desk whether she would be willing to serve as a witness at a civil marriage ceremony the next day. The woman tilted her head thoughtfully.

"Tomorrow is Sunday," she said, "so the justice of the peace won't be able to do it. Why don't you come here instead? I'll ask my minister if he'll do it."

At noon the next day when Esther arrived with Oda at the YWCA they were surprised to see a large smiling group of people waiting to greet them. The YWCA receptionist had brought along some friends from Sunday morning church services. As the organ played the wedding march, the bride and groom exchanged their vows with the blessing of these cordial strangers. Even though it was Sunday, Oda had only a half-day pass, so he had to return to Camp Shelby as soon as the service ended. It all happened in March 1943 as the fresh-smelling green Southern spring was beginning.

After the war Oda stayed in the army. His memory of that wedding ceremony may have been behind his strong Americanism. Oda's nostalgic memories of Hattiesburg were like those of the 100th Battalion veterans about Sparta, but he was an exception among the Japanese Americans stationed at Shelby. Even today most will talk only about the unaccustomed racial discrimination they encountered in Hattiesburg. The only name they remember with fondness is that of Earl Finch, who owned a store in town and had a 350-acre cattle ranch ten miles north of town. He was in and out of the Aloha USO in Hattiesburg nearly every day, so Mary knew him well. Every day he got a thick packet of letters from 100th Battalion soldiers at the European front.

It was the 100th troops that Finch got to know well first. Finch saw two lonely-looking Japanese American soldiers standing in front of his store window one day, evidently with no place to go, so he invited them to come home for Sunday evening supper. A close friend who had been sent to England in the army had written him that English people had invited him to their homes and helped him get over his homesickness. Or at least that is what Finch told the FBI agents who later came to investigate him.[1]

The two Japanese American soldiers, who finally accepted his invitation hesitantly, smiled all the while as they gorged themselves on the hearty Southern supper—fried chicken, mashed potatoes, black-eyed peas, and apple pie—that Finch's elderly mother prepared for them. When Finch came home from work the next day, he found the two soldiers laughing and chatting with his mother, who had been paralyzed for several years and was confined to a wheelchair. The parlor, usually quite plain, was filled with flowers. The soldiers had brought some red American Beauty roses as a thank-you gift.

Finch was still young, only twenty-eight years old at the time. A local woman visiting the Aloha USO one day mused, "I wonder if that is the same Earl Finch who was my classmate in elementary school." She told Mary that Earl had been so poor he had not even worn shoes to school. He started working when he was ten years old, and with a lot of effort he had made himself comfortably well off. Some townspeople called him an upstart.

Earl Finch had a graceful and gentle Southern manner. His head was already starting to get bald, but his eyes were youthful and soft almost in a feminine way. His only entertainment was going to church on Sunday. He neither drank nor smoked, and he was very kind to his mother. For a Southerner he seemed to have very little racial prejudice. Mary recalled that she often saw him chatting with the local blacks.

When Finch heard that the local girls in Hattiesburg would not date the Japanese American soldiers, he put up money to hire a bus and invite Japanese American girls from the relocation camps at Jerome and Rohwer to a dance. He invited more than three hundred Japanese Americans to his farm where they ate watermelon and watched a rodeo. When he heard that they missed Japanese food, he brought soy sauce and tofu back from business trips to New York or Chicago. Once he slaughtered a cow to hold a sukiyaki party for the soldiers.

Some soldiers were suspicious of this "one-man USO" who paid for everything out of his own pocket. There were rumors that Finch persuaded the soldiers to make out their wills to him in case something happened to them. Some soldiers thought he was trying to swindle them out of money before they went overseas, or wanted to use the Japanese Americans to make money for himself some other way.

The rumors even reached the Emergency Service Committee back in Hawaii. Hung Wai Ching, the Chinese American director of the YMCA at the University of Hawaii, had gone to Hattiesburg to help get the Aloha USO started. The ESC sent him out again to see what kind of person Finch was. The FBI and the army G-2 questioned Finch several times. It was said that some of Finch's neighbors who did not like seeing Japanese Americans around all the time reported that Finch was using the Japanese Americans as part of an espionage plot for Japan. But none of the investigations uncovered any motive other than that Finch had taken a liking to the Japanese American soldiers who were so kind to his mother.

"He was really a good person at heart," says Mary firmly. "He couldn't have had bad intentions." Even though he had succeeded at business, she adds, it seemed as though the local people looked down on him somehow. Perhaps he got some kind of self-satisfaction, hard for anyone to measure, from his association with the Japanese Americans who showed their gratitude so directly.

Although his neighbors continued to look askance at him, Finch kept on helping the Japanese Americans. In March 1946, after the war ended, the Japanese American community in Hawaii invited him for a visit. After he stepped off the Pan American airliner, he was treated to a twenty-five-day festival of parades, ceremonies, and parties on every island. Several years later Earl Finch moved to Hawaii for good. He helped to pay for the education at the University of Hawaii of a young Japanese who came to Hawaii as an intercollegiate boxer and later became an economics professor. Finch died in Hawaii at the age of forty-nine.

After she became known as "Bill's Mary," Mary got to know the other men in Bill's unit—Company K, Third Battalion. Even after she moved to Hattiesburg she could not date Bill often, but she always sent him a message through the other Company K boys who came to the USO. Her second cousin, Pfc Calvin Saito, was in Bill's company. He died right after he was sent to Italy.

Fights between mainlanders and Hawaiians continued. Some broke out even at the Aloha USO dances. Mary never forgot one at the dance just before the 442nd went overseas. A group of Caucasian soldiers, usually friendly to the Japanese Americans, dropped by to say hello. One drunken Hawaiian soldier charged into them as soon as he saw their faces.

Mary was dancing with Bill when the fracas began. She escaped outside with his protection. It was as though she was watching scenes from a Western movie being played out in front of her. A soldier reeling from a punch crashed through the glass; one fell from the handrail on the second-floor balcony. Mary wrote letters to apologize to the three badly injured Caucasian soldiers who were carried to the hospital that night. One of them wrote back, "You don't have to apologize. This is army life."

Rudy Tokiwa, the volunteer from the relocation center at Poston, was in Company K too. Other veterans from the company remember him well—lying on his bed quietly writing while everyone else was cleaning rifles or listening to music on the radio. He was writing an English composition on the topic "Why I Volunteered for the Army." The camp high school teacher who gave him the assignment was an understanding woman in her fifties. Tokiwa, whose attendance record showed too few days at school, went into the army without going to his graduation ceremony. The teacher promised him a graduation certificate if he would send a five-thousand-word composition from Camp Shelby. Tokiwa spent so many evenings out with his buddies that the composition never seemed to get done.

Rudy rarely wrote his parents, but news often came from his mother at Poston. She wrote simply about their slow-paced life, with no worries about food, liberated from the heavy farm work that had often brought tears to her eyes. With time passing by so slowly they felt they had become old. Perhaps intentionally, she wrote nothing about the disturbances that broke out in the area around the relocation camp at Poston.

On November 30, 1943, the *Los Angeles Examiner* ran a sensational headline: JAPS SWARMING INTO THE STATE; EVACUEES SUPPLIED WITH GUNS. Below it was a picture of a Japanese American in a phone booth with a caption that suggested he might be getting in touch with enemy agents or saboteurs. The next day the paper reported, "Arizonans are ripsnorting mad about the Jap situation. They don't want a wartime, a peacetime, or any other time invasion by them."[2]

The *Los Angeles Examiner* was an affiliate of the Hearst chain that often mounted anti-Japanese campaigns before World War II. The paper was trying once more to stir up public feelings against the immigrants from Japan and their children. It had picked up news of what was going on at the relocation camp at Poston, a former Indian reservation near the California border.

The life of the internees seems to have differed from relocation camp to relocation camp, and much depended on the outlook of the camp director and his staff. At Poston camp inhabitants had more freedom. Since there was an acute shortage of farm workers, some internees were asked to help out with the cotton and vegetable harvest on nearby farms. While they were off the camp, some would run errands in the nearby town. That upset the anti-Japanese American elements among the local inhabitants. What if the Japanese Americans were to settle down in the area, with their wives and children in the fields working without a day of rest even on Sunday, producing inexpensive crops that competed with their own? The local inhabitants did not want Arizona to become a "dumping ground" for Japanese Americans, reported the *Examiner*. It quoted the publisher of the *Phoenix Republic and Gazette* as saying that "our state is the kind of country that the Japs would more or less like to take over."[3]

While the *Los Angeles Examiner* and the *Phoenix Republic and Gazette* bristled with concern over a "Jap" takeover, Japanese American boys continued to die in Europe. On the day the *Examiner* displayed its sensational headline, Private Toshio Miura of Company A, 100th Battalion, died on the Italian front. Although he was a full-fledged American citizen, the War Department had difficulty finding out where to send his death notice. Miura had no relatives in the United States. He had been drafted after his parents and the rest of his family had returned to Hiroshima before war broke out. Several of his friends got together to hold a simple funeral for him. For the anti-Japanese elements in California in 1943, Private Miura was just one more "dead Jap."

Coincidentally, the first funeral service for a mainland nisei killed on the European front was held at the relocation camp at Poston. Sergeant James Shiramizu, a medic with the 100th Battalion, had been killed in battle at about the same time that Masaharu Takeba was hit. He had grown up in Salinas, and he had been drafted a few months after the war began. He was one of four mainland Japanese Americans assigned to the 100th Battalion at McCoy. His wife Shizuko was at Poston when she received the telegram announcing his death. His son Mikio was still too young to go to school.

By late 1943 nearly twenty thousand Japanese Americans had left the relocation camps with the help of the War Relocation Authority (WRA) to work in Chicago, Minneapolis, and other eastern cities. Since the psychological condition of the Japanese Americans tended to deteriorate into a kind of spiritlessness, Dillon S. Myer, head of the WRA, was looking for an opportunity to return them as soon as possible to their homes on the West Coast, especially California. The military authorities charged with defending the security of the West Coast continued as before to oppose the idea as premature.

The army took the hard line it had two years before when the Japanese Americans were sent to relocation camps. The "disloyal" Japanese Americans, the so-called No-No Group who had chosen to return to Japan, were segregated in a separate relocation camp at Tule Lake, California. Disturbances broke out there when a truck carrying men to help with the harvest on nearby farms turned over and several were killed or injured. The army responded by sending tanks into the camp and declaring martial law.

The attitude of the military authorities on the West Coast was no different toward the Japanese American soldiers wearing their country's uniform. Several days after Joe Takata was killed, Corporal Hideo Uchida of Company B, 100th Battalion, barely escaped with his life when shrapnel hit him in the chest just a fraction of an inch from his heart. His Caucasian wife, Helen, had followed him from Honolulu to

Sparta. Six days after he left for Camp Shelby she had given birth to their son, Greydon, at the hospital in Sparta. After secretly seeing the 100th Battalion off for Europe from New York harbor, she had rented an apartment to wait for him there.

For several weeks Uchida hovered between life and death. Judging from the news she got from the army doctor, Helen could not help thinking that there was almost no chance that he would return home alive. In February 1944, just as his buddies were fighting at Cassino, Uchida was sent back to the United States on a hospital ship. Still in serious condition he was sent to an army hospital in northern California. His wife wanted to follow him there, but the West Coast Defence Command refused to grant permission on the ground that her fourteen-month-old son Greydon was half-Japanese. It would only grant temporary permission for a brief visit as she stopped off on her way back to Honolulu. Uchida was reunited with his wife and son only several months later when he was moved to a hospital in Honolulu.

Army treatment of the Japanese Americans reflected the general feelings of the public. Newspapers and radio carried daily reports of the fighting on the Pacific front. Even more than before, the Japanese Americans were "Japs" in whose veins flowed the same blood as the enemy soldiers who were shooting at American boys on the Pacific islands. Letters opposing the return of the "Japs" to the West Coast continued to appear in the newspapers. On April 23, 1944, the city of Sunnyvale, a small town south of San Francisco, formally passed a resolution urging the "ban of Japs permanently from our city and state."

But more and more voices were being raised outside the West Coast criticizing the relocation camps. In response to a report issued by Lieutenant General DeWitt on January 25, 1944, the *Washington Post* editorialized: "However necessary the evacuation may have been, it was essentially tragic. They [the Japanese Americans] were accused of no criminal act and no disloyalty." Taking off from General DeWitt's famous pronouncement that "a Jap is a Jap," the editorial bore the title "A Man Is a Man."

In April 1944 *Fortune* magazine addressed the relocation camp problem head on for the first time in an article on "Issei, Nisei, Sansei." Earlier *Time* had run an article that commented with irony on the achievements of the 100th Battalion in Italy and the relocation camps in the United States.[4] When Japanese American soldiers like Uchida, badly wounded in Italy, returned home on the hospital ships, willy-nilly they became news.

In February 1944 *Life* published a full-page picture of Turtle Omiya. "Blind Nisei American hero," read the caption, "loses his sight at the crossing of the Volturno." The picture showed Turtle sitting cross-legged in his pajamas and gown, his head tilted to one side with his hands thrust between his legs. A gauze head bandage hid his eyes. It was held in place by two strips of white tape from his forehead to his cheeks. A faint smile seemed to play over his lips as he looked at the photographer he could not see, as if to say that he was able to bear his pain. There was a childish apprehensiveness in his look, like a baby who had lost its sight. This one photograph must have left an impression about the Japanese Americans that went far beyond words. When it finally became clear that there was no prospect that Omiya's sight would be restored, it was Earl Finch who went out to get Turtle the best seeing-eye dog he could find. Mary tried to visit wounded soldiers like Omiya who were spread out in hospitals all over the mainland. And it was Earl Finch who paid her way.

Doc Kometani was worried about what would happen to disabled veterans after their return to the United States. He had written a friend in Hawaii about the problem. "There will be quite a number of our boys returning before the war is over. . . . What are you fellows doing to cope with this great problem of our wounded boys—permanently wounded and physically handicapped?" While hospitalized for a light wound in Italy, he heard a Japanese American in a bed across the aisle begin to bawl like a baby when he heard Kometani's voice. "Captain! Captain! What am I going to do now? They cut my hand off. I can't go home to Hawaii now."[5]

Twenty-five-year-old Sergeant Ben Kuroki was another Japanese American fighting man whose name became known in the States at about the time Turtle Omiya's did. He was not a member of the 100th Battalion, though.

Kuroki had grown up in Hershey, Nebraska, a town of a little less than five hundred people in the western central part of the state. His father raised potatoes on a farm about a mile north of town. After Ben graduated from high school, he started to work for his father, driving a truck carrying produce to market. When the Japanese attached Pearl Harbor, his father urged him to join the army. "America is your country," he said.

Three days after the war began, Ben and his younger brother Fred drove 150 miles to Grand Island, Nebraska, to enlist. They were refused because they were "Japs," but they did not give up. Two months later they tried to enlist again at a recruiting station in North Platte, and this time they were accepted.

When they arrived in high spirits to start basic training in Texas, the two Japanese American brothers got the cold shoulder from the Caucasians in camp. "How did a Jap get in here?" they asked. At night both brothers wept quietly on their bunks, faces pressed into their pillows. It was the first time that either of them had encountered the cruel face of racial prejudice. "We were the loneliest soldiers in the U.S. Army," said Kuroki later.[6]

After basic training Fred was sent to combat engineering school, and Ben went to clerical school. Ben was the last of forty clerks to be assigned. He was assigned to the Army Air Force but spent most of his time doing KP. The Air Force motto was "Keep 'em Flying," Kuroki later said, but his was "Keep 'em Peeling." He spent his days restlessly wondering whether he would ever have a chance to show what he could do in combat. He was finally assigned to a bomber group formed at Barksdale Field in Louisiana.

Just before his unit was to be sent to Florida for final training before being shipped overseas, the commanding officer of his squadron called Kuroki in and told him that he was not going. Kuroki was to be transferred to another outfit. "That was about the worst news I had ever heard," he later recalled. "I told him pretty bluntly about the prejudice I was encountering, and that I didn't even go to town because I couldn't enjoy a minute of it when I did." Kuroki was tenacious, and he managed to stay with the squadron.

Three months later when orders came for the squadron to go to England, only Kuroki's name was omitted. Kuroki was desperately anxious not to miss his only chance to see combat. Once more he went to the squadron adjutant's office, tears streaming down his cheeks, to ask that he be taken along. The adjutant, moved by Kuroki's appeal, went himself to negotiate with headquarters, and he came back with permission for Kuroki to go.

In August 1942, two months after the 100th Battalion arrived at Camp McCoy, Ben Kuroki was sailing across the Atlantic on the *Queen Elizabeth*. As soon as he arrived in England he volunteered to become a turret gunner. The Army Air Force, finally giving in to his entreaties, made him a gunner. He was assigned to the crew of a B-24 Liberator, the long-range heavy bomber used early in the war.

For more than six months before the arrival of the 100th Battalion at Oran, Kuroki fought as a tail gunner in the skies over North Africa, flying out of a base in Libya. During the land battle from Sicily to the landing at Salerno, Kuroki had been in air combat a step ahead of the 100th Battalion. He was well liked by the rest of the crew who called him "Honorable Son" or "Harakiri."

During the raids against the Ploesti oil refineries in Romania, Kuroki was assigned as top turret gunner. The oil field supplied about a third of the German army's petroleum and nearly all of the Italian army's. The low-altitude bombing attack was extremely dangerous. Fifty-four planes were shot down in the raid. Only Kuroki's and one other in his squadron returned home from the thirteen-hour flight.

Most of his crew had completed twenty-five raids and were at the end of their tour of duty. Kuroki had been on twenty-four, but the day after his twenty-fifth he asked his commanding officer if he could go on five more. His final mission, a raid on Münster in northern Germany, was nearly his last. A shell exploded over his turret, smashing the dome, ripping off his helmet, and tearing away his oxygen mask. His buddies pulled him out of the turret, and he got home safely.

Many Japanese Americans who did not volunteer for the 442nd say they did not like the idea that the new regiment was to be made up entirely of Japanese Americans. There was strong resistance to a racially segregated unit. If, as President Roosevelt said, every American had a right to fight regardless of ancestry, then why was it necessary to have a unit made up only of Japanese Americans? Some argued that the achievements of an all-nisei unit on the battlefield would attract more public attention, but would those achievements have any meaning after the war was over? Wouldn't it be better, these critics insisted, for the Japanese Americans to fight side by side with other American soldiers, so that when the war ended and everyone went back home they would carry in their living memories a true understanding of the Japanese Americans?

The example of Ben Kuroki is a good case in point. After he returned to the United States with a chestful of decorations, Ben became an instant celebrity. Stories about him appeared in *Time* and other major magazines, he was interviewed on the radio, and he made speeches all over. "I have the face of a Japanese but my heart is American," he told one newspaper.[7] His story—a Japanese American "given equal opportunity to fight as an American"—was superb propaganda for American democracy. The War Department decided to send Kuroki to visit the relocation camps.

After the outbreak of war the Japanese Americans had been given 4-C draft classification, the same as aliens, which effectively shut them out of the draft. On January 1, 1944, they were once again included in the selective service system. Since this change coincided with news of casualties suffered by the 100th Battalion in Europe, army authorities were at pains to prevent any public misunderstanding about the move. A memorandum of the Operations Section of the War Department dated December 22, 1943, urged caution: "Coincident with recent lengthy casualty lists of the 100th Bn and the current feeling over incidents at the segregation center at Tule Lake, [it] might lead to the interpretation that the reinstitution of selective service was designed as an 'exterminating' measure for Japanese Americans." Publicity releases, the memo warned, would require "extreme caution."

Reconsideration of whether or not to reinstitute the draft for Japanese

Americans began after the 100th Battalion had fought their first battle. On October 12th, 1943, Assistant Secretary of War John J. McCloy expressed his views on the matter in a letter to Major General M. G. White, assistant chief of staff: "I think that the experience of the 100th in Italy should prove that Americans of Japanese descent, properly screened, are no menace to our security, and that our army can function perfectly well with them fighting side by side with us, at least in the theatres where we are not opposing Japanese. . . . I believe we should immediately consider whether we ought not reinstate selective service for all Americans of Japanese descent, adopting the procedures which are necessary to safeguard our security. I am convinced that these men will make good units." And, he concluded, "the propaganda value is tremendous."

The Operations Section memorandum of December 22, quoted above, recommended that the new Japanese American draftees be assigned exclusively as replacements for the 442nd Combat Team and the 100th Battalion. It goes without saying that reinstitution of the draft was prompted by the military achievements of the 100th Battalion troops risking their lives on the battlefield.

After the organization of the 442nd the Japanese American Citizens League had presented several petitions with the aim of reviving the draft for Japanese Americans. In a petition to McCloy, the Japanese branch of the Los Angeles YMCA pleaded, "We have borne the stigma of the 4-C classification. We are still 'enemy aliens' unwanted by our government for military service."[8] On the other hand, many in the relocation camps could not understand the rationale behind the reinstatement of the draft for Japanese Americans. It was an individual choice to volunteer, but how could the government justify drafting young men from relocation camps where they were treated like enemy aliens?

When Ben Kuroki returned to the United States the army authorities were still trying to bring under control what they called a "Jap revolt" at Fort McClellan in Alabama. Only a few mainland soldiers drafted before the war had been sent as cadre to help train the 442nd. The rest were given menial duties, cleaning latrines or collecting garbage at bases in the continental United States. When the draft was reinstituted for the Japanese Americans about six hundred prewar draftees were assembled at Fort McClellan for retraining.

On March 20, 1944, shortly after this training began, the nisei draftees, who had put up with discriminatory treatment for more than two years, laid down their rifles and staged a sit-down protest. They were not refusing to risk their lives as Americans on the battleground. This is still widely misunderstood today, even among Japanese Americans. Rather, the striking Japanese American soldiers were worried about the safety of their mothers and fathers, their brothers and sisters, their wives and children, who remained in the relocation camps. If they left for the front would the government guarantee the security of their Japanese parents, especially after the war ended? When one kibei asked this perfectly natural question, the Caucasian commanding officer provided no answer. One hundred and three of the soldiers, unflinching even in the face of strong threats, said they would continue the sit-down strike until an answer came from Washington. The 442nd, fearing that they might be lumped together with these mutinous soldiers, dispatched a military chaplain from Camp Shelby, George Aki, a mainland nisei, to persuade them to change their minds and end their strike.[9]

On May 24, 1944, Army G-2 sent a memorandum to G-1 recommending that "action be taken to prevent repercussions." Twenty-eight of the soldiers, assuming responsibility for the incident, were court-martialed. Seven were acquitted, and twenty-one were sentenced to five to thirty years of hard labor at Fort Leavenworth. All were given dishonorable discharges in June 1946. This was a black mark making it difficult for them to get jobs, but their names were finally cleared in 1982. The rest of the strikers were sent as replacements to the 442nd and the 100th Battalion.

At a time when rumor said the Japanese American draftees were to be used as bullet shields *(tamayoke)*, Ben Kuroki must have appeared to the army authorities as a heaven-sent hero. The camp newspaper at Heart Mountain Relocation Center in Wyoming headlined his arrival as "War Hero's Visit." During the week or so he spent at the camp in late April 1944 he was feted at public meetings, banquets, and informal gatherings. According to the camp paper, he was "honored and respected by the residents."[10] Although there were 1,970 youths of draft age in this camp, only 45 had volunteered for the 442nd.[11] Most nisei at Heart Mountain were negative about the reinstitution of the draft. At the time of Kuroki's visit fifty young men were in jail waiting to be tried for resisting the draft.

Moved by Kuroki's appeal to "fight for our country, America," a number of young men at Heart Mountain eventually joined the army and went off to the European front. Kuroki signed more than two thousand autographs while he was there. Many who mobbed him were bobby-soxed teenagers. Mary Kochiyama later recalled that he was idolized like a movie star.

But no matter how much he was treated as a war hero, in Denver another passenger refused to ride in the same taxi with him. The local newspaper report on his speech to the Commonwealth Club headlined: JAP SPEAKS IN SAN FRANCISCO. Much to his disgust, Kuroki realized that his own battle against discrimination had not ended at all. He requested that he be sent to the Pacific theater to fight the Japanese enemy. He was turned down time and again, but he did not give up. After appealing to his congressman in Nebraska, he finally got through to Secretary of War Stimson. In 1944 when long-range B-29 bombers based on the island of Saipan began regular night bombing raids on the major cities of Japan, Sergeant Ben Kuroki was the only Japanese American airman among their crews.

VII

"Little Brown Soldiers"
in the Dark Forest

BOBBY Chain, then fourteen years old, but later to become mayor of Hattiesburg, delivered newspapers inside Camp Shelby. The day the 442nd Regiment left the camp he sat watching on his bike. It was unusual enough to see Japanese American faces, but there was something else different about them. Bobby had watched other units leaving for overseas, and usually the GIs who always kidded with Bobby at camp seemed gloomy as they rode off in their crowded trucks. But he vividly remembered how differently the Japanese American troops reacted. "They were overjoyed at the thought," he recalled. "It was as though they were going off to a picnic instead of the warfront."[1]

The Japanese American volunteers, who had been training at Shelby for nearly a year, left the camp on April 22, 1944, just about the time that the 100th Battalion, tempered by the heavy fighting at Cassino, was moving to the Anzio beachhead. Their 442nd shoulder patch showed the hand of the Statue of Liberty in white holding her torch against a sky-blue background surrounded by a red and white border. The regimental motto was "Go for Broke." The high-spirited unit had chosen as their slogan a phrase often heard during crap games.

As training and maneuvers had continued day after day, week after week, in a never-ending monotony, the troops' morale sometimes wavered. They were sick of playing war at Shelby while hearing news about the real exploits of the 100th Battalion in Italy. It was a relief finally to get orders to move out.

When the 442nd boarded troopships at Hampton Roads, Virginia, at noon on May 1 they presented a spectacle to the onlooking Caucasian troops. Loaded down with heavy knapsacks and weapons, the slightly built Japanese Americans seemed ridiculously small, some barely able to see out from under their huge helmets. But they marched up the gang-plank smartly singing out the numbers loud and clear.

The Atlantic crossing took nearly a month in a huge convoy of one hundred vessels. Bill Kochiyama wrote Mary his first report on ship-board.

"How have you been? . . . In the States while training, we used to gripe like hell and bitch our heads off, but a funny thing has happened. Here . . . I've yet to hear boys complain."[2]

After disembarking at Naples, the 442nd moved north of Rome to Civitavecchia where they were reunited with the 100th Battalion on June 10. The 442nd was attached to the Thirty-fourth Division, and the 100th Battalion was assigned to the 442nd to replace the First Battalion left behind at Shelby. Since Anzio the 442nd had already sent the equivalent of about two replacement companies to the 100th so the regiment was at full strength again.

The 100th Battalion did not change its numerical unit designation even though attached to the 442nd. General Ryder and General Clark gave the unit special permission to retain the name it had honored with its battlefield accomplishments.

The troops of the 442nd did not accept this easily. On average they were much younger than those in the 100th, and many felt that since they had volunteered to go to war they were different from the draftees in the 100th. It was not only the enlisted men who felt this way. When the 100th headquarters offered to hold a seminar for the 442nd officers to share what they had learned in battle, Colonel Charles Pence, the regimental commander, turned the offer down. (Pence, incidentally, had been stationed in China in the late 1920s and early 1930s when the Japanese were expanding into Manchuria and northern China. He was regarded as an expert on the Japanese and the Chinese, and for that reason he had been assigned command of the 442nd.) There were even some 442nd officers who said they needed no advice from the 100th at all. From the start it was clear the 442nd felt in competition with the already famous 100th. They were going to show they could fight harder and better.

The day after Rome fell the Allied armies moved north and began fighting once again. The Germans, their manpower increased by the infusion of new troops, planned to build up the Gothic Line north of Florence and hold that position through winter. The 442nd moved north along the west coast of Italy. On June 22 the regiment moved to a new bivouac area near Grosetto where the troops continued to train. On June 25 the unit moved up to a final assembly area, and on the following day joined the battle line for the first time near the town of Belvedere.

Since the Second and Third Battalions wanted to win their first engagement without any help from the 100th, Colonel Pence decided to keep the 100th in reserve in the rear. The Second Battalion moved out first at about 6:30 on the morning of June 26, but it soon ran into trouble. Communications were not good, and by late morning the unit was pinned down by enemy fire from the direction of Belvedere and the surrounding high ground. Company F, which was lured into the midst of an enemy trap, suffered so many casualties that it was nearly useless as a unit for some time afterward. Company E and Company G were pinned down most of the day, and Captain Ralph Ensminger, the well-liked former commander of Company E, who had become operations officer (S-3) of Second Battalion, was killed in the fighting.

In the midst of the debacle General Ryder found himself surrounded by enemy troops in a town 442nd headquarters had assured him was occupied by friendly forces. The general's jeep was captured, according to the 442nd unit journal, as well as that of a colonel accompanying him. The general's driver and the colonel's radio operator were both wounded.[3] Though he had lost his helmet, General Ryder managed to escape. Shortly afterward, his face red with anger, he stumbled onto the 100th Battalion. As Colonel Singles looked at him with puzzlement, Ryder shouted in a voice tight with emotion, "Singles! Clean up this mess!"

It was sometime after noon. The 100th Battalion moved eastward and forward in a wide circle to the east and north of Belvedere. When they reached the high ground north of the town they saw to the west below them an SS motorized battalion attacking the Second Battalion with tanks. Under the command of Sakae Takahashi, Company B, unprotected by artillery support, launched an attack with split-second timing on the Germans' exposed flank. Company A, commanded by Mits Fukuda, moved north to take up a position cutting off the enemy's escape route, and Company C, which had been in reserve, pursued the fleeing enemy soldiers into a nearby olive grove. By 3:15 in the afternoon the enemy positions along the road west of Belvedere, which had been expected to take several days to capture, had fallen to the surprise tactics of the 100th attacking unexpectedly from their eastern flank. During the battle, as well as during the battle for Sassetta the next day, all the units in the 100th Battalion meshed their movements superbly like the parts of a precision watch. In just three hours the unit had taken the town, killed at least 178 enemy soldiers, wounded about 20, and captured 73, while suffering only four dead and seven wounded. In addition to taking enemy weapons the 100th had also captured nineteen jeeps, thirteen motorcycles, two amphibious jeeps, eight trucks, two tanks, and some artillery pieces.[4] The Germans had been so surprised that they retreated in disorder leaving nearly everything behind. Three times the 100th Battalion received a presidential citation, the highest honor for an individual unit, but the first was awarded for this engagement at Belvedere and Sassetta.

From then on the 100th became the pivot of the 442nd, covering for the inexperience of the other units in battle. Colonel Pence, unlike the other officers in the regiment, accepted this fact right away. Although the 100th undertook the most difficult operations, its superb conditioning and excellent timing rolled back position after position held by the enemy. The unit took many POWs but its own casualty rate was unbelievably low. Yet rivalry continued with the rest of the 442nd. When the Third Battalion moved to the front for the first time on the night of June 26, the unit journal reported: "Good. Stop the 100th at Sassetta."

Newspapers all over the United States carried headlines about the 442nd's exploits in Italy: 442ND INFANTRY SURGES AHEAD ON ITALY FRONT.[5] But it was the 100th Battalion that occupied the port of Leghorn, the most important supply base for the Allied army after Naples, while the rest of the 442nd was fighting south of Florence. The 100th Battalion was given the job of securing the port and providing local order while the city's inhabitants returned from the hills where they had fled during the fighting. The unit was placed under the direct command of the Fifth Army headquarters in Rome. Although the care of Leghorn was not as big news as the fall of Rome, it was the 100th Battalion that marched into the city first behind General Mark Clark's jeep. This was clearly a way of recognizing the 100th Battalion's battlefield achievements.

Shortly after the battle for Sassetta, Secretary of the Navy James Forrestal visited the front lines for an inspection. During the parade ceremony General Ryder clapped Captain Sakae Takahashi lightly on the back and turned to Forrestal. Like a proud father, he said, "My best outfit." At the time most of the 100th was in the midst of battle. Colonel Pence had objected to the battalion being in the honor guard at the parade, but General Clark insisted so Pence sent Takahashi and a detachment of soldiers to represent the unit. Several weeks later when King George VI visited the front, Clark again insisted that the 100th also be included in the review ceremonies. The king, apparently quite fascinated, chatted for a while with the Oriental-looking American soldiers. And when Prime Minister Winston Churchill visited the Thirty-fourth Infantry Division in August 1944 he was careful to include in his greeting "the Americans of Japanese ancestry and your American officers."

General George C. Marshall, the U.S. Army chief of staff, had the highest regard for the Japanese American soldiers, especially the 100th Battalion. He later recalled, "I will say this about the Japanese fighting men in these units we had. They were superb! That word correctly described it: superb! They took terrific casualties. They showed rare courage and tremendous fighting spirit. Not too much can be said of the performance of those battalions in Europe, and everybody wanted them."[6] Before the 100th Battalion was sent overseas Marshall had asked General Eisenhower whether he wanted the Japanese American unit. Eisenhower's reply was, "No thank you." But Mark Clark had replied that he would welcome anyone who wanted to fight. Now all the commanders wanted the Japanese American soldiers fighting for them.

On September 27, 1944, the 442nd (including the 100th Battalion) left the port of Naples to sail for the new front in France. About a month earlier, on August 15, Allied armies had landed on the southern coast of France. The American army, in hopes of drawing enemy forces away from the front in Normandy, where the initial Allied invasion was to take place, had proposed a simultaneous invasion in the south, but the British army opposed the plan, so the landing took place two months after D-Day.

According to General Clark's recollection, command of the operation in southern France was to come to him, but his views were close to those of the British and he saw no advantage in it, so he asked Eisenhower to be allowed to remain with the Fifth Army in Italy. In return he agreed to send three divisions to southern France. When a request came to send the Japanese American units to southern France as well, Clark says that Fifth Army headquarters was reluctant to do so.

The 442nd was positioned west of Florence at the time, face to face with the enemy's Arno Line. As at the Anzio beachhead both sides simply monitored each other's movements, and the battle was marked by long periods of waiting. Fifth Army headquarters had not expected the fighting on the northern Italian front to be so drawn out. A compromise was finally reached, and the Fifth Army agreed to give up the Japanese American units. (Six months later, when the 442nd returned to the Fifth Army command, there was still no progress on the Arno Line. The 442nd, as expected, became a vital element in penetrating the enemy line.)

During the three-day voyage from Naples to France the Mediterranean was flat and calm. Reverend Masao Yamada, chaplain for the Third Battalion, took it easy. During the battle for the Arno his jeep had hit a land mine while on a mission to pick up the dead. His driver was killed instantly, and another officer riding with him died several days later in the hospital. Yamada's wounds were not yet completely healed, but he did not want to be left behind so he had left the hospital earlier than he should have. He spent most of the voyage to France on his back. From his bed he proudly wrote to his wife that even though many had lost their lives in the bitter fighting at Hill 140 (nicknamed "Little Cassino" or Pupule Hill, which means "Crazy Hill" in Hawaiian) and in the assault on Luciana, the spirit of the volunteers was still high.

There was news that the Seventh Army was doing some heavy fighting in the mountains of northern France. Some said that the enemy was about to collapse. There were even optimistic rumors that the war would end in the middle of October. It was said that General Eisenhower hinted that the American boys might be home for Christmas. Some of the 442nd troops were worried the war might end before they had a chance to prove they could fight just as well as the 100th Battalion.

On September 30 the regiment landed at Marseilles. On the dock nearby were several dozen Oriental-looking stevedores. When they saw the Japanese Americans they came running over chattering among themselves. The men of Company K, with the same look of curiosity on their faces, crowded around for a better look at the dockworkers.

The men had seen other Asians in Europe. During the battle of the Arno a Brazilian unit had taken up a position near the 442nd. Some Oriental-looking Brazilian soldiers had called out to the Japanese Americans. At first the Americans did not understand what they were saying since the Brazilian soldiers were speaking Portuguese. But soon both sides fell into Japanese: *"Papa wa Hiroshima ka?"* (Is your papa from Hiroshima?) In this unexpected encounter they reverted to their forefathers' tongue. The Brazilians were nisei too. Shaking hands eagerly the Americans and the Brazilians wished each other good luck as they parted.

The Oriental-looking stevedores in Marseilles, however, did not speak any Japanese. When Reverend Yamada squatted down and wrote with his forefinger the Japanese characters for "father," "mother," and "Japan," their smiles suddenly faded. Even though it occurred to them that the dockworkers were probably Chinese or Indo-Chinese, some veterans recall that they could not understand right away why the stevedores turned their backs on the Japanese Americans.

As soon as the 442nd landed the unit was moved north where it was attached to the Thirty-sixth Division. The Thirty-sixth, also known as the Texas Division, had fought with the Thirty-fourth Division at Salerno. During the battle of Cassino the Thirty-sixth had tried to cross the Rapido River just before the 100th Battalion moved into their position and had lost nearly an entire regiment. In mid-August the Thirty-sixth Division had been transferred from the Fifth Army to General Patch's Seventh Army, which moved north along the Rhone River to the Vosges Mountains.

The main force of the American army advancing from Normandy had reached the Aachen district, historically the gateway to Germany, but there its advance had bogged down. British forces advancing through Belgium were trying to break their way into the heavily industrialized Ruhr district on the banks of the Rhine. They had met heavy resistance and were unable to move farther. The Seventh Army, as it entered the Vosges Mountains, also met with stronger enemy resistance than before. The German army was staking its all to defend the entire Rhine region. It is said that Hitler gave orders that no one was to retreat from the border region. If the Allies broke through they would be in the German Fatherland.

The main railway and road linking the two largest cities in the Vosges region, Épinal and St. Die, passed through the little town of Bruyères. The enemy's resistance stiffened as Allied forces focused on Bruyères as their objective. For three weeks after the 442nd arrived in the area the Thirty-sixth Division was not able to budge from its position.

The people of Bruyères, who lived for the day when the Allied armies would liberate them, had been under German occupation for four years. When the radio reported that Paris had fallen to the Allied forces on August 25, 1944, they knew that their days of humiliation were near an end.

It was on September 1 that the townspeople began to hear the sound of heavy artillery fire. The Americans occupied Épinal, the capital of Vosges province. But it was not until September 24 that word came that Bruyères was to be liberated in two days. When Dr. Collin heard the news in the town's only hospital, he rushed home, scarcely able to control his excitement.

Eleven people, including the doctor's family and some neighbors, were living in the cellar of the Collins' house. They had not changed clothes for days. Since the power station had been blown up several days before there was no electricity and not enough water. The Collins' daughter, born soon after the occupation began, was named "France." Already nearly four, she had gone for days without enough bread or milk.

Mme. Collin, whose father's house they had inherited, had studied English at Sacred Heart School in Metz. When she learned from her husband that the American army was getting closer, she cut up the cloth she had secretly been saving for the day. Hiding the cloth under her apron she ran over to the nearby cellar of the tailor and asked him to sew the pieces into an American flag. But when dawn broke the next day there was still no sign of the Americans.

The town of Bruyères was under the control of the much feared Waffen-SS troops.[7] Dr. Collin was anxious. He had heard a rumor from the town hall that the SS troops planned to round up men in the town to help destroy the railroad line between Épinal and St. Die. The Germans wanted to deny use of the line to the Allied forces. It was clear that once the railroad was destroyed, the men would be sent to Germany as forced laborers. About thirty Jews from the town had already been sent to the death camps in Poland. (Only three were to return alive.) But on September 29 the Germans, without bothering the local townsmen for labor service, blew up the tunnel to Épinal as well as the platform and set fire to the local station.

The American attack began the next day, September 30. At the hospital all the patients were moved into the cellar. The artillery barrage continued all the next day. Fires broke out throughout the town. A housewife who had climbed up from the cellar to the kitchen to make her family some soup was killed instantly by a direct hit. By evening the number of wounded was mounting. Dr. Collin, one of the town's four doctors, worked the whole day without rest.

An artillery round fell on the hospital morgue, scattering the bodies about crazily. Day after day the American artillery bombardment continued. On October 3 a young girl, not yet fifteen years old, who had resisted a rape attempt by a German soldier, was brought to the hospital seriously wounded. That evening she died.

In the cellar where Mme. Collin sat hugging her beloved daughter France the ground rumbled and shook all day. A shell struck the nearby church, and next door Jean-Marie Thomas tried his best to comfort his usually strong mother, who had opened the little photography shop that Jean-Marie later ran himself. "It doesn't amount to much," he told her.

Jean Soulier, the only son of the neighborhood baker, was a classmate of Jean-Marie. The Germans rounded up all young men born in 1922—an unlucky year, it was said—for forced labor service. Jean-Marie Thomas was in the group sent off by train to Stuttgart, but the baker's son went into hiding. Jean-Marie, luckily, was put to work at his trade, developing photographs. Compared to his friends who were forced to do road work, he had an easy job. All the young men in Stuttgart seemed to have been called up for military service, and only old people and children remained in the city. But the Allied bombing raids that began pounding Stuttgart as the war raged on were terrifying. Jean-Marie wondered whether every day would be his last. Compared to the air raids, he says, the bombardment of Bruyères was not all that frightening. In Stuttgart the tap water was sometimes tinted with blood. When Jean-Marie returned to Bruyères for a holiday, his mother arranged for a doctor to write out a false health certificate so he could remain at home.

Day after day Jean-Marie waited in the cellar for the final Allied attack. Several days before the bombardment began he and his family hid a German deserter in the cellar. Strictly speaking he was not a German but a Pole forced into military service by the Germans. The soldier pleaded with Jean-Marie in broken French to hide him until the Americans came. A neighbor also living in the Thomas's cellar was worried about being involved with a deserter and objected to helping him hide.

After listening to her complaints for two nights Jean-Marie could stand it no more. He led the deserter to an empty house behind the post office.

On the evening of October 5 a Yugoslavian soldier and a German soldier deserted to the hospital and asked the nuns there to help them. The German soldier apparently had been anti-Nazi.

On October 7 a shell struck a cellar where thirty people had taken refuge. Nearly all were badly hurt. With only three operating tables in the hospital, the surgeons had to work all day to take care of the wounded. The windows of the operating room rattled constantly as the artillery fire pummeled the town.

On the outskirts of town German army trucks sending up sprays of mud constantly sped along the road that ran by M. Robert's farmhouse. The rain came down without cease. The Robert family was living in their cellar, but being farmers at least they had something to eat. In the town nearly all the foodstuffs were gone. There were only raw potatoes to chew on.

Near the village of Champ-le-Duc, to the south of Bruyères, a group of fifty townspeople were hiding in a cellar. There was nothing left to eat from the day before. When the shelling stopped, the men ventured out to dig up potatoes in a nearby field. Sixteen-year-old Serge Carlesso, whose father had moved to the town from Italy after World War I, went with them. His broad tanned boyish face made him look much younger than he really was. The rest of the men quickly dug up the potatoes and ran back to the cellar at full tilt. Serge was farthest in the rear. Suddenly a shell exploded right in front of him.

Serge was flung into the air by the force of the explosion. His body was covered with blood and his left leg was bent in a peculiar way, but he crawled as hard as he could in the midst of the barrage to the protection of a nearby wall, desperately clutching a bag filled with potatoes for his family. Two German soldiers patroling the street had been hit by the same explosion. One was killed instantly, and the other lay wounded and motionless in the street. Other German soldiers who came running to rescue their wounded comrade noticed the French youth. Loading him along with the wounded German into the horse cart, they made their way through the bombardment to the town hospital, where Serge was anesthetized with chloroform. When he woke up two hours later he knew right away that his left leg was gone. The German soldier rescued with him died that evening.

As the days went by, the sound of aircraft mingled with the sound of the cannon. On October 14 a massive bombing attack rained down on Mont Avison, the hill overlooking the town of Bruyères. The watchtower on its summit was destroyed. But about 6:00 P.M. the cannon suddenly ceased their roar. Silence descended on the darkening town. German troops marched about town beating drums, ordering the townspeople not to set foot outside their houses. If anyone laid a hand on the retreating German soldiers, they were warned, the entire population would suffer the consequences.

On October 14 the 442nd arrived at the front lines in the Vosges. An information bulletin issued by the Thirty-sixth Division headquarters described the terrain as follows:

> In the Vosges mountains there are a great many paths which in the heavily wooded terrain are extremely deceptive. The forests in this area, being composed of pine with little underbrush, may be penetrated at any point by infantry. . . . Orientation by compass is vital throughout the Vosges, where paths winding through wooded areas cause even people who know the sector to lose their way.

From a distance, though, the landscape rolled on like a beautiful painting. The red tile roofs of the scattered villages sat cozily in green valleys. Reverend Yamada, who had once spent a year in Japan at the invitation of Toyohiko Kagawa, the famous Japanese Christian leader, said the Vosges scenery reminded him of Nara in the autumn.

The Vosges mountains do not soar majestically. They are covered with conifer forests reaching up toward the sky. Even at midday the sun hardly shines through the thick forest cover. After the German occupation began, no one had bothered to take care of the forests so the ground was covered with underbrush and bushes.

When 442nd veterans talk about the fighting in the Vosges, their most frightening recollections are of "tree bursts." There was nothing like this deadly rain in the Italian campaign. Shells exploding when they hit the tops of the tall conifers scattered fragments through the air with terrible force, splintering the trees and branches. This effect multiplied the destructive power of one shell many times. No matter how deep a soldier's foxhole, it was useless as protection unless there was a firm heavy cover over it.

The 442nd began its advance into the forest on October 15. The scheduled artillery bombardment began at 8:00 A.M. Their objective, the village of Bruyères, was two and a half miles to the east. The town was surrounded on three sides by low hills. To the south the terrain was flat. If the hills (designated Hill A, Hill B, Hill C, and Hill D) overlooking the town were taken, the town would fall. The Second Battalion was to take Hill B directly north of the town, and the 100th Battalion was to take Hill A to the west. The Third Battalion was held in reserve in the rear. Each battalion had several members of the local Resistance as guides.

Hill A, much higher than Hill B, was the key to taking Bruyères. Moving in files through the underbrush, the 100th Battalion advanced along a ridge through the forest west of the town and continuing up Hill A. At 9:15 A.M., after they had advanced less than a hundred yards, Company B, in the lead position, was pinned down by heavy machine gun fire.

Along all the paths leading to their position the German forces had made dugouts, skillfully concealed with brush, and set up machine gun emplacements. Their camouflage was superb, using twigs, branches, and pine needles as concealment. It was impossible to detect the enemy without stumbling right onto them while pushing through the underbrush. Mines were laid all over the area too.

Captain Sakae Takahashi, commander of Company B, and Captain Young Oak Kim, the battalion operations officer, were right behind the forwardmost squad. "I thought so," said Takahashi to himself, turning to Kim. Two days before, Major General John Dahlquist, commander of the Thirty-sixth Division, had assured Colonel Pence, the 442nd commander, that there was no sign of the enemy in the forest and that the going should be easy for the regiment. When Pence relayed this report to 100th Battalion headquarters, its officers intuitively knew even without sending out patrols that the division commander's assessment was unlikely.

Kim and First Lieutenant James Boodry, the new battalion intelligence officer, immediately set out on a reconnaissance patrol. Carefully, the two of them made their way through the brush to make contact with the Forty-fifth Division, scheduled to attack from north of the regiment. When they reached the unit's first foxhole, Kim was about to call out to the second lieutenant lying in it but the other man hurriedly gestured him to be quiet.

"Shh! The enemy's right in front of us," the lieutenant whispered. In a slightly self-deprecating tone the lieutenant reported that he was the company commander. Company G of the 179th Regiment had been there for only a week but all the other officers were either dead or wounded. Even though replacements were sent in every day, he said, only thirty-five men were left in the company. The lieutenant's mud-smudged face was drawn with fatigue. He looked as though he had hardly slept at all. Boodry, not quite believing what the lieutenant had said, reported that he had been informed the enemy had retreated from the entire area.

"I don't know who told you that," said the lieutenant with a sarcastic smile, "but I'd like to see the big liar's face. I haven't budged from this spot for a week."

Kim reported back to Lieutenant Colonel Singles, who immediately got in touch with Colonel Pence by wireless, but the division commander took no heed of the report when Pence passed it on to him. The Thirty-sixth Division had been in the Vosges since September 20, more than a month. Intelligence from division headquarters was not supposed to be that much off the mark. Pence called Singles on the field telephone. "I want to believe Kim's report myself," he said in a flustered voice, "but the division commander insists that we advance ten kilometers a day, and he won't back down." Singles had a bad premonition. Mutual disagreements with the division commander began that day.

In fact the situation was as Kim and Boodry reported. From the first day of the attack the enemy lay waiting for the American troops in the forest. Fortunately there were few casualties either in Company B or Company C, and battalion headquarters breathed a sigh of relief, but Company A, supposed to be in reserve in the rear, received concentrated enemy shelling. A tree burst killed one man and wounded nineteen others. First Lieutenant Sam Sakamoto, the company commander, later taken POW by the Germans, had replaced Mits Fukuda. Fukuda, who had struck it lucky, was on his way back for leave in the United States, where his wife and five-month-old son, David, born after he left for Europe, were waiting for him in Milwaukee. While the Second Battalion just barely managed to turn back the enemy counterattack, it advanced no more than 150 yards.

That day the Allied shelling of Bruyères became even heavier. About noon a shell falling on the hospital richocheted against the church bell, which pealed out reverberating chimes. Fires broke out. The nuns, their heads covered with cloth, ran helter-skelter trying to put them out. The water main had been hit so only a dribble came out of the faucets.

At 5:30 P.M., even as the sky outside was darkening, the artillery barrage continued. Serge Carlesso and the other patients were alarmed when a shell fragment hit the door to the cellar where they were hiding. Black smoke began to spread. An old man, maddened at the sight, began screaming, and babies howled. For eight days there had been no milk available, and bread flour had run out three days before. The town hall sent biscuits to the hospital for rations, but they smelled of mold and no one could eat them. That night the sky over the south side of town glowed red. The 141st Regiment and the 143rd Regiment, also units of the Thirty-sixth Division, had attacked that day.

On October 16 the 100th Battalion and the Second Battalion met enemy resistance as heavy as the day before. By the time the 100th Battalion made its way into the forest at the base of Hill A it was already growing dark again. With the silhouette of the hill always looming before them, the troops hurriedly dug their foxholes. At about 4:00 P.M. night descended on the forest. Almost in an instant it grew so dark the men could barely see their rifles in front of them. It was an eerie and ominous darkness. The wind whistling through the treetops sounded like demons piping. Even the sound of a falling pinecone sent shivers down the spine. The darkness was unreal, as though everything had suddenly faded away.

The Vosges forest was cold too. Foxholes filled with rainwater before they were completely dug out. If the men sat motionless, the cold would pierce through the body. Even if the soldiers snatched a few moments of sleep during the night, by the time rays of the early morning sun peeped through the overhead leaves and branches, rain had soaked through their jackets and their tightly laced boots. Soldiers began to suffer from trench foot, a kind of frostbite that left them unable to walk.

On the morning of October 17 the Second Battalion came under a serious enemy counterattack on Hill B. Companies E and F suffered heavy casualties. On Hill A, Company B of the 100th Battalion led by Takahashi twice launched attacks but could not get any closer to the base of the hill. Without tanks too many men would be sacrificed.

There were no roads in the forest suitable for the passage of tanks. The slope made it impossible to use them. Somehow or other, though, the enemy had managed to get their tanks on the high ground. Captain Kim decided to try using several strands of heavy steel cable to lower tanks and antitank vehicles from the high ground the battalion had just taken. Even here, he thought, tanks should be used to protect attacking foot troops.

Just as the tanks were being brought down from the high ground, there was a message for Kim from Lieutenant Frank DeMaiolo, the communications officer in the rear. DeMaiolo's muffled voice was hard to hear.

"There's someone who wants to talk to you," said DeMaiolo.

"Who?" asked Kim.

"Guess," replied DeMaiolo.

Kim suddenly realized who it was. As soon as he heard a new voice replace DeMaiolo's, he pulled out the telephone wire with all his strength. There had been ten phone wires. Most of them had been hit, and Kim had pulled the only one remaining. Singles, standing beside Kim, looked at him with surprise.

"I guess the last line got blown up," said Kim. The voice he had heard coming on the line was that of the Thirty-sixth Division commander.

During the Italian campaign General Ryder, the Thirty-fourth Division commander, had often visited the front lines during the fighting. But he never gave orders to the men on the spot. He did not interfere in the tasks he had assigned them. He trusted their abilities and left everything to them. He only questioned results. But whenever Major General Dahlquist made his way up to the front lines, he issued orders to whichever unit or officer he encountered.

The general was a big husky man with a thick neck set firmly on broad shoulders. Before the war he had a tour of duty in the Philippines. Later he was with Eisenhower's headquarters in England and was said to be one of Eisenhower's favorites. He had joined the Thirty-sixth Division only after it landed in the south of France and had served as its commander for less than three months. Unlike Ryder, he was not hardened by battle experience. He had received special training as a qualified air observer, but he was better at desk work and did not know much about infantry tactics.

When DeMaiolo's message came in, Kim thought it would take another hour to get the tanks down from the high ground. Several times since morning orders had come from the division commander to attack immediately. Kim was trying to buy time by pulling out the phone line. About twenty minutes or so later sounds of an attack being launched suddenly came from the forest where Company C was supposed to be.

"What idiot is that?" blurted James Boodry, unable to understand what was going on.

It can't be any of our men, thought Colonel Singles. Kim, the battalion S-3, had not yet given any orders for an attack.

In fact, a lone platoon from Company C had launched an attack against the enemy. The division commander, taking only a first lieutenant who usually served as his aide, had made his way into the forest looking for Kim. Along the way he had stumbled across a platoon of Company C, led by Second Lieutenant Masanao Otake, waiting in reserve. The division commander ordered Otake to attack immediately and stood looking on as if to supervise. Otake did not even stop to get in touch with his company headquarters. He and his men, just one small platoon, set off by themselves toward a waiting enemy machine gun nest. When the report of Otake's death came back to battalion, someone heard Kim blurt out, "Was that suicide or murder?" Neither Jim Boodry nor Colonel Singles tried to conceal their anger.

Twenty-four-year-old Masanao Otake had been given a battlefield promotion at Anzio. He was regarded as one of the most promising second lieutenants in the battalion. He had been heavily wounded twice. He had spent a good deal of time hospitalized in northern Italy, but at his own request he had gone back to the 100th Battalion. He was one of the few original members of the unit still left.

Otake had been born on Maui. Since his father died early he and his older brother had to work to help their mother. Otake had also made a reputation for himself as a baseball and football player. He had been a member of the Aloha Team. On the battlefield he had shown not only exceptional ability as a marksman but was also capable of making decisions fairly and calmly. Otake's younger brother, Masayuki, a sergeant in Company H, was on Hill B when his brother met his death.

Once the tanks had been brought down from the high ground the advance of the 100th was speedy. The tanks moved forward under a smoke screen toward Hill A. The farmhouse at the foot of the hill was a sturdy stone structure like so many others in the region. Firewood was stacked on both sides of the house. The farmhouse windows were not large but the enemy had no trouble seeing the movements outside.

Kenneth Kaneko, who had been promoted to second lieutenant during the fighting on the Arno, was leader of the Third Platoon of Company B. Under orders from Sakae Takahashi, the company commander, he and his men quickly surrounded the farmhouse. Inside all was quiet. At a word from Kaneko, Sergeant Yozo Yamamoto moved forward a step at a time with his rifle in hand. Since returning to the unit from hospitalization for wounds received at the battle for the Volturno, Yozo had been Kaneko's assistant platoon leader. The two men, buddies on the Aloha Team, went everywhere together.

A machine gun rattled. I must have lost my footing, thought Yozo to himself, struggling to his feet. Then suddenly he fell right down again.

"Don't move, Yozo," said Captain Takahashi, who came to grasp him from behind. Yozo's consciousness suddenly faded. Takahashi saw countless bulletholes in Yozo's helmet.

By the time Kaneko and several of his men broke down the front door of the house and rushed inside, the enemy had disappeared. Cowering in the cellar were only the middle-aged couple who owned the house. They were clearly surprised and frightened at seeing these American soldiers who did not look like American soldiers.

Kaneko gestured to the husband to bring some water. He came back right away with a glass of fresh clear liquid. Desperately thirsty Kaneko poured it down his parched throat. Suddenly he felt a burning sensation in his stomach. It wasn't water but some kind of potent potato liquor. He went outside to clear his head and look for Yozo's stretcher. Suddenly he was knocked flat by the blast of a heavy mortar shell. Heavily wounded in his left leg, he was unable to move.

There was a deep gash stretching from Yozo's face to his scalp. The skull was smashed in as well. With several massive blood transfusions the medics just barely managed to save him. It took a long and intricate operation to remove a piece of shrapnel from his head. Both Yozo and Kaneko recuperated at a hospital in Naples. The 100th Battalion had lost two more of its original members.

On October 16 the rain continued to pour down. It seeped into the cellars where the inhabitants of Bruyères sat huddled waiting for liberation. Shells hit the hospital again, first the maternity ward, then the operating room where a leg amputation was proceeding. Surgery continued in the hospital corridor. The previous evening, news reached the hospital that the American army had entered the town. Children lying in their beds sent up a cheer. But when dawn broke the next morning the Americans still had not arrived. The patients in the cellar of the hospital were in a state of panic. Two wounded German soldiers had been brought in. One of the nuns noted in her diary that they looked like "hunted animals."[8]

At 6:00 P.M. at last the noise of the German withdrawal could be heard outside mingled with the rattle of machine gun fire. Fighting had begun inside the town. In the cellar of the Souliers' bakery, everyone spoke in a hush, but there was a palpable feeling that the moment of liberation was at hand. The baker's son, hidden away for nearly a year, was seized by the extraordinary thought that soon he would be able to walk freely in the sun once more.

It was early on the morning of October 17 that M. Drahon, the French Resistance guide for the Americans, had pounded on the door of M. Robert's farmhouse, southwest of the town, beyond the end of Rue Léopold. The "strange American soldiers" with tan skins whom M. Robert had met that day were probably troops from the Third Battalion held in reserve until the day before. As M. Robert looked on, unable to conceal his surprise and curiosity, the shelling of Bruyères continued. German shells landed in M. Robert's fields and garden. The trees on the slope behind his house were riddled with shrapnel, and he was never to make a penny out of them again. The day was one M. Robert would remember all his life.

That evening the strange American soldiers disappeared across the wheat fields toward Bruyères. M. Drahon was the guide for Company L. Several 100th veterans still remember "Jean," so he must have helped guide other units of the 100th Battalion as well. To Drahon all the soldiers looked Oriental. He could not tell them apart.

At 6:25 A.M. on October 18 Kim sent a message to regimental headquarters from Hill A. His face was so numb from the rain and cold he could hardly make himself understood. Headquarters asked him to repeat himself several times. Kim had been up until 2:00 A.M. squatting on a poncho, looking at his maps by flashlight and planning tactics. He had barely managed to get a few winks of sleep.

The attack was to begin at 10:00 A.M. sharp.

"Have you started yet?" The message came to Colonel Pence from division headquarters. The 143rd Regiment had been attacking the town from the south for about thirty minutes. The shelling of the town had stopped but it continued on the high ground surrounding the town.

On Hill A the 100th Battalion laid down a heavy rain of fire before advancing into the forest. The roar of the tank guns was so close it was frightening even to the American troops. As soon as the firing stopped, two figures emerged out of the smoke screen on the small flat area just at the forest's edge. Facing in the direction of the unseen enemy they beckoned with their hands as if to say, "Come out." Kim and Takahashi were making a dangerous gamble. Even though they had no idea whether or not the enemy's guns were pointed at them, the two officers, in apparent disregard for their own lives, called out to the enemy. Sakae Takahashi was an exceptional officer. He did not talk much and his manner was rather brusque and unemotional, so he was not loved by his troops the way Mits Fukuda was. But whenever he was given a job, he got results quickly and efficiently, keeping the sacrifice of his men to a minimum. He and Kim were quite close, instinctively understanding one another without words.

Silence returned to the forest. For several minutes it was so quiet the troops were afraid to draw a breath. Then Kim and Takahashi stepped back into the smoke screen, and once more the hideous tank barrage began. The troops in Company B ducked their heads and put their hands over their ears. They thought to themselves that no enemy soldier could possibly survive in the midst of the exploding shells.

Once more Kim and Takahashi exposed themselves to the enemy's vision.

"Come on! Come on!" they cried, waving their arms in a gesture of invitation.

There was no sign of movement in the forest. Seeing that there was nothing to do but attack in force, the two men started to turn back. Suddenly an enemy soldier, hands raised over his head, came fearfully out of the forest. Then came another, and another, until more than forty enemy soldiers surrendered. All that was left to do was to charge Hill A. By 2:47 P.M. the 100th Battalion had reached the summit. On the way they managed to capture over seventy German soldiers. For the successful assault on Hill A the battalion received its second presidential citation.

Although the fighting in the Vosges was difficult, both Kim and Takahashi say it was nothing compared to the fighting in Italy. The German forces were not of the same caliber as the hand-picked elite troops at Cassino. A 442nd interrogation report remarked that the German prisoners appeared to be war weary. Morale among the German troops was low. One German general was reported to have slapped men on sick call and ordered them to return immediately to the lines. "The men of the 19 SS Pol Regt," said an American intelligence report, "have been told by their SS officers that they have no alternative than to hold to their last man. They were told that they could never desert because [they] would be executed by us [the Americans] immediately."[9]

The Germans also appeared to be running short of manpower. An interrogation report noted that POWs taken on October 15 had "been posted to their present units only recently. Among them are recruits with little infantry training and former policemen. They are not security minded and appear to be happy in captivity."[10] They knew little about troop movements or troop dispositions. Many were from special engineer units rarely sent into battle. There were also retired soldiers and officers recalled for service, merchant seamen, and downy-cheeked boys. Sakae Takahashi even remembers capturing a seventeen-year-old with his father, who tried to shield his son with his body.

Karl Schmid, an artillery sergeant captured by 100th Battalion soldiers during the battle at Bruyères, and today a lumber merchant in his native Stuttgart, remembered such recently recruited units in his own division. Schmid himself had first seen two years of action on the Eastern Front in Russia before his unit was sent to the Pyrenees to fight guerrillas under de Gaulle's command. After Allied forces landed in southern France, Schmid's unit had retreated immediately to avoid being cut off, and then had been ordered to fight in the Vosges. Schmid was captured in the middle of the night as he was trying to move his artillery piece to the rear. It was so dark that he could not see his captors even though he felt the muzzles of their rifles at his chest and sides. When he first saw their faces the next morning, he had trouble controlling his fright. They must be headhunters from the Philippines or some other South Seas island, he thought to himself. He found it hard to believe he had not been killed on the spot. In talking about the Japanese American troops another German POW said, "The Vosges must be like the jungle where they were born, I guess. They were perfectly used to moving around in the forest, and we were just no match for them."

That same day, October 18, the Second Battalion had captured Hill B by 4:25 P.M. and taken sixty-three prisoners. As night fell troops from both battalions began to dig their foxholes in preparation for the dark. At about the time that Hill B fell, the first Japanese American soldiers, rain dripping down their helmets, entered the town of Bruyères. Moving in from the west and the north they made their way carefully from house to house flushing out enemy troops.

Today Rue Léopold cuts through the center of town just as it did during the war. The street runs past the Souliers' bakery, and past the town hall to the main square. If you turn left at the main intersection, you will find Dr. Collin's office and M. Thomas's photography shop. If you turn right and go up the street a little way, you will find yourself in front of Monique's barber and beauty shop. Monique, who runs the shop today, married Serge Carlesso, and their recently married son Dominique is now in his late twenties.

Monique was only eight years old when the town was liberated. That day she climbed to the second floor of the house behind her father and older brother. When she peeked out from the huge hole a shell had ripped in the side of the wall, the first thing she noticed was the acrid smell of explosives and smoke bombs. The cobblestone street below was almost narrow enough to stick your hand out and touch the house across the street. As Monique looked down she saw the body of a dead German soldier sprawled in the middle of the street, a grenade still clutched in his hand.

Then she noticed a Japanese American soldier, holding a rifle in one hand, talking in a low voice into a walkie-talkie in the other. He was joined by two more Japanese American soldiers, their rifles at the ready, who walked into the house. After searching the house high and low for enemy soldiers they left. A little later five or six more soldiers came in and sat down on the floor. One of them fished a chocolate bar out of his knapsack and gave it to Monique, who stood watching transfixed with curiosity. Another gave her a piece of leftover bread. It was just a piece of ordinary American white bread, but Monique, who had grown up when there was so little food to eat, never forgot its taste. "It was soft, just like cake. It was so sweet it tasted heavenly," she recalled, almost with tears in her eyes.

The soldier whose rifle knocked on the door to the cellar of M. Thomas's shop was also an Oriental-looking soldier. *"Boche?"* he asked. M. Thomas was confused as he looked at the soldier's face, but he understood right away that he must be an American. There had been Somalians and Ethiopians among the German troops, and there were even Indians fighting against the English for national independence. M. Thomas says he was not all that surprised to see Orientals in the American army.

The Japanese American soldier pulled a Lucky Strike from his pocket and handed it to M. Thomas. With the cigarette dangling from his mouth, M. Thomas grabbed his camera and dashed outside. He thought he would compose a masterpiece to send off to the Épinal newspaper to which he occasionally contributed. As if suddenly remembering something he returned to the house and led the Japanese American soldier to the hiding place of the Polish deserter. The deserter looked apprehensive at the sight of the American soldier, but M. Thomas reassured him with a pat on the back. The Pole had only one possession left—a knife about a foot long. With a *"merci"* he gave it to M. Thomas.

By now there were several Japanese Americans on Rue Léopold. The sound of gunfire could still be heard on the eastern side of town, but here and there people were beginning cautiously to come out of doors. Dr. Collin's sister-in-law Ammie looked out of the bombed-out vestibule of their house. M. Thomas took a snapshot of her with a Japanese American soldier standing beside her in front of the house.

The baker's son found himself free again. In a photo M. Thomas took that day, he stands with an absentminded expression on his face, both hands stuck in his trouser pockets, wearing a necktie under the woolen V-neck sweater his mother had knitted for him, part of a group of towns-people surrounding a bashfully smiling Japanese American soldier. Even though the sky was growing dim, M. Thomas's camera captured a few moments of the liberation.

The troops staying that night at the bakery and the barber shop were probably from the Third Battalion. The soldiers at the bakery refused the wine their hosts brought out for them, but former Pfc Masaki Horiuchi of Company I remembers very well drinking the wine offered him in another house. A fire burned brightly in the fireplace where Sergeant Tadao Beppu of M Company stayed with several others. They dried out their waterlogged jackets and warmed their chilled bodies for the first time in days. They thought the house was empty, but a middle-aged man suddenly appeared from the interior. Beppu recalls he brought some beautiful peach-like fruit. Most of the town dwellers had been reduced to a diet of raw potatoes, but a few had managed to hoard other things. Company K, Third Battalion—Bill Kochiyama's unit—entered Bruyères smoothly in the wake of troops from the 143rd Regiment and spent the night in a mineral water bottling plant. The Vosges is well known for the purity of its water, and several famous brands come from natural mineral springs in the vicinity of Bruyères.

The hospital was on the eastern edge of town, near the village of Bel-mont, where Rue Léopold turns into Rue Cameroun. The Japanese Americans did not get that far on October 18, but at about 6:00 that evening the postman secretly brought news that the Americans had arrived. Serge Carlesso lay on his bed wracked with a high fever and groaning with pain. A sickening smell wafted from his amputated leg.

To cover their retreat the Germans for several hours held out that night at a barricade in the square between the main intersection of Rue Léopold and the hospital. But for all practical purposes the town was in the hands of the Americans. Troops from the 232nd Engineers dynamited the concrete barricades the enemy had erected near the town hall, and they began to clear rubble from the street with bulldozers. They used electric saws to cut through the logs strewn everywhere as obstacles to street traffic. For Monique's family, peering out of their window, the deft cleanup was a scene they never forgot.

The 442nd had taken 134 POWs. About fifteen percent of them were Poles, Yugoslavians, Somalians, and other non-German troops. (About twenty-three percent of all POWs taken in the Vosges were non-German.) About the same number of enemy dead were found in the town.

By 8:00 on the morning of October 19 the Japanese American soldiers had already left the bakery and the barber shop. At about that hour two

Caucasian American officers, probably from the 143rd Regiment, appeared at the hospital. They led off the two German deserters who had been hiding there. At noon shells once again began to fall on the hospital. Retreating German troops were firing from southeast of the town. Newly injured were brought to the hospital.

The Second and Third Battalions mounted an attack on Mont Avison, the high hill overlooking the town, which the Americans called Hill D. When Roman armies invaded the region in the fourth century it is said that they burned all the surrounding villages and set up camp on the summit of Avison, where they could see the terrain around them. The hill was to the northeast of town. Its round top, almost like an inverted bowl, is easy to see from the dining room on the second floor of Dr. Collin's house.

For Rudy Tokiwa and the other troops in Company K, which had been the Third Battalion's reserve company, this was their first real battle in the Vosges. The observation tower on the summit had already been destroyed, but it was uncertain how many enemy soldiers might be in position there. When the Americans finally reached the summit, only two German soldiers surrendered with raised hands. Having taken Hill D the Third Battalion moved on to secure the railroad line on the east side of town. They met unexpectedly heavy resistance from German positions on the other side of the tracks. With dark falling they found they could advance no further.

Leaving Company A to secure Hill A, the rest of the 100th Battalion descended to the houses on the north edge of town. Since they did not come into the town center, Dr. Collin and others do not know if there were any Japanese American soldiers left in Bruyères that day.

Colonel Singles and the 100th Battalion staff officers spent that night in a small schoolhouse on the northern side of town. Making his way there through the lightly falling rain Sakae Takahashi noticed a crowd of excited townspeople. Men who looked like policemen were prodding along a group of women with shaven heads. Surrounding them was a large crowd of men, women, and children, shouting abuses, even spitting. In the growing dark under the ashen grey sky it was clear that the women were terrified. Several were sobbing. Before the war there had been a brothel with four licensed prostitutes outside of Bruyères. After the town was occupied by the Germans, the so-called Milliciens, a Gestapo-like organization set up by the pro-Nazi Vichy puppet government, moved in too. These collaborators, wearing enemy uniforms, took over the best houses in town and requisitioned whatever provisions they wanted. They also brought women. Some probably sold themselves so that they could eat, and some may also have fallen in love with enemy soldiers.

"There are some women who sleep with anybody. With the Germans, and then later with Americans," says M. Thomas, shrugging the whole matter off. "C'est la vie." But the crowd Takahashi saw that day pursued the women with eyes filled with hatred. It is the only sight he remembers from Bruyères. Even now when he hears the town's name the unpleasant feelings he felt then come back to him.

On October 20 the American army set up a medical tent in front of the hospital. It was decided to send the sickest patients to another facility where they could get better care. When an American army doctor came down to the hospital cellar to tell the patients this in superb French, there was only anxiety and confusion on their faces. Even though there were holes in the walls, and the sky could be seen through the roof, their own hospital was the most reassuring for the inhabitants of Bruyères, who rarely went to the nearby city of Épinal.

"Is there anyone who wants to move?" asked the doctor.

The only one to reply was Serge Carlesso. In his fever he thought he would be going to America, a country he had always wanted to visit. When the ambulance came around to pick him up, he tried as hard as he could to raise the upper part of his body. His mother, who had been taking care of him, had returned home for a while. After Serge was loaded into the ambulance, he was not particularly surprised or shocked at the sight of the Japanese American medic in the ambulance with him. What worried him was not this strange companion but the pain in his wound.

No matter how slowly the ambulance moved down the shell-pitted street, it shook terribly. Blood from Serge's infected leg soaked through the bandage. He kept crying out. When the ambulance reached the intersection in front of the town hall, an artillery attack began. The vehicle pulled up on the sidewalk for cover. The Japanese American medic lit up a cigarette. When Serge smelled the aroma of cigarette smoke, wracked with pain though he was, he asked for a puff. The Japanese American medic reached over and put the lighted cigarette in Serge's mouth. As he drew the smoke deep into his lungs, for a moment Serge forgot his pain. Serge had started smoking when he was five. During the early days of the war, right after the French retreat, he, his older brother, and other neighborhood children played war with real weapons the French soldiers had thrown away, and lit up cigarettes they found too.

It was only the next day that Serge's parents, half crazy with worry about what had become of their son, made their way in an American jeep to the hospital at Épinal. The American doctor who had amputated more of Serge's leg told them that in one more day gangrene might have killed him. An American shell had blown off Serge's leg but American penicillin saved his life.

During the month before the liberation of Bruyères, twenty-one townspeople had died and more than five hundred, over ten percent of the town's population, had been seriously wounded. According to American records 35,000 rounds of artillery had been fired at the town, and about 15,000 had been direct hits inside the town. Of 494 houses 342 had sustained thirty percent damage and 23 had burned down completely. The damage done to the forests in the vicinity, the most valuable local resource, was incalculable. Some said it would take sixty years for the town to return to its original condition. Even though the trees look splendid and tall today, it may well be decades before the forest fully recovers from the wartime damage. But, despite all the destruction, the long days of shame and humiliation had come to an end for the people of Bruyères. Once again they were free men and women.

The war had not ended for the Japanese American soldiers though. After the fall of Bruyères fighting in the Vosges intensified.

VIII

The Battle
at Biffontaine

THE army public relations office often used a photograph to illustrate the achievements of the 442nd Regimental Combat Team. It shows a file of about ten German soldiers marching up a slope with their hands over their heads. In the background is a range of gently curving hills. Two Japanese American soldiers, one in front and one behind, escort the German POWs. The soldier in front has rolled up the sleeves of his khaki combat tunic, and unlike the soldier in the rear he does not have his rifle at the ready. He carries it casually in his right hand. The soldier was Private Rudy Tokiwa, who had volunteered against the opposition of his parents just a year before. His expression seems distorted somehow, much more bitter than that on the faces of the German prisoners. His face almost seems on the verge of tears.

Several days after the photograph was taken during the fighting in northern Italy, Tokiwa was wounded in both thighs. It was the first time he had ever been hurt. Three months later in the forests of the Vosges, where he had rejoined Company K, the expression on Tokiwa's face must have been even sadder. Many friends he had made during training had lost their lives in the Italian campaign. Tokiwa swore to himself that he would never again make a really close friend on the battlefield.

On October 19, 1944, after the town of Bruyères had been liberated, the Third Battalion sat in the darkness facing the enemy across the railroad tracks on the east side of town. Only on the afternoon of the following day did Company K and Company I finally cross the tracks to the opposite side. The Germans were retreating to the high ground overlooking the road to Belmont, a village to the northeast of Bruyères.[1]

As Companies I and K pursued the enemy into the Belmont forest, they ran into a minefield. It took time to make their way across. When they reached their objective, it was already dark once again. From the position held by the First Platoon of Company K it looked as though an enemy officer was trying to leave a farmhouse at the foot of the forest. The platoon leader, twenty-two-year-old First Lieutenant Robert E. Foote, a native of Connecticut who had just returned to the unit after recovering from a leg wound received in Italy, had struck up a friendship with twenty-five-year-old platoon sergeant George Nishi while in the hospital with him. Nishi called Foote *"Kodomo"* ("Kid") and Foote called him *"Ojisan"* ("Uncle"). They often talked about Japanese history and Buddhism, Nishi later recalled. Of the four platoon sergeants in Company K who had trained at Camp Shelby only Nishi of the Third Platoon had survived. Like him, the other three were mainland nisei draftees, but the Hawaiian volunteers admired them. None had ever been jumped in his sleep by the Hawaiians. On the battlefield all four were out in front of their men.

Ted Tanoue of the Second Platoon, a native of Los Angeles whose parents were in Rohwer relocation camp, died at Pupule Hill. Atsushi Sakamoto of the First Platoon, known as "Sako" to his men, who had grown up in San Pedro and whose parents were in Camp Poston, fell in the fighting at Luciana. George Iwamoto, assistant leader of the Fourth Platoon, was hit in the back by a shell blast and paralyzed from the waist down. When Pfc "Moon" Saito, the mail clerk, received word that his father had died in Honolulu, it was Iwamoto who passed his helmet among the men and collected two hundred dollars to send Moon's mother as a condolence. Iwamoto's family lived in Yakima, Washington. Since his father was regarded as pro-Japanese he had been sent to a special camp in New Mexico. Iwamoto nonetheless volunteered for service, hoping that the army might be kinder to his father if he did.

Seeing the German officer make his way out of the house, one soldier turned to Lieutenant Foote and asked, "Shall I get him?" Bill Kochiyama and Sanji Kimoto called this soldier "Trigger Happy." He was certainly a good shot, but even when it made more sense to wait quietly he would shoot right and left. Instead of hurting the enemy he often revealed the American position. ("I was afraid that if I didn't get them they would get me," he candidly admits today.) With a nod of assent from Foote, Trigger Happy dropped the German officer, a major, with a single shot. In his briefcase they found a map showing the deployment of the German positions in the area. They sent it off to headquarters immediately. Shortly afterward Foote received a severe wound.

A little before midnight on October 19 Colonel Pence had summoned Singles and Kim to the 442nd headquarters command post south of Bruyères. Pence seemed upset. General Dahlquist, the Thirty-sixth Division commander, had ordered the 100th Battalion to take Hill C by noon the next day. Kim was angry. It was an order that defied common sense. There was so little time. Kim had to stay up the rest of the night preparing a tactical plan. A frontal assault was certain to mean heavy losses. There was no alternative but to swing round behind the enemy position for a surprise attack.

On October 20, under the cover of a smoke screen that looked like mist, the 100th troops moved out. Shortly after 9:00 A.M. they broke through the enemy positions. Colonel Singles told the division commander that the "hill was ours but to clear it absolutely would take a long time." By noon they had occupied Hill C as ordered. At 2:15 P.M. a call came down to the battalion from Colonel Pence. General Dahlquist had issued another order. Instead of pursuing enemy stragglers and repulsing the enemy, the entire battalion was to move into reserve back in Bruyères.

Enemy tanks had appeared at the foot of Hill C. It was clear that the Germans were regrouping their forces for an attempt to recapture the hill. The battalion staff officers debated whether they should ignore the order for a few hours and destroy the counterattacking Germans before leaving the hill. A half-hour after the new order came in from General Dahlquist, Lieutenant Colonel Singles sent a message back to regimental headquarters saying that Companies A and B were in a firefight again and it would not be possible to move off Hill C right away.

"The hill is taken, isn't it?" asked the general when Pence relayed the report.

"Yes," replied Pence. "But on the farther slope, they'll slide up the hill again if we withdraw."

"I don't think they'll do that," the general replied. "Pull them off the hill and leave one company there."

This exchange took place at 3:20 P.M. Kim immediately got in touch with the regimental headquarters himself.

"That order from division is screwy," he said. "We're still fighting on Hill C. There's a hell of a lot of Jerries in front of us. We were going to make a squeeze play up there, but I'll call it off."

"I don't care what company you leave on top of the hill," replied Pence, "but pull back the rest of the battalion. General Dahlquist said it has got to be done." In a tone that did not really sound like him, Pence added, "Please, Kim, answer 'Yes, sir.'"

Pence's "please" sounded more like a supplication than an order. It is no surprise to find that part of the message missing from the combat journal, but Kim remembers it well. He does not think the combat journal accurately reported Pence's other words either. In fact as Pence was talking with Kim the general was standing right beside him. Naturally Kim learned this from Pence only much later.

By the time the 100th Battalion occupied Hill C, division headquarters had realized that the position was in a sector assigned to another division, just beyond the line the Thirty-sixth Division was supposed to hold. All the division commanders were competing to see who would cross the German border first. The general apparently did not feel like lending a helping hand to one of his rivals, even though holding the hill might be advantageous to friendly forces. Moving off the hill might have made sense had it been possible to leave one company, as indicated in the conversation between Pence and the general in the combat journal, but that exchange may have been inserted into the record by someone in the rear. When the order to withdraw from Hill C came it stated that they were to "immediately withdraw the entire battalion." Kim and Singles remember it that way, and so does Sakae Takahashi.

The next day when a regiment from another division tried to move up Hill C it was not the 100th Battalion looking down at them but German soldiers. It cost more than a hundred casualties to retake the hill.

But let us return to the events of October 20. The 100th Battalion descended from Hill C by 5:45 that evening. A message came in to Colonel Pence from General Dahlquist.

"Put a force in tonight under cover of darkness so you can jump first light in the morning. The men didn't move at all today and have to get in place tonight and get moving in the morning. Force has to get behind the hill tonight. Suggest that reconnaissance be made tonight."

Three hours later the division commander sent another message asking Pence if he shouldn't send four companies to help out the O'Connor task force. Enemy forces on the high ground overlooking Bruyères from the east were holding up the advance of the Second and Third Battalions. A special task force of two companies led by Major Emmet O'Connor, executive officer of the Third Battalion, was supposed to squeeze the enemy from the opposite side of the ridge. The task force had gone astray in the dark. The general wanted the 100th Battalion, just down from Hill C, to move in to support it.

"If we send a battalion, they have to go through a narrow path," replied Pence. "The enemy can set up a roadblock and stop a battalion as well as two companies [that is, the O'Connor task force]. I have my plan already formulated."

"I'm not going to stop you," replied the general, "but get to them where they least expect it. I don't believe you are using your force in the right place."

Unconvinced, the 100th Battalion left Hill C behind. By the time they got back to the houses in Bruyères where they had bedded down the night before it was already close to 11:00 P.M. After several hours the assistant division commander and his entourage suddenly appeared at the 100th Battalion command post. He ordered the surprised Colonel Singles to move out immediately in the direction of Biffontaine, a village northeast of the ridge where the O'Connor task force was advancing. The village was surrounded by forested hills.

Kim, who heard the order as he stood beside Singles, reached for the telephone to give instructions to the company commander. The assistant division commander, his face red with anger, shouted, "You don't have time for that!" A barrel-chested man, he rushed about prodding everyone to get going. Even Kim, who usually did not give in just because someone had higher rank, barely managed to grab the jacket he had just taken off. The next thing he knew he was out in the middle of the rain again.

It happened so quickly that Kim only managed to confirm what was going on with Pence after he was in his jeep. James Boodry, the battalion S-2 riding together with them, kept muttering over and over again, "This is crazy. This is crazy."

The 100th troops hardly had time to eat their rations before they put on their knapsacks again. They moved northeast in quite a different direction from the O'Connor task force. There was little enemy resistance. They moved fast, almost at a run, and before the light of dawn they had reached the ridge that was their objective.

At 10:00 A.M. on October 21 the division commander contacted Pence.

"Have they got to the hill yet?" he asked.

"Yes," replied Pence.

"Now one trouble you will encounter is communications for the 100th," said the division commander.

By then the battalion was already isolated. It had managed to pass through the enemy's defenses to capture its objective but then enemy troops closed in behind them. Units supposed to consolidate the 100th Battalion's flanks had not yet been dispatched, and liaison with regimental headquarters was no longer easy. At 5:50 P.M. the battalion notified the 442nd command post that they could not say much because their line was tapped. "All they could say was that they were where the general told them to go, and did what he told them to do." Telephone communication was poor, and the only way to keep in touch was by using code on the 284th radio.

Battalion supplies were low too. The troops had had no rations since the evening before. Some were lucky enough to eat their fill after capturing an enemy mess truck, but the rest had to endure empty stomachs as well as the piercing cold. The troops dug in on the ridge overlooking the town of Biffontaine, vulnerable to attack from the rear by the enemy standing between the 100th and the rest of the 442nd.

At 7:20 P.M. General Dahlquist sent another message to Pence: "I think we got the thing beat now. A very good job and a good dividend. Now get a roadblock up to Singles and get it set. A good job, Colonel, and well done."

The following morning the 100th tried to clear out enemy forces in front and behind them but it was not easy. Singles sent a message to Pence that the area was too big. The unit was being hit from three sides, and the supply situation was desperate. The battalion S-3 reported that "the 100th will have to be throwing stones if they don't get any ammo." Regimental headquarters replied with the news, "The general is particularly interested in the 100th."

It is a peculiarity of the countryside around Biffontaine that a heavy fog often rises when the ground is warmer than the air over it. Company A and Company B found themselves surrounded by a white darkness that floated upward every time a shell hit. They fumbled about trying to find hiding places, constantly fearing that they were about to be obliterated.

Then came orders to capture Biffontaine. The 100th battalion officers could not understand it. If they descended into the town they would be even further cut off from friendly forces and beyond radio contact or artillery support. It was almost meaningless to take a town in that position. It would make better sense for the 100th to hold the ridge until friendly forces moved in to take up supporting positions.

Kim took the transmitter from Singles to reply to the order, but Pence spoke quickly as if to forestall him. Kim realized that the division commander must be at the regimental command post. "This puts us beyond radio range and artillery support, and we are low on ammunition, so promise that you'll put another unit in our position by evening if we go down into Biffontaine."

"Absolutely," replied Pence.

Biffontaine was a small village with a population of about three hundred souls. It stretched for about two and a half miles in an L-shaped basin that opens up between the forested hills. The village center was a few houses clustered around the village church but it was so quiet the village looked deserted. The ridge overlooking Biffontaine was not very high but the descent was steep.

M. Gerard Henry, who later inherited his family's farmstead on the west side of Biffontaine, remembers very well how the 100th took the town. He was chatting with some neighborhood friends by a crater in the road in front of the house. With him was Romary, his bride of less than two weeks. Several days earlier the twenty or so German soldiers billeted in the Henry house, who requisitioned the family cow, pigs, and chickens for rations, had moved out. The enemy soldiers manning a machine gun emplacement by the village church had disappeared the night before. M. Henry was discussing this turn of events with his neighbors.

Suddenly a dozen or so figures scrambled down the forest slope in front of them. They seemed to be moving at almost unbelievable speed. Running at full tilt, and not even casting a glance in the direction of M.

Henry and his friends, they were suddenly in the middle of the field. Hurriedly they dropped to the ground, and without saying a word pulled up fresh cabbages and onions and began to munch them greedily. Only two or three minutes had elapsed since they appeared out of the forest.

"They were *tres, tres, tres petits*," recalled M. Henry. "They looked just like rabbits."

As M. Henry and his friends looked on dumbfounded, one of the "rabbits" turned a grime and mud-stained tan face in their direction. He waved his hand as if to say, "Why don't you join us?"

When the 100th entered Biffontaine they found only fifty or so German signal troops whose escape had been delayed. Battalion ammunition supplies were running extremely low. Captain George Grandstaff, the battalion S-4 was trying to make his way through the forest with troops from Company G, Second Battalion, carrying supplies for the 100th. They could not use jeeps or mules as they had in the hills of Italy, so everything had to be carried on foot. The supply party, followed by the prayerful eyes of Doc Kometani and Reverend Yost, had no idea where the road they were traveling through enemy-held territory would lead.

The Felber task force, an armored group, also set out along the mountain road between Belmont and Biffontaine to bring the 100th water and ammunition, but as soon as they entered the forest they met heavy enemy resistance. The Germans had moved onto the ridge just vacated by the 100th, overlooking not only Biffontaine but also the village of Belmont on the other side. The Second and Third Battalions also marched out to help the 100th but enemy resistance delayed their progress too. Company E and Company F spent the day in the forest battling one hundred or so German bicycle troops who had arrived the night before to cut off the 100th. Even though they fought desperately they could not move one step closer to the 100th.

Company K, Third Battalion, moved along the foot of the high ground, searching each farmhouse for enemy troops as they advanced. Several local people were casualties in the fighting. A ten-year-old boy had his leg blown off by an American grenade. One soldier pulled his trigger immediately when he saw the door of a farmhouse opening from inside. A middle-aged woman who looked like the wife of the house fell to the ground, her chest bathed in blood.

Even though the capture of Biffontaine had been easy, the 100th troops realized that they were completely isolated behind enemy lines. Kim rushed from company to company, making sure their defenses were firm against a counterattack that might come at any moment. The last command post he reached was a village house occupied by Captain Bill Pye, the commander of Company C. As he was about to leave, Pye said to him, "I don't like the look of that enemy tank they left out there in the field." To avoid showing himself Kim peered out over a door in the direction Pye was pointing. He steadied himself by holding onto the top of the door. A German soldier, hearing no more firing, came out of a cellar across the street where he had been hiding since morning. Seeing Kim and Pye standing there, he fired his machine pistol at them. A hail of bullets flew under Pye's extended arm, and three of them hit Kim's right hand.

Soon afterward enemy forces who had surrounded the 100th attacked from all four directions. The battalion ammunition supplies began to dwindle before their very eyes. Some soldiers had to use the rifles taken from the captured enemy signal troops. Casualties mounted. There was still no sign of the friendly troops that Pence had promised to send to the high ground overlooking the village.

As the enemy tightened their net, German soldiers began infiltrating between the houses occupied by the 100th troops. From a tank moving in on the area held by Company C came the voice of a German soldier speaking English.

"You are surrounded. Throw down your weapons and surrender."

In reply someone tossed a hand grenade.

Romary Henry was worried about her parents who lived by themselves in a farmhouse on the westernmost side of Biffontaine, about 100 yards away. They farmed a V-shaped wedge of flat land thrust into the forested slopes. The trees rose up beyond the wall of their stone house. When Romary ran over to see how her parents were, she found that most of their roof had been blown away by a shell. In the dirt courtyard attached to the house were several dozen wounded 100th Battalion soldiers. Her mother and father were hauling water from the well for the thirsty wounded.

On the early morning of October 23, still very dark, another group of eleven wounded 100th soldiers, including Kim and Sam Sakamoto, the Company A commander who was severely wounded in the back, were making their way to the rear with an escort of six guards and German POW stretcher bearers. The group had completely lost their way. As dawn broke they had discovered they were hardly any distance from Biffontaine. One of the guards, twenty-one-year-old Stanley Akita, recalled that just as they sat down on the slope to rest and get their bearings, he suddenly saw enemy soldiers moving on the terrain above them. As he looked about, he could see Germans, about a squad in number, with rifles on the right and on the left.

One German who looked like an officer called out, "Hallo!"

The German POW stretcher bearers made no attempt to move. They looked disgusted at the thought they might have to take up their rifles again. A Japanese American guard called out to the enemy soldiers surrounding them.

"Why don't you put down your guns and come back to America with us? That way you can save your lives."

It looked as though the Germans might respond, Akita later recalled, but then the officer who had called out earlier shook his head and shouted back, "No!" Sergeant George Hagiwara, Akita's superior, thought to himself, "This is it." He turned to Sam Sakamoto, lying motionless on his stretcher, to tell him as much. Sakamoto, his eyes fluttering open, told Hagiwara in a feeble voice to see whether Kim would agree to surrendering.

Wounds on the extremities can be exceptionally painful if they affect a tangle of nerves. Kim, who had lost a lot of blood, had been given several shots of morphine to kill his pain, and his consciousness was hazy. When Hagiwara came over to report the situation, Kim replied in a barely audible voice, "That's not for me."

"Give me a hand," Kim said to Private Richard Chinen, a medic standing nearby. Akita, who had been watching Hagiwara's movements, wondered what was going to happen. He thought Kim was unconscious, but Kim got up off his stretcher and rushed by Akita into the nearby bushes.

"What's going on?" asked Akita. Before his words had died Chinen and Hagiwara had disappeared too. Maybe I should get going too, Akita thought to himself, but by that time the enemy soldiers had closed around him.

Kim rushed headlong into the forest. He did not want to become a POW, and he did not want to die in the forest either. He simply wanted to get away if he could. The morphine made the trees whirl about in front of him, but as he stumbled along he moved with incredible lightness from thicket to thicket. Chinen had trouble keeping up after him.

The message from Lieutenant Colonel Singles came in that afternoon at about 1:18.

"Enemy is coming over big ridge that runs NE and SW. . . . We can't clear the hill mass because they come right back after we clear up. We had a party of litter bearers, also 20 PW's, and Kim was on the litter train and they met a superior force. Kim managed to escape but A Company commander, Lieutenant Sakamoto, is probably captured."

Captain Sakae Takahashi, commander of Company B, was seriously wounded in the arm by enemy machine gun fire. Earlier he had led ten wounded men to the rear. They should have arrived at their destination already, but they had lost their way in the forest. At about the time Singles sent his message to regimental headquarters they ran into soldiers from the 232nd Engineers. As Takahashi stumbled into the engineers' jeep, his face was gray from pain and the loss of blood from his arm. He remembers hearing Singles's report to regimental headquarters come in over the receiver.

"Is Kim hurt?" asked Pence.

"Yes, sir," replied Singles. "Captain Kim managed to escape but he was wounded on the head."

The combat journal reports the injury was to Kim's "head." The message came in over a scratchy and static-filled radio, so it is not strange that everyone thought that Singles said "head," not "hand."

Takahashi muttered to himself, "It's because he didn't have a helmet. I told him so many times. . . ."

So Kim had been hit, thought Takahashi. Kim, the indestructible man, whom bullets avoided, had finally gotten it. For a moment Takahashi forgot his own considerable pain, and an emptiness suddenly filled his chest.

That afternoon, as Pence had promised, the Third Battalion led by Company K reached the ridge overlooking Biffontaine. About the same time the armored Felber task force had broken through the enemy's defenses and moved up the ridge, while the Second Battalion mopped up the enemy forces on the flank. But by then the 100th Battalion had lost nearly all its key men.

By 6:00 P.M. on October 24 all three battalions of the 442nd had come down into Belmont, relieved by the 141st and 143rd.

The alert came at 2:30 on the afternoon of October 25. The division commander had appeared at the 442nd regimental command post with Lieutenant General Alexander M. Patch, commanding general of the Seventh Army. Dahlquist told Pence that he did not really want to send the Second Battalion out to the battlefield again, but he ordered Pence to move to the flank of the 141st before dark. The division commander also paid a visit to the 100th Battalion command post, where he explained to Singles that the First Battalion of the 141st had been surrounded by the enemy and the 100th should be ready to move out at any moment.

The 141st troops had run into trouble after they left the village of Belmont and moved northeast through the Biffontaine forest. Bill Hull, first sergeant of Company C, First Battalion, then twenty-seven years old, first realized that the unit had been surrounded when five of the thirty-six men sent out for supplies came back, reporting that they had just managed to escape. The trapped group consisted of Company C, Company A, and several men from Company B, as well as an observer from the artillery company. Altogether there were 275 men. They were barely able to maintain contact with the regimental headquarters by the transmitter belonging to Lieutenant Erwin Blonder, the artillery observer.

The Thirty-sixth Division was originally a Texas National Guard unit, but by late 1944 the majority of the troops were replacements from all over the United States. First Lieutenant Martin Higgins, Hull's superior, was from New Jersey, and Blonder was from Ohio. Very few soldiers were from Texas. Bill Hull, born and raised near San Antonio, was one of them, but he did not look like a tall rangy Texan. Of medium height and medium build, and rather calm and relaxed in manner, he was one of the handful of the original Thirty-sixth Division soldiers who had managed to survive the fighting in North Africa.

All during the night the men of the surrounded battalion took turns standing guard. At almost exactly 10:00 A.M. every day for the next several days the enemy sent a tank out for a frontal attack. The only reason the enemy did not attack in force, thought Hull, was that they did not know how many American soldiers they had surrounded. Whenever the tank advanced the trapped Americans responded with a barrage of machine gun fire. They could do nothing but try to gain time, hoping that the enemy would not learn their strength, hoping for help from friendly forces.

In Biffontaine Lieutenant Colonel Singles remembered when his own 100th Battalion had been surrounded in the town. He could imagine all too well why the 141st had been cut off behind enemy lines. Even so why did he and his men, just off the front lines, have to rush back again to rescue them? Colonel Pence had just told him the battalion would have at least two days' rest.

On the morning of October 26 the Second Battalion of the 442nd was ordered to move out on the rescue mission to a position just in front of the Third Battalion of the 141st. The closer they got to the "lost battalion," the tighter and firmer they found the enemy's line of encirclement. By dark they could not move forward any further.

According to intelligence reports, that evening several hundred enemy reinforcements had come in to surround the lost battalion. To judge by their insignia, which the 442nd troops had not seen before, the reinforcements were special elite troops trained for mountain warfare. All were strong, well built, and excellent marksmen.

At 2:00 A.M. on the morning of October 27 the 100th Battalion and the Third Battalion, which had remained at Belmont, received an alert to move out. It was still pitch-dark. The Third Battalion jumped off at 4:00 A.M. and the 100th at 5:00 A.M. As they entered the forest they passed by mess trucks and ambulances prepared for the moment when the lost battalion was rescued. Moving silently the Japanese American troops disappeared into the forest.

The first day: Friday, October 27, 1944, rain.
The mother of twenty-three-year-old Sergeant Noboru Fujinaka remembers well what her son's friends told her after the war about the

darkness of the forest. As a baby Matsuno Fujinaka emigrated to Hawaii from Fukushima in the northeastern part of Honshu. She still lives by herself in Honolulu. Her oldest son had not been able to join the army since he had just become a father, so her second son and her youngest son, Noboru, a sophomore at the University of Hawaii, had volunteered to represent the family in the military service. Mrs. Fujinaka displays the letters Noboru sent home from the front like treasures in her Buddhist household shrine right beside the family mortuary tablets. Noboru, who died in the rescue of the lost battalion, wrote his mother in Japanese.

"It has been a long time since I have been in touch with you. How are you, honorable mother and father? Is everyone in the family well? . . .

"Mother, thank you for your recent letter. I am spending the days in good health so please do not worry. . . . Father, can you read this letter? I have not used Japanese in a long time so I am wracking my brains as I write this letter. Mother and Father, I would like to write you a letter in Japanese every now and then, but since I am so inept please be patient with me."

Many soldiers, like Noboru Fujinaka, tried to summon up their long unused Japanese during the lulls in training so they could write parents who could read and write no other language. The military censors seem to have approved these letters in enemy script, and news of their sons got back to the Japanese immigrant parents.

"The forest was really dark, they say," said Mrs. Fujinaka. "I heard it was so absolutely dark that you couldn't see your hand if you stretched it out in front of you. They had to move through the forest slowly with one hand on someone's shoulder in front of them."

The forest was not only dark. The wet, muddy road was pitted with holes and hard to climb. If one soldier in a file slipped in the dark so did the soldiers below, falling down like a row of dominoes. When it became light enough to get a sense of the surroundings the Third Battalion came out onto the narrow road that led to the lost battalion's position. Their uniforms were soaked through to the underwear, and their boots and socks were covered with mud. The only dry thing most had left was a change of socks kept pinned under their underwear.

At 8:00 A.M. a steady barrage of long-range 88-millimeter shells began. More fearful of being separated and lost in the forest than of being hit by shrapnel the soldiers moved ahead following the man in front. From the shadow of the trees and brush enemy machine guns fired ceaselessly. In the first squad of Company K, Trigger Happy kept firing at the enemy he could not see. Suddenly he lost feeling in the tip of one of his feet. When he looked down he saw that there was a hole in the bottom of his boot. A bullet had passed through it.

From the first day the enemy directed their fiercest attacks on the

Third Battalion's position. The battalion was constantly showered by concentrated fire. On their right flank the Second Battalion had lost one of their tanks to a land mine, and the road was too narrow to use the other.

At 1:15 P.M. General Dahlquist appeared in the farmhouse the 442nd and the 141st shared as a command post. He issued detailed orders. He was annoyed that the Third Battalion had not advanced to its objective even though four hours had passed since the scheduled attack began. He kept in touch with Lieutenant Colonel Alfred Pursall, commander of the Third Battalion.

The main enemy counterattack force moving behind tank cover hit Company K full force. When the German tank began firing from a distance of about seventy yards away the men in Company K thought it was all over for them. Nineteen-year-old Sergeant Joe Shimamura calmly put the tank out of commission with a well-placed shot. The wide-eyed Shimamura had incredibly sharp vision.

The Second Battalion was in reserve on the division's outermost flank. It did not meet much enemy resistance and was able to reach its objective. At around 5:00 P.M., when dark had already fallen, an artillery barrage from another battalion in the division hit the ground in front of their position. Boiling mad, Lieutenant Colonel James Hanley, commander of the Second Battalion, called regimental headquarters and complained that he did not recall asking for artillery fire in that direction.

At 6:37 that evening Colonel Pence sent orders to Lieutenant Colonel Pursall, commander of the Third Battalion.

"We attack tomorrow at 0630. The division commander wants us to push and reach the isolated battalion."

Pursall reported that he had tried to close the gap between his unit and the 100th Battalion, but his men had run into heavy machine gun fire. Company K had found itself in "a hell of a fight." Company K and Company I, in a V-shaped defense position on the hill, were unable to move forward so they dug in.

Nineteen-year-old Private Harry Nakabe, who grew up near San Francisco, was a member of the Second Platoon of Company K. A slightly built young man, barely five feet tall, he had tried to volunteer for the service from Granada (also called Amache) relocation camp in Colorado but failed the physical examination. After spending two months working as a seasonal laborer in the nearby beet fields to build up his body, he volunteered again. As the eldest son in his family he was determined to get into the service so that his younger brothers and sisters, and parents too, could live proudly as Americans once the war was over. The army seems to have been moved by his resolve and inducted him. During training Harry became a buddy of Rudy Tokiwa. Harry's face had the round puffy cheeks of a boy, and he looked even younger than Tokiwa.

Nakabe dug his foxhole as deep as he could. Curled up in it he felt quite safe. Suddenly someone leapt into the foxhole with him. He could not see the stranger's face but to judge from his physique Nakabe thought it must be a Caucasian soldier. In the tight foxhole he could feel the heat of the other fellow's body. Perhaps he felt secure in having another human being at his side in the midst of the dark forest. Before he knew it he had drifted off to sleep.

The ground was so rocky that some soldiers did not find it easy to dig a foxhole. Twenty-year-old Private Richard Oda tried as hard as he could, but every time his shovel went into the ground, it hit a stone. His squad leader, Sergeant Joe Shimamura, came over to chew him out. Frustrated, tired, and angry, Oda shouted back at him, "It's rocks all over!" "Do your best," said Shimamura after feeling around with both hands.

That night Shimamura, half-asleep, heard a rattling sound in the dark coming from the direction of the enemy. German soldiers appeared to be repairing the tank that Joe had knocked out earlier that day. All night he heard the sound of tools against metal, and then the sound of the tank receding up the mountain road.

Private Henry Nakada, twenty-four, a member of the First Platoon, Company I, spent the night crawling about in the dark trying to find friendly forces. That morning he and two other soldiers had been ordered by his platoon leader, Second Lieutenant Richard Hayashi, to scout the enemy situation and terrain. (Hayashi, from Stockton, California, had been drafted before the war, but because his Japanese was good he had gone into Military Intelligence School [MIS] and interrogated Japanese POWs at New Caledonia in the Pacific theater. When the 442nd was organized he repeatedly asked for a transfer to the combat unit. He became the only Japanese American officer transferred from the Pacific to the European front.) As Nakada and the other two scouts were making their way through the forest they ran into machine gun fire directly ahead of them. Nakada dove into the underbrush and waited by himself until dark. When he made his way to the spot where he thought his company was, he found no one there. He did not know the password. Whenever he heard what sounded like the voice of a friendly soldier he whispered softly in Japanese. "*Shi-shi-ni* [442]." "*Oyaji* [Dad]." "*Meshi* [Food]." "*Bakatare* [Asshole]." When at last he found someone who understood him he was so drained of energy that he did not feel like digging a foxhole.

Nakada, who had been born in Los Angeles, was drafted while working at a harbor in Alaska. The fifth of twelve children, Nakada had one older brother in MIS in the Pacific and another in officers training school. Altogether seven Nakada brothers wore the uniform of their country. Among all the Japanese Americans the Nakada family gave the military service the most sons. Indeed in the whole United States there was only one other family—Caucasian—that could match that record. The Nakadas' mother spent the war years at the Gila relocation camp in the Arizona desert.

The second day: Saturday, October 28, 1944, cloudy, followed by rain.
"Father," wrote Noboru Fujinaka, "do not worry unnecessarily about me and my brother. And Father, I hear that you are working without resting even one day. Please do not strain yourself. That is my hope. If you have a hard day please get some rest. Mother, please take care of yourself in the same way. Please."

The Caucasian soldier who had spent the night in Harry Nakabe's foxhole left at dawn the following morning. "Good luck!" he said as he departed.

The attack began again at 6:30 A.M. During the night the enemy had spread out over the area overlooking the narrow valley, and more enemy tanks had been brought in. At 6:55 the division commander asked Lieutenant Colonel Pursall, the Third Battalion commander, whether he had advanced.

"Yes, we're moving out slowly," Pursall replied. "It's so dark you can't see your hand in front of your face. I don't want to walk blindly into them."

By 8:20 A.M. Company K and Company I had managed to move forward 350 yards. Private Kiyoshi Yoshii, twenty-six, a member of the Second Platoon, Company K, jumped into a hole that he thought the enemy had dug. It was about chest deep. Harry Nakabe was crouching in the underbrush a little behind him. Sergeant Etsuo "Etchan" Kohashi, age twenty-eight, in the lead, stepped from the shadow of a tree and shouted, "Keep on going!"

A native of Hilo, Etchan was the son of a fisherman who had immigrated from Hiroshima. He had a broad-boned face that at a glance might be mistaken for Polynesian. He often went on reconnaissance, moving through the forest with strong, long strides as if he had known it for years. Few of his buddies knew that Etchan had to put up with the sharp pain of a stomach ulcer.

Hearing Etchan's shout Yoshii quickly jumped into the hole in front of him, his rifle at the ready. A mortar shell landed to his left a few seconds later. When Harry Nakabe raised his helmet to peer out from the brush where he was hiding, he saw several of his buddies lying motionless on the ground.

Yoshii suddenly came to his senses. He saw blood pouring from both his legs. His left hand was hanging from his arm by a piece of skin. Yoshii was seized with fear. A medic, round-faced little Tadao Miyamoto, appeared and quickly tried to stop the bleeding with a tourniquet. He gave Yoshii a shot of morphine and stuck a sulfa tablet in his mouth.

"I'll be back," he said, moving to another wounded soldier.

Lying drenched in a pool of his own blood, Yoshii says that he suddenly thought of the parents he had left at the Topaz relocation camp in Utah. Immigrants from Yamaguchi prefecture, they had settled in Oakland where they ran a restaurant before the war. The face of Yoshii's younger brother also hovered before him. All he could think was that he had to return alive to see them. His consciousness was beginning to fade, but for the first time in his life Yoshii began to pray with all his heart. As he was being carried back to the aid station Yoshii, wracked by a delirious nightmare in which enemy soldiers were burning his arms, kept screaming, "What are they doing to me?"

When Etchan shouted, "Keep on going," Pfc Harold Fujita, twenty-five, from Kona jumped out of his foxhole. He was mowed down immediately by enemy fire. He had no idea where or how he had been hit. As he tried to get up he felt a numbness in his hands and legs. The numbness spread to Fujita's whole body. He had no feeling from the neck down. It was as though he had been sucked into the floor of the Vosges forest. A small fragment of shrapnel had struck his spine.

Fujita's Japanese name was Kenichi. His father, a native of Yamaguchi, had died when he was seven years old. His mother had to raise Fujita and his five older sisters by herself. By the time the war had begun Fujita had moved to Honolulu where he worked for a milk company. The company, apparently fearing that the Japanese American employees might sabotage the milk, fired them all after the Pearl Harbor attack. Without asking his mother, Fujita volunteered for the service. Afterward he learned that his nephew, Takeshi Kudo, the son of his oldest sister and only two years younger than he, had volunteered along with a younger brother. The uncle and his two nephews, brought up in a house where the emperor's photograph was proudly displayed, left Kona by truck for induction together.

Private George Abe, age thirty, a member of the First Platoon, came staggering toward Harry Nakabe, who was quietly watching over his wounded buddies. Abe's face was covered with blood. He had gotten out of his foxhole when he heard his squad leader, Sergeant Joe Shimamura, yell "Let's go!" Suddenly he felt as though he had been slugged near the eyes by a hard swung baseball bat. He dropped back down on his haunches into the foxhole. When he recovered himself, he saw the Vosges forest dyed blood red. He did not yet realize he had lost the sight of one eye. He simply thought he was dying. Suddenly he began to worry about his younger brother who had volunteered from the Poston relocation camp in Arizona and been sent as a replacement to the 100th Battalion where he was serving as Kim's signalman. Abe climbed out of the hole hoping to make sure that his brother was all right.

Sergeant George Nishi, Company K platoon sergeant, was the only noncom left in his unit. As he started to move on an order to withdraw to the rear a little, a hand grenade trailing a blue-white wisp of smoke came sailing into his foxhole. He threw it back. From behind him he heard a voice call out, "Good shot!" Another grenade came sailing over and exploded. The soldier who had just called out lay drenched in blood.

Nishi turned to Private Satoru Sawai, age nineteen, beside him. "Something wrong with my back?" he asked. Sawai looked goggle-eyed at him. Before Sawai made a move to check Nishi, Sergeant Tak Goto, twenty-two, turned to him and said, "Yup." At that moment Nishi began to feel a sharp pain in his back.

Sawai was hit in the chest and arm soon after. Like Sawai, Pfc Kenji Takubo, nineteen, was one of a group of four buddies from Oahu in the squad who were so close they had picked up the nickname "The Four Musketeers." While on leave in New Orleans Takubo had shown a Gypsy fortune-teller in the French Quarter a photograph of the four of them together. She told him, "You are the only one who will come back alive." Takubo could not hide his relief. It turned out instead that he was the first to go. Takubo was killed instantly after Sawai was carried to the rear by stretcher. Another member of the "Four Musketeers," Pfc Saburo Yamada, twenty-one, was seriously wounded several days later, and the final member, Pfc Sadaichi Kohara, twenty, was to die in Italy the day before the war ended.

At 11:00 A.M. in response to a call from General Dahlquist, Colonel Pence said that Company L, until then held in reserve for the Third Battalion, was in a holding attack.

"I don't want a holding attack," replied General Dahlquist. "That's the trouble. Get the men out of there crawling and get the krauts out of the holes."

A few moments later, he went on. "I want you to go up to C Company and see if they are in foxholes. If they are get them out and fix a boundary."

It was probably shortly afterward that a huge figure emerged out of the shadow of the trees in front of the foxhole where Private Sanji Kimoto, First Platoon, Company K, waited with his rifle at the ready. When Kimoto noticed there were two stars on the helmet he was so surprised that for a moment the strength drained out of the hand holding his weapon. What in the world was the division commander doing out here on the forwardmost battle line? He's got guts, thought Kimoto. At the same time he somehow realized for the first time how tense the situation was. The Japanese American soldiers still had not been told they were on a mission to rescue the lost battalion. They simply followed orders to move out and attack. In the midst of the continuing fire Kimoto soon forgot the two stars on the helmet and renewed a grip on his rifle.

Pfc Henry Nakada of Company I was sniping at an enemy machine gun nest hidden in the bushes ahead of him when his adversary stopped shooting for a moment. Nakada sensed someone watching him from behind. When he turned around in his foxhole, he saw a man with two stars on his helmet followed by a clean-cut young first lieutenant. The two stars shouted angrily at the startled Nakada.

"Why aren't you up out of your foxhole!"

Second Lieutenant Richard Hayashi, Nakada's platoon commander, was crouching in the shadow of the trees. The two stars came up from behind and gave him a kick that sent him sprawling forward.

At 11:20 Lieutenant Colonel Pursall, commander of the Third Battalion, sent a message to Colonel Pence at the regimental command post.

"We have tanks up here but there are mines in the road. We have only two tanks. I talked to Colonel Singles and we think we'd better place artillery."

But preparation for an artillery bombardment in the rear took time, and it was slow. The 100th Battalion was in position on the Third Battalion's right flank. By noon the enemy had begun to retreat to the next ridge.

Sergeant Yoshio Minami, twenty-five years old, had been envious when Akahoshi had gone to help Captain Kim capture the enemy POWs at Anzio. He and Pfc James Kubokawa, twenty-five, had continued to work in the S-2 section. The two of them, together with several other soldiers, stood guarding a group of German POWs who had been herded into a dugout. They were firing questions at the POWs to figure out where the enemy position was. A barrage of artillery shells suddenly struck, mowing down the Americans. All were killed instantly. The force of the explosion tore their bodies to pieces. Ironically not one of the POWs, witnesses to this hellish scene, was even slightly wounded.

By a stroke of good fortune Irving Akahoshi was in Honolulu on leave. He tried to cheer up Kubokawa's parents (Kubokawa was an only son) when he visited them. "He works in the headquarters, so he doesn't have to go anywhere that's dangerous," he told them. "He'll be back soon, for sure." He told the same thing to Minami's widowed mother when he visited her.

The next day he got a phone call from Minami's sister about Minami's death. Akahoshi was at a total loss over the death of his two close friends. The army had given the original 100th soldiers who had returned on leave at the same time the choice of transferring to the local army garrison, but Akahoshi, alone among them, refused. Not long afterward he was on a military plane going back to the European front.

First Lieutenant James Boodry, the 100th Battalion S-2, succeeded Kim as S-3. Kubokawa and Minami had both worked for him a long time. Shortly after he heard they had been killed, Boodry was huddled with First Lieutenant Bill Pye, the commander of Company C, to put the finishing touches on plans for the next move. An explosion burst over their heads. Boodry fell to the ground as though stamped upon. The top of his head had been split open.

Pye, blood streaming from his own hands and arms, looked in disbelief at Boodry's shattered body. The six foot two Pye was skin and bones. He had shrunk to about 110 pounds over the past several days. A native of Texas born in San Antonio, he says that when he learned that the 100th was being placed under the Texas Division—the Thirty-sixth Division—somehow or other he had a disagreeable feeling about it. On the Italian front the 100th had always been made to haul the division's chestnuts out of the fire.

Pye moved quickly when he saw Boodry go down. "Hard to wait any longer," he thought to himself. "If I have to get it, get it done sooner." Heedless of the enemy shrapnel, he moved forward. Less than a half-hour later he was sprawled in the forest unable to move, his leg shattered by an enemy shell.

No matter how often they were warned Reverend Yost and Doc Kometani both kept moving closer and closer to the dangerous front line. Even after dark fell they hurried about, helping to tote stretchers and taking care of the wounded. Yost recalled that Kometani could not bear to sleep safe and sound in his foxhole while his "boys" were falling in battle. Although he usually started snoring as soon as he laid his head down, he had trouble sleeping in the Vosges forest. For the first time his bulldog face seemed to have lost vitality. How many of his "boys" had survived since they left Honolulu more than two years before? The glorious record of the 100th Battalion, built as they had given their lives one after the other since Salerno, was being destroyed before his eyes. Doc had explained to them why they were fighting as Japanese Americans, and he had urged them on. Now he seemed beaten down, thought Yost, as he looked at Doc's suffering eyes. Even Yost felt as empty as he felt angry when he saw how the 100th was being squandered in the Vosges.

Veterans have many unforgettable memories of Reverend Yost during this time. In the roofless field hospital, the doctors could see the figure of Reverend Yost kneeling beside a prostrate ashen-faced youth. "Takao, I'm praying for you." He did not say he was praying for recovery. Even in the rain the medics and the doctors took off their hats when they heard those words.

"Our Father who art in Heaven hallowed be thy name . . ."
The ashen-faced youth had stopped breathing.

Shortly after Jim Boodry was killed Lieutenant Colonel Singles, who had gone to the very front of the line, assembled all the company commanders on his ridge. Standing before him were only two second lieutenants and two sergeants. The 100th had lost so many troops that only men of this rank were left to command companies. Singles, doing his best to reassure them, was explaining the battle plan when a signal soldier reported there was a message from the division commander. Singles used all his strength to pull the field telephone wire loose. He knew that if he opened his mouth he would say something to the division commander that would get him court-martialed.

The jeep Colonel Pence was riding in was hit by an enemy shell as it moved toward Singles's position. One of the passengers was killed instantly, another was seriously wounded, and Pence himself was injured in the leg. When Reverend Hiro Higuchi, chaplain of the Second Battalion, met Pence earlier as he was getting in his jeep, the colonel had told him dispiritedly, "Hiro, I'm really tired." It was the only time that Higuchi had ever heard the usually bold Pence say anything so weakly.

Even after dark a stream of messages continued to come into regimental headquarters from the division commander. At 6:40 P.M. the general was angry when he heard that Lieutenant Colonel Pursall of the Third Battalion had stopped forward movement on account of the thick darkness.

"I think if [the enemy] have pulled back you ought to push and find what is ahead of you."

He gave detailed orders, down to the movement of individual platoons, to Lieutenant Colonel Virgil Miller, the regimental executive officer who had taken command of the 442nd when Pence was wounded.

"Drive the Jerries out, rescue the First Battalion [the lost battalion], and drive Jerry south of the ridge. Your objective really is that ridge and push out to the south."

At 7:30 P.M. Dahlquist sent a message to Lieutenant Colonel Pursall of the Third Battalion telling him to send out a patrol.

"You need a good man and if he can get out that First Battalion he can have a Distinguished Service Cross. You personally interview the man who is going."

The general's message betrayed his anxiety. If an entire battalion was wiped out the division commander's competence inevitably would be called into question. The patrol was sent out from Company L. They were not able to get anywhere near the lost battalion.

About the same time a party of volunteers from Company K was making its way to the rear to get ammunition and rations. Sanji Kimoto, unable to lie in his foxhole because of the cold, volunteered but was not chosen to go. Harry Nakabe did not volunteer, but when orders were issued to prepare gas masks he joined the group. He had left his gas mask in his foxhole the night before since it was a nuisance to carry around.

There were twelve men in the party. Their eyes perhaps now used to the darkness of the forest, they walked through the night, less cautious than before, certain of where they were headed. Suddenly an 88-millimeter shell hit. Two of the group were killed, the rest all wounded. The soldier picked instead of Sanji Kimoto was seriously hurt.

Also wounded was Sergeant George "Matsu" Shigematsu, age twenty-two, who had grown up in New Mexico, near the border where many Mexican Americans lived. His was the only Japanese American family in the area. His father, a repairman for the Santa Fe Railroad, had moved there from California. (Matsu, who now works as a mailman in his old hometown, says what he missed most on the battlefield was hot Mexican food.) Japanese Americans living in New Mexico were not sent to relocation camps, but when Shigematsu applied for a job on an airbase he was refused on the grounds that he might be a spy. That was what led him to volunteer.

When Matsu came to after the explosion he heard someone laughing in the darkness. It was annoying. He kept thinking to himself, who is laughing like that? But the laughing sound was coming from Matsu himself as air leaked out of a big hole in his chest. The blood and air accumulating in his lungs made Matsu feel as though he were drowning.

Harry Nakabe had felt a sharp pain in his thigh when the shell exploded. When he reached down to touch it his hand was slippery. After putting a tourniquet on his leg, he started to walk. He wanted to get away from the shrieks and cries of his wounded buddies. With faltering steps he made his way down, half conscious, half delirious, as if pursued by the whole dark forest.

IX

The Rescue of the Lost Battalion

FOR several days wounded soldiers were carried to the house of Romary Henry's parents near the edge of Biffontaine forest. About six hundred yards away the humble two-room Voirin cottage was so closely packed with wounded from the 442nd Regiment that it was hard to walk among them. Josephine Voirin had a surprising kind of strength. Her husband had returned as a hero from World War I with several medals, a small pension, and piece of shrapnel in his head. Ever since, he had been nearly a complete invalid seized by splitting headaches several times a day. During the fighting in the forest of Biffontaine his headaches were worse than usual because of the artillery fire and the general tension. Josephine could not let him out of her sight.

Even so, Josephine tried to give the wounded Japanese Americans water. A shell had hit the water pipe, though, and the water only dribbled out. She wet the lips of one soldier who whispered "Mama" in a voice she almost could not hear. It was the last word he spoke. When she pulled back the blood-soaked blanket covering him, she could see exposed intestines.

Today Josephine, now widowed, lives by herself, even though heart trouble confines her to bed most of the time. Her soft voice, almost at a whisper, still sounds youthful. "There is one thing you ought to see before you go," she said, getting out of her bed in her nightgown and pushing open the door to the shed attached to the house. Inside the light was dim, and sound muffled. Josephine had kept there a mattress covered with rust-colored stains, where many wounded and bleeding Japanese American soldiers had lain.

Farther along the edge of Biffontaine forest in the direction of Belmont, other wounded soldiers were carried to the Tarentzeff farmhouse. On the road in front of it was a stone cross about ten feet tall put there more than two centuries before. Some veterans remember an apple tree growing on one side of the house.

Alexander Tarentzeff, a former Cossack, had come to the Vosges as a Russian army officer during World War I. When he learned that his father, a landowner, as well as his mother and siblings had been killed by the Bolshevik revolutionary army he decided not to return to his homeland. He married a local girl whose father taught the trade of making wooden shoes to earn a living. The Tarentzeff house was where his wife had been born.

The outside of the two-story stone building is almost unchanged since the war. Long since a widower, M. Tarentzeff is in his late eighties and lives with his son, daughter-in law, and their two children. His broad-jawed face and straight-backed torso still give a hint of how he must have looked when he was young. In a high-pitched nasal voice he apologized that he could not do a Cossack dance anymore, and as he talked about the Japanese Americans his voice rose even higher.

About a month before the arrival of the Japanese Americans, he said, he helped a group of a dozen or so Indian soldiers fighting with the British army, who had escaped from a POW camp near Épinal. He hid them near a big stone in the forest, where every day his eleven-year-old son, George, took them food. Today the locals call it the "Hindu stone." The day after Tarentzeff gave the Indians some old clothes and sent them on their way German soldiers arrived at the house to set up a command post. During the next three weeks German officers slept inside the house as if they owned it, and wounded German enlisted men lay outside.

One day the Germans left hurriedly. Soon afterward a company of Japanese American soldiers emerged out of the forest. (There are many soldiers in Company E and Company G of the Second Battalion who remember the stone cross.) Like the Germans, the officers slept inside the house and the rest of the men dug foxholes in the field. In one corner of the field stand several crude grave markers made of two pieces of wood put together in the form of a cross. George says that the German soldiers told him to bury their comrades there.

In a corner of the storehouse in the backyard there is a lathe for making wooden shoes. The Japanese American signal troops set up their equipment beside it. The sound of voices could be heard there all night long. The smell of coffee wafted from another outbuilding used as a field kitchen.

So many wounded Japanese Americans were brought down out of the forest there was hardly room inside the house. George remembered that the German wounded were noisier. They screamed like animals, he said. But whether it was the Germans or the Japanese Americans the memory of soldiers crying out in pain always remained in the ears of the young boy. The bodies of the Japanese American soldiers were wrapped in canvas and laid out in the field until a truck came around to pick them up. More and more were carried off as each day passed.

On the evening of October 28, the second day since the 442nd was ordered to join in the rescue of the lost battalion of the 141st Infantry Regiment, the commander of the 143rd Infantry, Colonel Paul Adams, complained to the division commander that none of the rest of the 141st was fighting that day. To the men in the 442nd, however, even the 143rd Infantry did not seem interested in risking their all to save the lost battalion. According to the combat journal of the 442nd the following conversation took place on October 22 between Colonel Pence and Lieutenant Colonel Hanley, commander of the Second Battalion.[1]

HANLEY: I talked to Akins and the patrol has taken off. This thing makes me mad. Akins said the 143rd sat all day long, and he saw them 200 or 300 yards away. He sent someone over to them but they wouldn't budge.

PENCE: They stayed in their safe place.

HANLEY: Yes, we had a platoon go 800 yards NE and cleared out the Jerries in their dugout with hand grenades. The CO of F Company of the 143rd came up to us when there was no firefight at that time and asked if they could plug into our line. Akins asked him for help in case of a firefight, and this 143rd F Company CO said they were going to stay where they were.

After leaving the Vosges the 442nd officers speculated that none of the other regiments in the division moved because their officers had already figured out General Dahlquist's way of doing things. They had had plenty of experience with his constant drive to move forward, never consolidating a position. They knew that the battle in the Vosges was a minor operation, not a major front in the Allied drive toward the German border, and they did not want to waste lives in such a place. A radio message from one commanding officer, Colonel Paul Adams, complained, "If the general doesn't find out the right information I'll have him busted and the company commanders will have to go up to the front and give the right information."[2] To judge from that, the opinion of the 442nd officers may not have been mere speculation.

On the evening of October 28 a 105-millimeter artillery shell packed with chocolate was fired into the perimeter of the lost battalion. According to Bill Hull, nearly all the chocolate was buried so deep in the rain-soaked soil that it was impossible to dig out. Though their food supplies had run out several days ago, the surrounded 141st troops had no trouble getting water. Just outside their perimeter was a small pond. When they found out the Germans were using the pond too, they took turns sneaking out under cover of darkness to draw water.

All day long the men of the lost battalion talked about nothing but food. Milk shakes and ice cream, popcorn and chocolate cake. And when the talk turned to ham and eggs, some of the troops could almost smell them frying. They argued about which restaurant had the best food.

Through it all they never lost hope. Bill Hull never doubted that eventually friendly forces would come to rescue them.

The surrounded unit even took a prisoner. One enemy soldier who had lost his way stumbled into their midst. He curled up in a foxhole with two of the American soldiers, thinking they were Germans, and dropped off to sleep soundly. That is how close the enemy was.

The third day: Sunday, October 29, 1944, fog and rain.

"Mother and Father," wrote Noboru Fujinaka, "please don't worry about us. I am careful about everything so please set your minds at ease. I will not die a needless death. As Mother said, anybody can die. The real achievement is to give one's all for the country, and then to come home alive."

The 100th Battalion and the Third Battalion waited for dawn to begin their attack. The circle of enemy forces surrounding the lost battalion showed no sign of crumbling. The ridges in the area were extremely narrow and fell off sharply like cliffs to the left and right. Land mines were planted everywhere.

Lieutenant Colonel Pursall's Third Battalion planned to cut the enemy off on the left flank without waiting for engineers to clear the minefields, but the Germans, spearheaded by tanks, counterattacked relentlessly. Casualties were especially high in Company K.

The enemy might have been cleaned out by artillery, but it was impossible to adjust the fire among the tall trees and the sloping terrain. Shells might land inside friendly lines or sail beyond the enemy position into the lost battalion's perimeter. It was like trying to hit a nail on the head without seeing it.

The 100th Battalion circled to the right of the minefield to attack the enemy's flank, but the casualties mounted. The first message of the day came from General Dahlquist at the 442nd command post at 8:00 that morning.

"Keep them going and don't let them stop. There's a battalion about to die up there and we've got to reach them."

"Yes, sir," replied Lieutenant Colonel Singles simply.

The general, accompanied by his aide, a handsome young first lieutenant, left the regimental command post at 9:45. Four hours later a report came in that his aide had been killed.

Lieutenant Colonel Singles had been crouching on the slope of a ridge cautiously looking at an enemy machine gun nest about forty yards away in the forest when the general suddenly appeared from behind and kneeled down beside him.

"Have you got a map?" he asked.

First Lieutenant James Boodry, who had been killed the day before, had kept the 100th's military terrain map, and Singles replied that he did not have one. The division commander ordered that a map be brought right away from the regimental command post. As Singles moved back several feet toward his transmitter to send the order, the general's aide called out, "I've got one." He stood up and stepped one pace in front of the division commander to spread the map out. The enemy machine gun fired. The lieutenant fell forward as though crushed. Without emotion Singles kept walking back into the forest. The division commander came up from behind and knelt down beside him. The front of his uniform was covered with the young lieutenant's blood.

"Lewis is dead," he said.

"I saw that," replied Singles.

"Did you know? He was Sinclair Lewis's son," said the general as though all his energy had left him. Slowly he lifted himself up and disappeared toward the rear.

Sinclair Lewis, the author of *Main Street, Arrowsmith,* and *Elmer Gantry,* was the first American to receive the Nobel prize for literature. His eldest son, twenty-seven-year-old Wells Lewis, a Harvard graduate, his father's pride, was on his way to making a name for himself as a journalist when he had been drafted. General Dahlquist wrote Sinclair Lewis a personal letter of condolence on October 31. "I was near enough to catch his body as it fell. He was dead before I laid him on the ground. . . . I was present at the services, and it was as though my own son was being buried. I had known Wells only since July of this year, but in that short period he had endeared himself to me as a real man."[3]

Although Singles thought the general had gone to the rear, suddenly the general appeared at his side again. "Have you got the map?" he asked. Singles suddenly remembered that one of the men had given him a map after Boodry's death. He found it in his pocket. The general followed Singles looking at the map, but his mind seemed to be somewhere else. Ignoring him Singles continued to move along. His chest was filled with anger. It was hard for him even to speak. The general, not showing whether he was aware of Singles's anger, kept following.

It is clear from the 442nd combat journal how deeply the general was shaken after Lieutenant Lewis's death. At around 2:00 Lieutenant Colonel Baya Harrison, commander of the 522nd Field Artillery, sent a message to regimental headquarters.

"We had a call from a forward observer that the general wanted some shoot [*sic*] on Hill 345573. Isn't that right in the middle of the lost battalion? I wish you would check."

"Yes, it's right in the middle of the lost battalion," came the reply from regiment.

The road at the foot of the hill had been turned into a muddy swamp. The 232nd Engineers Company was busy laying down logs so that ambulances and trucks could get through.

Suddenly enemy forces appeared at the rear of the 100th. One medic was taken prisoner and the field telephone line was cut. Ahead of the battalion enemy tanks continued to counterattack. It was difficult even to get the casualties out. Singles assembled his three companies for an attack to get as close as possible to the trapped battalion. The enemy retreated a bit, leaving nearly sixty dead behind. The Germans were evidently ready to die before being taken prisoner.

General Dahlquist insisted that the main push be made from the position held by the Third Battalion. When Rudy Tokiwa, the messenger for Company K, arrived with a message for Lieutenant Colonel Pursall, he saw the general upbraiding the battalion commander.

"Why aren't you moving forward?"

"If you think it's that simple," said Pursall, "I'd like you to come with me for a look." Urging the general to follow he made his way through the trees. As Tokiwa watched, the two figures continued arguing beyond the trees in front of him.

Company K's assault from the left flank had failed, and the unit was pinned down unable to move further. The enemy held a position on the slope above them. Uninterrupted machine gun fire seemed to come from all directions. The men jumped even at the rustle of the branches.

Orders came to make a charge, advancing under the cover of tanks, against the enemy above them. The troops listened grimly. An uphill charge was like asking to be shot. Only that morning the troops had learned they were being sent to rescue the lost battalion. As long as we save them, thought some of the men, nobody cares what becomes of us.

Companies K and I were to begin an attack simultaneously. Tanks moved up the slope firing constantly. The troops did not make a move. Lieutenant Colonel Pursall sent a message urging the Second Platoon, Company K, the forwardmost unit, to move out. Second Lieutenant Edward Davis began to climb up the slope. He was the only officer left in Company K who had not been wounded or injured. He stumbled forward clutching his stomach. Many of the soldiers, bolting down cold rations in the wet and cold, had developed severe diarrhea, almost like dysentery. Davis had been in severe pain since the day before.

Company K had not been lucky with its company commanders. Their first commander, a tough-talking officer while at Camp Shelby suffered shell shock after the first battle, and his successors had not been much improvement. In tight situations they seemed to find some excuse or other to stay in the rear. Many of the troops thought the white officers were a cowardly bunch. They were more than surprised to see Davis leading the charge in such a dangerous situation where most men would flinch at moving. Some like Chika Nitahara, a signal sergeant from Honolulu, even thought the second lieutenant must have gone out of his head.

Before moving forward Davis turned to Sergeant Etchan Kohashi and asked, "Follow me?"

Kohashi picked up his rifle, let out a bloodcurdling cry that seemed to well up from the bottom of his lungs, and began to follow Davis. Hearing him, the rest of the troops, as if trying to rouse their own spirits, started to yell all at once. They began to move from tree to tree taking cover. A hail of machine gun bullets splattered over their heads. An anti-tank rocket exploded against a tree trunk and fragments flew mercilessly in all directions. Ear-shattering noise cut through the flash of explosion. The smoke was so thick it was hard to see ahead. The Japanese Americans moved as though maddened with anger.

Second Lieutenant Davis was carrying only a hand grenade. He did not throw it. Etchan recalls that Davis, for religious or some other reason, had never fired his rifle. Davis fell suddenly, his leg bone shattered by a hit.

Sergeant Fujio Miyamoto, twenty-one, also in the Second Platoon, had been wounded that morning in the right arm. He moved forward cradling his rifle in his left arm. All around him other soldiers were stumbling and falling. His nerves and body were tattered, his mind benumbed. Miyamoto had a reputation like Bill Kochiyama. Almost every day he got a letter from his fiancée in Honolulu, and whenever he had a chance he wrote back a detailed reply. His buddies knew him as a gentle soft-spoken person. But as he strode across the forest floor the glare in his eyes belonged to an entirely different person. Everything had vanished from his head—getting back alive, his fiancée, his father from Hiroshima. He didn't even think about his mother, a nisei, who wept when he told her he was volunteering. All he could think of was killing the enemy who had killed his buddies. Kill and kill again—that was the only thought running through his head.

The division commander was close at hand watching the charge. Jim Tazoi, twenty-two, a radio soldier in Company K, fell forward when the division commander came up behind him and gave him a kick. "Move out!" he shouted. Startled out of his wits by surprise, Tazoi trotted across the pine needles, lugging on his back the heavy battery for the transmitter.

Shouting war cries the soldiers moved forward, stumbling and falling as they went. The trooper helping Tazoi was shot through the shoulder. The company mess sergeant, pressed into combat service because manpower was short, fell to the ground dead. Tazoi, still feeling the imprint of the division commander's kick, moved forward firing his rifle. It was as though he was being pushed from behind. He moved toward a tree trunk knocked down by an artillery burst, hoping to protect himself. An enemy soldier who had taken cover behind the trunk fired a shot that tore through Tazoi's shoulder and buried itself in the radio battery. Tazoi, knocked to the ground by the bullet, was hit again in the stomach by fragments from an enemy grenade.

Suddenly Tazoi began to hear the most beautiful music in his life coming from the other side of the hill. In the next moment Tazoi was brought up short by a voice inside his head whispering desperately that he should stop listening to the inviting music. As he regained consciousness, he looked down and saw intestines protruding from his abdomen. This is it, he thought. Then he saw the Red Cross on the helmet of Doc Miyamoto, the tiny medic, working desperately to staunch the flow of his blood.

The company had moved only a third of the way up the slope. The troops stopped their advance all at once, as if by agreement. Their legs suddenly became cramped and feelings of fear seized them. Shells were bursting all around. Suddenly Sergeant Joe Shimamura of the First Platoon saw Lieutenant Colonel Pursall leap out in front of him.

"Okay, boys, let's go!" he shouted. Brandishing a .45 caliber pistol in each hand, like an actor in a Western, the burly Pursall strode forward in huge steps, seemingly heedless of the enemy fire. He wasn't even wearing a helmet. Pursall was not a bad fellow, Shimamura had thought, but he did not have much guts, and he certainly would not cross any dangerous bridges for the Japanese Americans. Shimamura realized that he had underestimated the "Old Man." There he was up front. "I guess he is going to die with the rest of us," thought Shimamura.

Clutching his light machine gun Shimamura began to move forward again, oblivious to himself, screaming in English, in Japanese, in Hawaiian, "You *baka*, you *bakayaro! Make, Make, Make!*" (*Make* means "death" in Hawaiian, but in Japanese it means "lose," so the word had a double force.)

Pfc Bill Kochiyama and Private Sanji Kimoto, also in the First Platoon, began moving forward screaming, "Bitches, sons of bitches, die!"

The soldiers fired and threw grenades at anything that moved, even the pine tree branches. Hiding in the shelter of the tanks, now scrambling into enemy dugouts, now moving from tree to tree, the men climbed up the slope screaming and shouting curses.

George Henry, now the mayor of Biffontaine, was down in the valley below the forest where the lost battalion was surrounded. His father, a World War I veteran, straining his ears to hear the sound of battle, turned to him and whispered, "It must be a fork." That was what his father called a bayonet charge. The young Henry had often heard him tell stories about the war. M. Henry believes that he must have heard, however faintly, the cries of the "banzai charge."

Doc Miyamoto, today an optometrist in Kona, Hawaii, witnessed the charge. He was wounded in the back and leg. As a medic he did not carry a rifle, but the enemy fired even on helmets with a red cross. The only thing protecting him was the stitched talisman *(senninbari)* that his mother had made for him, wrapped around his waist.

Often Miyamoto heard his buddies murmur, "Mama, Mama," as they lay injured or dying. Even now, he says, there are nights when he can hear that word echoing if he strains his ears. "Mama . . . Mama." One kibei soldier who fell during the "banzai charge" closed his tear filled eyes, whispering in Japanese, *"Kachan, itai, itai"* (Mama, it hurts, it hurts).

Company I joined the "banzai charge" too. The men moved forward screaming at the top of their lungs, many falling as they went. The First Platoon commander, a Caucasian second lieutenant who had replaced Richard Hayashi when he was wounded, had been killed instantly the day before. The assistant platoon leader had been killed too, so the platoon was taken over by Sergeant Takashi "Tak" Senzaki, twenty-two, a native of Los Angeles who had volunteered for the service from the Rohwer relocation camp in Arkansas.

When Company K and Company I reached the top of the slope fear and dread filled the faces of the Germans who had been left behind.

It was 3:45 P.M. by the time the regimental command post received a message from Lieutenant Colonel Pursall. The "banzai charge," which began around 2:30, had taken little more than one hour. Pursall had come through the fight without so much as a scratch.

PURSALL: We have no officers left in K Company. We are up on the hill but we may get kicked off. There is a roadblock, and we are having a lot of casualties. . . .
REGIMENTAL S-3: Blue [Third Battalion] of 141st is on your left flank.
PURSALL: They are nowhere near us. We have to get that roadblock knocked out.

General Dahlquist suddenly interrupted Pursall on the telephone wire.

DAHLQUIST: Blue [Third Battalion] 141st started a patrol. . . . They say they are getting tank fire. Is it yours?
PURSALL: It could be but we have to shoot up our way. Enemy tank is coming up from the south.

Pursall explained that a captured German soldier reported the enemy defenses ahead of them were even tighter.

PURSALL: We lost K Company CP [command post] and have many casualties. How about some infantry help?
DAHLQUIST: I can give you only engineers.

As evening fell things quieted down, but men still died. Captain Joe Byrne, Company I commander, was respected by all his men. A native of New York, nearly six foot six, he had the reputation of being the lankiest officer in the 442nd. Caucasian officers usually found it difficult to remember the strange-sounding names of their Japanese American troops, but Joe Byrne could remember a name even if he only heard it once, and he pronounced it without any accent. He had a reputation for never losing his composure. His only defect was that he had no sense of direction at all, a failing that became even more pronounced in the Vosges forest. Fortunately Sergeant Tak Senzaki had a superb sense of direction. Whenever Byrne, ordinarily calm and collected, was puzzled about where he was, he would call on Senzaki, the top of whose head hardly reached Byrne's chest.

That evening Byrne asked Senzaki to go on patrol to pick up supplies. Senzaki set out leading a party of fifteen. Almost immediately they ran into trouble with an enemy patrol. Senzaki heard the sound of a land mine exploding in the distance. For some reason or other that bothered him strangely. By the time Senzaki and his men returned with the supplies it was after midnight.

"Byrne got it," someone reported to him in a whisper. Hearing the sound of firing in the dark, Byrne had worried about Senzaki's patrol. Unable to stay put, walking in the direction they had left he had stepped on a land mine. That was what Senzaki had heard.

Bill Kochiyama of Company K, looking for a foxhole to spend the night, had made his way through the underbrush, only dimly able to see. An enemy soldier who had been hiding in a foxhole right in front of him suddenly stood up, his face and body covered with blood. The fingers on both of his raised hands had been blown off. Blood trickled down his arm.

"*Kamerad*. Help. Help," he said in broken English, sucking his breath in pain.

With a violence that surprised him Bill pushed the wounded German aside. He kept on going through the brush until he found a foxhole and plunked down into it. Overcome by anger racing through his whole body Bill even forgot the cold. The only thing that kept him under control was a rage that seemed close to madness. How many of his buddies had died, one after the other? He had survived, sustained by his anger at the ruthlessness of an enemy who shot down even medics. Sorrowed by the death of his buddies and never knowing when he too might die, he realized somehow that his nerves would never be what they had been. He let himself become giddy with rage.

Bill could hear the sobs of the German soldier. In the deep still of the forest night they beat on his ears. "Help. Help. . . . ," the German kept calling. He was dying in the cruelest fashion, second by second, as the blood trickled from his body. Bill Kochiyama, crouching in his foxhole, stared into the dark shivering. Gradually the sobs grew weaker, then finally stopped altogether. Forgetting about sleep Bill waited for dawn, looking out into the dark in front of him. The night was cold. There was ice in the foxhole.

The fourth day: Monday, October 30, 1944, rain.

"Well, take care of yourselves, Mother and Father," wrote Noboru Fujinaka. "Please make Yaichan, Etchan, and Hisakosan study as hard as they can. What worries me the most is Mitchan. Please take care of her. That is my last request. Please have a wonderful wedding for Big Sister too.

"Mother and Father, please don't worry about us boys. I am being as careful as I can. I am not doing anything foolish. With luck we boys will be able to receive your beloved affection again. Until that auspicious day, *sayonara*.

"From your beloved Noboru, to my beloved Mother and Father."[4]

That morning the forest was still dark even at 7:00 A.M. At 9:00 A.M. the Third Battalion and the 100th Battalion renewed their attack. According to the morning report their unit strengths were as follows: 100th Battalion, Company A (77 men), Company B (76 men), Company C (80 men); Third Battalion, Company I (71 men / 2 officers), Company K (78 men / 2 officers transferred from Company I), Company L (85 men / 3 officers), Company M (102 men / 5 officers). The normal strength of a company is 180–200 men. Since the figures above included everyone, even the noncombatant headquarters personnel as well as supply soldiers and medics, fewer men were available for combat than the numbers suggest.

From the very beginning of the day the men had to face the danger of artillery fire concentrated on the ridge in front immediately between them and the lost battalion. Many of them were hit, but compared to the day before the troops made a speedy push forward. Once the roadblock and minefield had been cleared, Company I and Company K of the Third Battalion overran a machine gun nest softened up by friendly artillery. Worrying that they might get caught in sniper fire from the 143rd and 141st Regiments in their rear, the Japanese American troops continued to advance.

At 1:50 P.M. General Dahlquist asked regimental headquarters what the situation was.

DAHLQUIST: Any contact with the 141st?
S-3: Yes. Our Blue [Third Battalion] is in contact. B Company is on the right flank of the Third Battalion and they have contact with them.
DAHLQUIST: Okay. Keep pushing.

Sergeant Bill Hull, a member of the lost battalion, recalls the enemy attack that morning was much fiercer.

"I was worried when a P-47 dropped rations and ammunition to us by parachute the previous day. That's how the enemy found out what a tight situation we were in. The attack usually came a little after 10:00 in the morning. But it was different from previous attacks. They mounted a terrific attack on three sides of our broken perimeter. They attacked right in front of Company C's machine gun emplacement—that was my company —and from the left and right too. I thought to myself, 'This is the last fight.' It was like the enemy was determined to wipe us out one way or another. That was the first time I thought I was going to die. The only thing in my head was: if I'm going to die then I'm going to take as many of them with me as I can.

"I kept shooting not worrying about saving my ammunition. I don't know how much time passed. Well, it's all over, I thought. Then suddenly there was a lot of noise from behind me. They're finally coming in from the rear, I thought, and when I turned to look I saw this little Japanese American soldier jumping into the dugout.

"I just can't put in words what I felt then. . . . I was so proud to see that little fellow moving along so fast with his rifle and his eyes scowling ahead of him. Even though it wasn't somebody from our own regiment. . . . It was the Japanese Americans who broke through the enemy and saved us. I was giving thanks to God, and that Japanese American soldier looked real special to me."

As he talked tears welled up in Hull's clear blue eyes. Pulling in his jaw, reconstructed some years before after cancer surgery, as he fought back his tears, he continued, "I had two sons then—one five years old and the other two."

The first Japanese American soldiers to break through were from the First Platoon of Company I. Only six men were left in the First Platoon, and only two in the Second Platoon. These eight men, led by Sergeant Tak Senzaki, finally reached the lost battalion.

The point man, Pfc Matt Sakumoto, twenty, who had grown up on the same Waialua plantation in Oahu as Mits Fukuda and Sergeant Joe Takata, was the first to jump into the dugout. A Caucasian soldier, his unshaven face covered with mud, stared at him in disbelief. The soldier's eyes were dark and hollow from lack of sleep, and his lips quivered as though he were holding back tears. Sakumoto hurriedly reached into his pocket for a pack of cigarettes.

"Want a smoke?" he said.

Henry Nakada jumped into the foxhole of a Caucasian soldier who yelled at the top of his lungs and hugged him. One war correspondent reported that the rescued soldiers said, "We never thought we'd be this happy to see Jap faces," but none of the eight Company I soldiers who got to the lost battalion remember hearing anyone say that. The Caucasian soldiers were yelling excitedly at the top of their voices, happily embracing one another.

Glancing at Sakumoto and Nakada, Tak Senzaki angrily shouted, "Don't stop! We keep on moving!" Senzaki says that he did not exchange a single word with the soldiers of the lost battalion. He looked right past them, his eyes on the enemy in front. Nakada and the rest of the squad followed in a flurry.

Sergeant Joe Shimamura, Bill Kochiyama, and other men from Company K appeared from the right flank soon after. By then the soldiers of the lost battalion realized that they really had been rescued. Sergeant Tak Goto, twenty-two, of Company K, who had volunteered from the Manzanar relocation camp, refused to hand over his canteen when one of the rescued members of the lost battalion called out to him for water. "No," he said, simply.

The rescued soldiers made their way down the hill an hour later. The division commander and a group of war correspondents were waiting for them. So were warm chow and showers. But the battle was not over for Goto and the other men of the 442nd. After receiving a report about the rescue General Dahlquist, without a moment's delay, ordered the Japanese American troops to take the next hill. The war in the forest continued.

Bill Kochiyama, Sanji Kimoto, and two other soldiers had to take care of another job first. Right after the rescue, they had been assigned to carry the bodies of four Company K men and one Caucasian soldier downhill on a stretcher. It was a dreadfully painful task for Bill and Sanji. They both thought they would rather brave battle again. Silently, they took their mutilated burden down through the wet forest. One of the bodies was that of Pfc James Okamoto, who had always gone to the movies or to the PX with Sanji while they were at Camp Shelby. Another was Pfc Matsuichi Yogi, a bunkmate of Sanji on the voyage across the Atlantic; both had gotten seasick. Then there was Private Fred Okada from Hawaii and Private Ko Tanaka, a replacement soldier who had been drafted out of relocation camp.

The bodies were heavy. It was as though they had soaked up the cold, heavy rain. Each man carried one corner of the stretcher, stumbling now and then as they made their way down wordlessly. They did not retch or vomit. There was nothing in their stomachs. They felt beaten down, drained even of energy enough to feel sad. By the time Bill and the others had finished the job and rejoined their buddies in Company K it was already evening.

On October 31, the next day, the division commander once again prodded the Japanese American troops to advance. The Third Battalion was in the lead. A white officer dispatched to Company K after the successful rescue insisted on going by himself to take a look at the ridge that was their objective. He died instantly in an artillery blast. It almost seemed the shell had been aimed directly at him.

The rain of enemy artillery fire continued, and so did enemy bombing runs. Despite that, the Third Battalion finally took the ridge. Company K, bereft once again of a company captain, was in the lead. Detailed orders kept coming down from the division commander.

On November 1, Lieutenant Colonel Pursall reported that there were only two hundred men (about the number in a company) left in the Third Battalion. He told regimental headquarters that if he did not get more men from somewhere he would have to give up the hill. No, said General Dahlquist, stay there.

At 5:20 P.M. on the evening of November 2, Lieutenant Colonel Pursall called regimental headquarters to ask who had reported that the Third Battalion of the 141st was a thousand yards ahead on the left flank. Pursall was supposed to move into contact with the unit, but it had not been there. The division commander had supplied the information, replied the regimental S-3.

"Is there anything we can do to help you?" asked the S-3.

"Yes," said Pursall, "relieve us."

The rain continued to fall, and the cold grew more severe. The enemy stepped up its artillery bombardment. Tension continued day after day with no respite, no opportunity to relax or let down one's guard. The young soldiers, pushed beyond the limits of their physical strength and subjected to the continuing inhuman conditions, were no longer young. Their faces, hidden by unshaven stubble, showed the fatigue of the aged, tired even of living. There was no joy or sadness or hatred or even despair in their eyes. They seemed hollow and dried out.

In a letter to his wife Reverend Masao Yamada, the chaplain, observed that battle fatigue, until then relatively limited among the 442nd soldiers, was on the increase. Most were serious cases. Constantly confronted with fear and grief as their buddies fell one after the other, their bodies strained from the lack of opportunity even to sleep, the men were under incredible stress. According to Yamada, unlike the Caucasian soldiers, who moaned, cried, yelled, and became almost impossible to control when their nerves collapsed, relatively few Japanese American soldiers showed these symptoms. Sometimes a soldier would just forget everything or start to jump or twist whenever he heard a sharp sound.[5]

The fighting in the forest was like an unending nightmare. The endless hours the men spent waiting in their foxholes only intensified the strain. As the days dragged by they were often overwhelmed by the feeling they were isolated and alone. And sometimes as they waited they had to gaze at the cold bodies of their fallen buddies or the dead enemy.

The forest was shrouded in a dim light even at midday. Now and then the sunlight would reach the ground, enveloping the soldiers with a soft feeling of well-being as they stared ahead, their rifles at the ready. Often they dozed with their eyes open. Private Sanji Kimoto, who lost his eyesight in Italy six months later, found himself in a reverie hearing the sound of the wind rustling through the sugarcane fields. The third son among seven siblings, Sanji was always kidded about his name. In Japanese it was a homonym for "three o'clock." *"Nanji? Sanji?"* "What time is it, Sanji?" or "What time is it? Three o'clock?" He was really a sansei—third-generation Japanese American. His grandfather had come rather early to work on a sugar plantation near Hilo.

For as long as Sanji could remember, Grandpa—his face lined by sun and weather—had lived with the family. When they were little Sanji and his brothers and sisters had worked in the canefields with Grandpa. His grandfather had a savings account in the Honolulu branch of a Japanese bank. Little by little he had put aside his money, dreaming one day of returning home, happy and prosperous. It was on the morning of the third day after the attack on Pearl Harbor that Grandpa had gone into the field back of the house and hanged himself from a tree.

Pfc Bill Kochiyama had other thoughts as he sat in his foxhole cradling his rifle. In the foundling home where he had been raised after his mother died he was the only Japanese American. Everyone had paid special attention to him. When the Caucasian friends he had grown up with went off to war, he thought it the most natural thing in the world to volunteer for the service. But now for several days seeds of doubt had sprung up in his mind for the first time. So many men had been sacrificed in the two and a half mile advance to rescue the lost battalion. Why, even after the successful rescue, had they once again been sent into the forest with orders to keep on advancing? He could not understand. A voice kept whispering inside his tired head: "Are we being used? Are we expendable goods? Are we cannon fodder?"

Ever since the regiment had entered the forest Rudy Tokiwa had been in terrible pain. He was wounded in the back and hands by an artillery blast. But it was even more painful to be separated from the few buddies who remained. He kept scolding himself, "Aren't you Japanese? Why be bothered about a little thing like that?"

Since coming to the Vosges Rudy had lost two assistants. That morning he lost a third, a kibei who had been sent to the unit as a replacement two days before. The kibei could not speak English very well. Rudy called him "Japan Boy." As a child the kibei soldier had gone to Japan with his parents and sister. Shortly after he returned to the United States to attend the University of Idaho, he had been drafted. When the kibei told Rudy he had planned to go back to Japan after graduation from the university, Rudy had to speak his mind. "If me was you, me would become a conscientious objector or anything and just not go into the service at all. Why risk your life for America?" he said. Even now Rudy doesn't remember whether he ever knew Japan Boy's real name.

There were other replacement soldiers like Japan Boy who arrived from the States and went straight into battle in the Vosges as soon as they joined a company. It was not at all unusual for such soldiers to meet their deaths after just a few hours in the forest. One veteran, who prefers to remain anonymous, was such a replacement. He remembers the Vosges as a place where his fellow Japanese Americans killed as if they were crazed.

Once when a cease-fire order came, and the white gunsmoke had cleared, the men saw a German medic kneeling to tend a wounded comrade. To judge from his insignia the fallen German was an officer. Suddenly one of the Japanese American soldiers began to yell.

"You did a fine job, you son of a bitch! You son of a bitch, you murdered my buddies!" A hail of bullets riddled the wounded officer and the unarmed medic. Not one of the other soldiers tried to stop the angry soldier. A Caucasian officer who happened by noticed the Red Cross on the medic's helmet. He simply said, "Better tear that off."

From the beginning some soldiers showed no emotion at all about killing. Others, who under different circumstances could not have wrung a chicken's neck, did not change expression even as they fired on the enemy. Although it is not an easy part of the war for them to talk about, some veterans witnessed needless killing by their buddies.

Soldiers sometimes stripped the enemy dead of their insignia or small arms to take home as war souvenirs. Orders were issued not to, but it went on anyway, as it did in other units.

Only after the rescue of the lost battalion did other things begin to happen for the first time. Pushed to the limit on the battlefield, the soldiers' feelings blazed into rage at the enemy. Pierre Poirat, a French Resistance fighter from nearby Belmont who served as guide for the Japanese Americans during the rescue of the lost battalion, remained with them afterward. Several times he saw the Japanese American soldiers shoot down enemy soldiers surrendering with hands raised. The German soldiers were extremely afraid of the Japanese Americans. They preferred to surrender to Caucasian troops.

Sergeant Karl Schmid, who was captured by the 100th Battalion before the rescue of the lost battalion, lives a comfortable life today in his native city of Stuttgart. An artillery sergeant, he was trying to move his unit's cannon by horse when he was taken prisoner. He had feared that his captors were headhunters, but they turned out to be quite kind to him. Since he was wearing riding pants and leather boots they nicknamed him "Cowboy." They passed a helmet around to collect rations and chocolate and cigarettes for him. "The war is over for you now," they told him, patting him on the back. After the war Schmid returned home, married his fiancée, and became the father of nine children. Today he says he is thankful from the bottom of his heart that he was captured by the Japanese Americans. He owes his happy family to them. He was lucky to have been captured early.

One veteran, not intending to make excuses but simply to set things straight, said, "In the middle of peace today how are you going to judge the right and wrong of what happened on the battlefield some thirty years ago? Isn't that a little too easy? There were fewer of us left than there were prisoners. There weren't even any troops left to escort the prisoners to the rear."

At 9:20 A.M. on November 4, Lieutenant Colonel Pursall got a message from regiment: "The general called up and wants to know if you're going to get down off the hill to those houses. He says it's good for the men." The day before, Lieutenant Colonel Miller, the regimental executive officer, had reported the regiment was at less than half strength. General Dahlquist proposed to boost their morale by letting them come down from the hill to take hot showers.

When he heard the general's suggestion about moving off the hill, Pursall replied, "Ask him who is going to hold the hill while we get down in those houses? As soon as we get off the hill the Jerries would swarm all over it and drop everything on us. I sure would like to be in those houses and I realize it is good for the men but I'm not that foolish."

There was no way that the 442nd, made up solely of Japanese Americans, could be brought up to full strength by replacements right away. Pursall reported that there were only forty-four men in Company I, seventy-six in Company K, and ninety-seven in Company L. Even so the regimental headquarters kept forwarding orders from the division commander to move to the foot of the hill. Pursall gave up trying to resist. The unit began to descend, but they immediately ran into a minefield and were unable to move farther. By that time it was already dark.

Late that night Pursall once again got a message about showers for the men. The men could take showers platoon by platoon but there were no fresh dry clothes for them. Pursall replied it would be hard to arrange with an attack coming up again in the morning. "Postpone the shower deal," he said.

On November 5 the fighting continued. Late in the afternoon Colonel Miller reported to General Dahlquist, "G Company has made slow progress. I Company is short with only thirty-four men. K made only a little progress. I talked to [the Third Battalion commander] and he said they have no offensive power left." The strength of the 100th that day was as follows: Company A (67 men/5 officers), Company B (41 men/5 officers), Company C (66 men/4 officers), and Company D (65 men/7 officers); the strength of the Second Battalion was as follows: Company E (74 men/5 officers), Company F (80 men/4 officers); Company G (87 men/5 officers), and Company H (75 men/3 officers). There was a big increase in the number of men suffering from trench foot, with purple feet swollen to twice normal size, and unable to walk.

On November 6 Company A and Company C of the 100th Battalion were finally ordered to come down off the hill. Without warning the 143rd artillery mistakenly began to fire at the position occupied by Company B and Company D. Lieutenant Colonel Singles was boiling mad.

On November 7 in the evening snow fell for the first time.

On November 8 the Third Battalion had lost more manpower as a result of enemy shelling the previous day. Company I had dwindled to four enlisted men. The officers sent from other units to Company K were wounded one after the other. Sergeant Tak Goto and Sergeant Ralph Yamaguchi had to take command of the unit. No matter how heavily they were bombarded the enemy stayed put, dug in like moles. At around noon division headquarters called to find out what the situation was. The regimental S-2 reported that Companies G, I, L, and K were running into stiff resistance, and Companies E and F were being shelled.

DIVISION G-2: Are they pushing in the south?
REGIMENTAL S-2: I might call it patroling, not pushing, when one company has four men and another seventeen men.

On the morning of November 9 the long awaited order to pull back finally came. The regimental S-3 put in a message to division G-3 to make sure: "Will you check with the colonel and find out when we will come back? It makes a difference with us for if it's only one or two days we'd rather stay where we are."

"I checked and the general says he wants you to move out for you need some rest up there too," replied division G-3. "He thinks you will be out longer than you think."

That evening the Third Battalion moved down to the village of Le Planges, and the Second Battalion to the village of Fays. The 100th Battalion had already moved to a position near Bruyères. Sergeant Joe Shimamura of Company K came down on a stretcher, his feet puffed up with trench foot. The wounds that Rudy Tokiwa had let go for several days had become septic, and his whole body felt as though it was glowing with fever. Even so he made his way down without help from anyone. Bill Kochiyama and Sanji Kimoto, who remained in Company K along with Sergeant Goto, were so fatigued that they seemed to have no strength left.

On November 12 at 2:00 P.M. the troops of the 442nd stood lined up at attention for an assembly called by General Dahlquist to honor them for their achievements. The sound of the bugle echoed through the forest. A military band played the "Star Spangled Banner" dispiritedly. The general, walking along in front of the troops, turned to Lieutenant Colonel Miller with a dissatisfied look on his face.

"I ordered that all the men be assembled," he said.

"Yes sir," answered Miller firmly. "All the men are what you see."

When the 442nd had entered the Vosges a month or so before, its strength was 2,943 men. Of those 161 had died in battle, 43 were missing, and about 2,000 were wounded (882 of them with serious wounds). Of the dead 13 were medics. The regiment had dwindled to less than a third of its authorized strength.

Reverend Hiro Higuchi held memorial services for the dead that day. "As we began playing the first few numbers," wrote Technical Sergeant Ed Kanaya, a member of the military band, a few days later, "a very light fall of snow began descending upon us from heaven and it seemed as if God were caressing us and giving us courage to carry on. As Chaplain Higuchi read the names of the honored and the last echo of taps died away in the distance followed by three volleys of rifle fire, tears welled into my eyes and I could no longer see clearly. I wanted to flop in the snow and begin bawling like a baby. . . . In the list of honored men was one that was dear to me. He was my lifelong companion, and I'll meet him up in the great beyond some day."[6]

The soldiers liked Hiro Higuchi because he was always jolly, but as he read the names of the fallen who would never return to their native land, his face was drawn. He seemed a changed person. He remembered how he had gathered with some of the men for prayers in the early morning before the unit had left Belmont to go on its mission to rescue the lost battalion. One soldier had asked earnestly, "You know, Chaplain, up to this moment, all the time you've been talking about helping others, help-ing the poor, doing missionary-type things, carrying the flag for peace, so to speak. Now, I'm not concerned about the man-to-man relationship and brotherhood and all that kind of stuff. I'm interested in the vertical. What is God to me? What am I to God?" For a moment Higuchi could not find words for an answer. The soldier disappeared into the forest mist without getting a reply.

On October 30 in the midst of the rescue of the lost battalion Rever-end Masao Yamada, another 442nd chaplain, had written a long letter to his friend Colonel Sherwood Dixon on the staff of the War Department in Washington. Dixon had commanded the Third Battalion at Camp Shelby but had been too old to go overseas.

"The major general is quite concerned and has commanded the 442nd to push. It is quite a strain to go forward, regardless of machine gun nests and their well-prepared defense. . . . The cost has been high. I admire the courage and the discipline of our loyal men. . . . [But] I am spiritu-ally low for once. My heart weeps for our men, especially for those who gave all. Never had combat affected me so deeply as has this emergency mission. I am probably getting soft but the price is too costly for our men. I feel this way more because the burden is laid on the combat team when the rest of the 141st is not forced to take the same responsibility."[7]

There were 275 men in the lost battalion when they were cut off by the enemy; when they were rescued there were 211. Considering how many 442nd men were sacrificed to rescue these 211 men it is not hard to imag-ine the pain felt by the Japanese American soldiers. Ironically the 141st Regiment, including those who had survived the enemy encirclement, suffered heavy losses a month later near the German border, and the unit was nearly annihilated.

In reply to Yamada, Colonel Dixon, who had a deep rapport with the Japanese American soldiers (and later became lieutenant governor of Illi-nois in Adlai Stevenson's administration), tried to console the chaplain by pointing out that things too close to understand at the front were easy to understand at a distance in Washington.

"The best troops," he wrote, "are called upon to do the hardest fighting. Whenever a general finds himself up against a tough proposition he sends for the best troops he has. In a critical situation he can't take chances with anything less than the best. So—when you are called upon again and again it is really a kind of backhanded compliment. A man who is being shot at daily has a hard time recognizing it as a compliment when, dead tired, bruised and battered, he is called upon to make one more effort to risk his life another time—but it is a compliment, nevertheless."[8]

Dixon was certainly right. In Italy General Ryder, the commander of the Thirty-fourth Division, and General Mark Clark, the commander of the Fifth Army, both used the Japanese American troops as a spearhead unit in difficult combat situations. Their reputation as a strong fighting unit was made there, and they felt warm ties to General Ryder.

Several years later Lieutenant Colonel Singles, who remained in the army and was promoted to colonel after the war, attended a military ceremony where he met General Dahlquist, four stars on his shoulders. When the general recognized Singles, he offered his hand and said in a friendly voice, "Let bygones be bygones. It's all water under the bridge, isn't it?"

Singles, who thought the general knew he had pushed the Japanese American unit too hard in the Vosges forests, acted as though he had not heard. He made no effort to shake the general's extended hand. While everyone stared at him, Singles stubbornly continued saluting.

War's End

AFTER leaving the Vosges forest the 442nd Regiment spent four months in southern France, near the Côte d'Azur, a winter watering hole for the rich and famous known for its brilliant sunlight. The Japanese American soldiers dubbed their time in southern France the "champagne campaign." To be sure it was a war front, but the main task of the 442nd was to guard the border between France and Italy. There was really no need for the regiment to move. The men spent their days quietly. It was a period of recuperation for the unit, which had lost so many men in the Vosges that it could no longer be used as a regiment-sized force.

Almost all the Japanese Americans I talked to tried to put aside their memories of the war forty years ago as something that was over and done with. When I interviewed many of them I often felt like an intruder barging into their past with muddy feet. It was always a relief when the veterans who survived the battle in the Vosges forest turned to their recollections of the four months they spent in southern France. They would start to smile again. It was the "champagne campaign" that they talked about most freely. Indeed the only war stories many of their families had heard were about the months in southern France.

The Côte d'Azur had suffered little damage during the war. The 100th Battalion was assigned the job of securing the area from the Italian border to Monte Carlo. Since the town of Menton was off limits to French civilians, the 100th had the place to themselves. Battalion headquarters was set up in the best hotel in town. Doc Kometani even had time to set up a dentist's chair to work on the soldiers' teeth, but most of the troops, aware that they might soon be going back to the battlefield, did not seem to be much interested in free dental service.

Soldiers from the Second and Third Battalions were assigned to defensive positions in the nearby hills. Jealous of their time they went down to Nice to enjoy themselves on their days off. There were still minefields along the seashore so they could not get near the water but every evening many Japanese American soldiers were to be seen in the nightclubs of Nice. Only officers were supposed to be allowed into Monte Carlo but some of the cleverer soldiers, unwilling to put up with that restriction, sneaked in at night by bribing the locals with cigarettes. One veteran recalled that when he ran out of pay, he plucked oranges from a nearby orchard while on duty and exchanged them for cognac. The bar proprietors liked it even better when he brought olives they could press into oil.

In France licensed prostitution was legal, and the going rate for a girl was about ten dollars. A private's pay started at $21 a month, and a Pfc's at $36, so even with overseas pay into the bargain consorting with prostitutes was not cheap entertainment. Wherever the U.S. Army went, its commanders were always nervous about venereal disease. In spite of surprise checks every month, the VD rate among Japanese American soldiers was exceptionally low when compared with other units. According to the 442nd officer responsible for VD control, there were even inquiries from other units about the 442nd's secret of success in keeping the rate down.

The reason was not that the Japanese Americans avoided the prostitutes. In both Italy and France soldiers enjoyed themselves when the opportunity presented itself. But the Japanese American community was a narrow one. All the soldiers knew that if word got around at home that they had come down with VD, it would bring shame on their families. They were very careful to take care of themselves after the fact.

When Reverend Hiro Higuchi recalled his experiences in the Vosges Mountains, he could not hide the pain in his face, but as soon as the subject turned to southern France he became voluble. He would always remember Room 206 in Hotel H, he said. One day a soldier came to regimental headquarters with a request to get married. "My girlfriend is pregnant," he said. Since the unit had been in southern France for only a few weeks the regimental commander asked Higuchi to investigate the matter. When Higuchi arrived at Hotel H, the "girlfriend's" house, he walked past a long line of soldiers to knock on the door of Room 206. From behind he heard a voice complaining, "Doesn't the chaplain have to wait his turn too?"

Inside the room Higuchi found a number of women. The amply built madam of the establishment called the "girlfriend" from a nearby room. As Higuchi stood talking with her, the other girls mockingly pressed their attentions, and their bodies, against the chaplain. Despite the harassment he managed to straighten matters out. Some young soldiers were often serious about marrying girls whom they met only a few times in establishments like this, said Higuchi, even though they could not speak the same language. So desperate for human affection were they after putting battle behind them, they could think only of the moment and not the future.

The sunny Côte d'Azur is protected from the strong winds of the Alps by the Maritime Alps, a mountainous region that towers over the coastline. About an hour by train from Nice sits L'Escarene, a town of about a thousand inhabitants wedged between the mountains. Mme. Jeanette Zeller, who still lives there with her family, recalled how different was each group of soldiers who occupied the town.

"The Italians were always running after the girls. The Germans ignored the local people and did not have anything to do with them. The Japanese American soldiers wanted to become part of your family. They were really friendly."

At Christmastime in 1944 the soldiers of the Second Battalion held a party for the children of the town at the little church in the town square. They decorated a huge Christmas tree about twenty feet tall. It was hard to decide who should play Santa Claus, but they eventually decided to drop Santa from the festivities when they found out the French had never heard of him. The soldiers sang carols to the accompaniment of an organ backed by guitars and ukuleles and handed out candy, chocolate, and other gifts to the children. They had contributed a week's ration of white bread and their Christmas ration of candy to the party.

Among those standing by the Christmas tree watching the unexpected Japanese American visitors were Mme. Zeller and her seven-year-old son, Maurice. Mme. Zeller was then only twenty-three. Maurice was the child of her husband's first wife, who had died. The Japanese American soldiers often came to visit their house. It was her husband's mother whom they liked to see. She had grown up in Alsace when it had been annexed by Germany, and as a result she was unable to sing the *Marseillaise* very well. One Hawaiian often teased her. "You must be a Communist grandmother," he said. Then he would sing the French national anthem himself while plucking at his ukulele.

Among the Hawaiian soldiers Mme. Zeller best remembers Chiyoto "Hoppy" Kaneshina because of a handmade card he gave to Maurice. It was cut out in the shape of a pineapple, and on it was written, "When you grow up, come to Hawaii some time, and let's pick pineapples together." Kaneshina was a cook from Company E. He had grown up on the Wailuku plantation on Maui. As a junior in high school, he had raced through the canefields with his friends to the recruiting station. Hoppy later recalled that whenever an American soldier went into L'Escarene he would be followed by a crowd of children shouting "Joe! Joe!" and holding their hands out for chocolate. He always noticed that Maurice simply stood to one side looking on. Somehow Hoppy liked that reserve. When the unit got its orders for Italy, he made the pineapple card and a little package for Maurice, but the day the unit moved out Maurice was not among the crowd of children who gathered to see them off. Hoppy gave the package to a child standing nearby. In fact, the child was a retarded little girl, but she remembered Maurice's name and faithfully delivered the package. Inside were cans of candy, applesauce and peanuts, some butter, and a bar of soap.

Mme. Zeller's elder daughter, Marion, drove me from L'Escarene over the narrow winding mountain roads to Sospel, a town of 2,200 facing the Italian border. During the war Mme. Zeller for a time had hidden a young Jewish couple from Lithuania, who then escaped to Spain after the birth of a baby daughter. From there they were to go on to the United States, said Mme. Zeller, but she never found out what finally happened to them. In the hope that they had survived, she named her own daughter after the young couple's baby girl.

The "champagne campaign" had not been without its casualties. Many veterans recall that it was always nerve-racking to go on duty on the defensive line since they could never tell when they might get shot at. After living as human beings again during visits to town, they had to sit waiting for an enemy hidden across the border in Italy. The apparent peacefulness, some said, made the occasional moments of fear even more grueling.

On the wall of a stone building facing the courtyard of the middle school in Sospel is a marble memorial tablet. Underneath the crossed flags of France and the United States can be seen the following inscription: "A la memoire des Militaires Hawaiiens tombés pour la liberation de Sospel, en Novembre 1944. Larry Mivra [sic]. Senti [sic] Sugawara."[1] Both men were from headquarters of Company K.

According to former Sergeant Tak Goto, who had survived the battle in the Vosges without being wounded, it was a little before noon on November 30. After writing a letter to his parents at the relocation camp in Manzanar about his Thanksgiving dinner, complete with turkey and cranberry sauce, he walked out into the courtyard of the middle school where he was bivouacked. Even though it was the beginning of winter, the midday sun was warm in southern France. Smiling at Corporal Larry Miura and Sergeant Kenji Sugawara, who were sunbathing there, Goto walked over to the stone steps opposite them and sat down. He pulled off his shirt to bare his chest. The warmth felt good. He closed his eyes and turned his face toward the sky. Before he knew it, his thoughts drifted back to the Vosges forest. It had all happened only two weeks before, yet somehow it seemed out of focus like a nightmare from long ago. The battle faded like mist as he tried to remember. Well, anyway, I survived it, he thought, and as if to make sure, he quietly breathed in the mountain air. Suddenly, he heard the roar of an explosion.

Signal Sergeant Chika Nitahara, who was on the second floor of the schoolhouse in front of his equipment, looked out the window when he heard the noise. He saw a German tank disappearing from view on the hillside across the Italian border. At the same time he heard moans from below. On the courtyard lay three bloody bodies. By the time Nitahara had run downstairs and out into the courtyard, several other soldiers were already there desperately trying to do something for the fallen. Nitahara hugged Sugawara, whose intestines were spilling out, then realized it was to late to do anything. Miura lay on the ground covered with blood.

When Goto recovered consciousness, someone's face was close to his looking down at his body. By the time he realized it was the mess sergeant, he noticed that there was blood on both the sergeant's hands. He seemed to be trying to staunch the flow. As Goto was thinking about that, he noticed that blood was pouring from his own arms and hands. His right foot had been blown off with his boot, and his left foot hung from his leg by a strip of skin.

In the ambulance on the way to the hospital in Nice, Miura died. By the time it arrived Goto had lost so much blood that it was hard for the medics to find a vein to give a transfusion. Thinking Goto would die anyway a doctor somehow pulled a vein out of the wound with his bare hands and stuck the transfusion needle into it. By a chance in a million, Goto survived. Both of his feet were gone, though. After Nitahara saw the ambulance off, he noticed Goto's boot still lying in the schoolyard. When he picked it up he felt Goto's foot still inside. He called over a private who was loitering nearby and handed him the boot. "Burn it with the trash," he said. The youthful-looking soldier took the boot with both hands, and then suddenly fainted. Only then did Nitahara realize that he was a replacement sent to the unit right after the Vosges campaign who still had not witnessed the horrors of the battlefield.

Miura and Sugawara were both in the quartermaster, and unlike infantrymen they were usually in the rear area far from enemy fire. Under normal circumstances, the chances were that they would return home safely. But they had survived the battle in the Vosges only to be felled by an unlucky shot in relatively peaceful southern France. The two men were not the only ones killed or wounded. Every day the Germans fired several rounds into Sospel, mainly to intimidate the enemy, and there were casualties every month. (In December 1944 there were twenty casualties, in January 1945 thirty-one, and in February nine.)

Two men from Company G were killed on the morning of January 16, 1945. While on a reconnaissance patrol along the Italian border, a platoon leader had been shot in the leg. While trying to rescue the Caucasian captain, Second Lieutenant Minoru Kurata and Pfc Herbert Kondo were killed instantly when they strayed into a friendly minefield. Kondo was the grandson of Sakuma Yonekichi, a member of the first group of contract laborers who went to Hawaii in 1867—the so-called *gannenmono* ("first year of Meiji immigrants")—and the only one to keep a diary of his voyage there.

"Are you Indonesian?"

The first Japanese American soldier who happened to catch sight of Lily Luong and call out to her as she was walking down the street in Nice was a Hawaiian from an antitank unit. Before the day was over, he and several of his friends arrived uninvited at Lily's family's house. Her tiny mother, who wanted to feed them something, stood in her kitchen kneading homemade *udon* noodles for them.

Mrs. Luong, as the soldiers called Lily's mother Imi, was born in Gifu prefecture in central Japan. While she was working in Nagasaki as a maid for the wife of the French consul, her mistress took a liking to her. When the consul and his wife returned to France, Imi married their cook, a Chinese from Hainan Island, and the two of them went home with their employers. Even after the consul retired they continued to work for the couple.

When the Japanese Americans visited them, the Luongs were living in basement rooms of a magnificent villa. They had five children—one boy and four girls. The oldest daughter had gone off to work in Paris, and the two youngest daughters had been evacuated to the countryside. Only eighteen-year-old Lily and her twenty-year-old brother remained at home. When Pfc Roy Kobayashi, a 552nd Artillery Battalion soldier from Maui, first met Lily, he blurted out, "Will you be my bride?" Everyone laughed, but ten years later he married her.

This was probably the first time in the twenty-seven years since her mother arrived in France that her mother was able to speak Japanese, says Lily. At home the family spoke French so Lily herself did not know her mother's language. Even so, when the children were small, their mother sang them Japanese songs, and Lily could entertain the soldiers with lullabies and other children's tunes.

From the day the first Hawaiian met Lily there was a constant stream of soldiers to her house, carrying coffee, sugar, flour, and other supplies. They gave Lily's father cigarettes, which at the time were almost as good as money. Lily's mother responded to their generosity by making sashimi from fish freshly caught in the Mediterranean. She braised fish for them in soy sauce and sugar, and she even made tasty fish-paste cakes (*kama-boko*) to feed these young men who were all about her son's age.

On New Years Day 1945 Reverend Yamada was invited to sample Mrs. Luong's cooking. He and his driver, Eddie Yamazaki, a soldier from Kauai, were treated to a feast of *ebigohan* (rice with shrimp) and pickled eggplant. Yamada later wrote to his wife that even though he had been surprised at how many times Eddie asked for second helpings, afterward he was ashamed to realize how much he had eaten himself. Later he took Lily and her mother along to visit some of the soldiers who had been wounded in the Vosges.

"The MPs stopped us at two points," he wrote to his wife. "They looked at me and then at the civilians in the back. Then they looked at me again, and let us go on. I didn't say a word, but twice the MPs saw that they were Orientals and didn't question. Lily was cute. She smiled and won the MP's favor." The men in hospitals were delighted with the visit. "Our men were so touched, some of them sat in their beds speechless. They couldn't talk Japanese or French, just smiled and almost wept. Mrs. Luong wept a couple of times, sensing how the men appreciated their visit. She talked in Japanese, and of course some of our men answered."[2] Lily reminded the Japanese Americans of their kid sisters, and Mrs. Luong of their mothers, far off at home. For the wounded soldiers, Yamada concluded his letter, their visit was like a blessing.

The men who had been wounded in the Vosges were in military hospitals all over the map—not only in France, but also in England and Italy. Of the wounded, 265 men eventually returned to the 442nd. In the meantime 1,214 new replacements had joined the unit. Like the 672 replacements who had been sent to the unit a month before the fighting in the Vosges, the majority were draftees from the relocation camps on the West Coast. They were no longer just eighteen and nineteen-year-olds. For example, Harry Iwafuchi, a draftee who joined Company C in the 100th Battalion, was thirty years old and had three children. Since his two younger brothers had already been drafted and assigned to MIS, he never imagined that he would be drafted himself.

After the Pearl Harbor attack, as we have already seen, the American government had put Japanese Americans in the same draft category as aliens even though they had been born in the United States. On January 1, 1944, they were once again made subject to the selective service draft on the condition that they "only be used as replacements for the 442nd." The War Department, far from refusing to draft Japanese Americans, forced their rights as American citizens on them.

At Gila relocation camp in Arizona Sam Hamai, twenty-six, asked that he be deferred since he was an only child and had to look after his ailing parents. His father was bedridden with paralysis. The government refused his request. The American government was taking care of his parents at the relocation camp, the official reply came, so there was no ground for a deferment. Hamai was later sent to the Pacific.

A family interned at the Topaz camp in Utah had requested through the neutral Spanish consulate that their son be given an exemption from the draft since they planned to return to Japan with their son even if that meant he had to give up his citizenship. The parents were fearful that their son was simply going to be used as cannon fodder. The War Department replied on March 28, 1945, "As your son was born in the United States and is a citizen of the United States, there is no way by which he might be discharged for the purpose stated."

On that same March 28, the 442nd, brought up to strength by replacements, departed for Italy once again at the request of General Mark Clark, commander of the Fifth Army.

On April 8 the *Stars and Stripes* carried the headline: THE 45TH'S ATTACK SPEARHEADED BY 442 NISEI REGIMENT. The following story said that the return of the 442nd to the battlefield was a well-kept secret. "They remained within carefully guarded bivouac areas until last Wednesday. Then under cover of darkness, they moved into the line and hid within mountain villages until the attack was launched. German prisoners said they had been caught completely by surprise. . . . Boasting an average age individual IQ highest of any infantry unit in the U.S. Army, the 442nd men have won an impressive list of decorations."

The army paper was effusive in its praise of the 442nd on its return to the Italian warfront. The unit's division headquarters announced that the 442nd had performed "brilliantly" in mopping-up operations near Mt. Belvedere to the east of Massa.

The 442nd, however, was now attached to the Ninety-second Division, an all-black division officered by Caucasians. Colonel Miller, the regimental commander, wrote to Colonel Dixon: "This, as you can well imagine, was not very popular with the men or officers."[3] On the other hand, William McCaffrey, then the division chief of staff and now a reserve brigadier general, says that when division headquarters learned that the Japanese American unit was joining them it was overjoyed. The Japanese Americans, perhaps because they were with the division for only about a month, did not bother to sew on its buffalo insignia patch.

The black troops tried to be friendly toward the men in the 442nd, but the Japanese American troops for the most part ignored them. Even today many veterans do not try to hide their contempt for the black soldiers.

"They always turned their backs to the enemy and ran. They never covered our flanks," recalled one veteran. On the first day of battle the regiment that was supposed to be on their left flank was more than three miles away.

"The ones that I saw at the emergency aid station when I took a buddy seriously wounded on the verge of life and death were black soldiers with headaches and stomachaches," recalled another.

In April 1945 Reverend Yamada wrote to his wife, "We have been associating with the Negro troops. One of the boys asked why they were pushed back so often. The Negro soldier replied, 'We weren't pushed back, we ran back.' They are unfortunately poor fighters. They don't have the determination nor the understanding of their part in the scheme of things. . . . Our casualties are not too large here, but enough to startle the division. The Negroes never had so many as we had in this campaign."[4]

The military authorities recognized that the morale of the black soldiers was very low. The black troops were always saying it was "whitey's war," and they wondered why they should shed their blood when a white officer gave them orders. In a way their main enemy was not the Nazis but the white society back home.

The illiteracy rate in the Ninety-second Division was a little over thirteen percent, and many of the troops had no more than an elementary school education. It is said that more than half the troops could not read military regulations satisfactorily. The reason undoubtedly was the Southern school system which denied blacks opportunities for an adequate education.

In retrospect it is difficult to insist that the young Japanese American soldiers on the battlefield should have had enough sensitivity to understand the problems the black soldiers faced. Yet, even though both minorities suffered from racial discrimination, the roots of prejudice toward blacks were far deeper than toward Japanese Americans. In contrast to the black soldiers, who had little hope of any gain from proving themselves in battle, the Japanese Americans believed they could demonstrate that they were loyal Americans by shedding their blood for their country. Perhaps that reveals how greatly different their experience was.

Fighting ended in Italy on May 2, 1945, and the war in Europe ended on May 7. In the Pacific the struggle was also coming to a close. American troops had landed in Okinawa, part of Japanese home territory, and a decisive battle had begun there.

When I began my research, I was told that hardly any mothers of men killed in battle were still alive. Even so I was able to find several Gold Star mothers. The first I met was Ushi Nakamine, whose oldest son was Pfc Shinei Nakamine (Company B). As I talked with her in Honolulu, she sat with a serene face speaking Japanese slowly in a voice so low it was almost a whisper. She showed me her hands. I was surprised to see that all her fingers, except her thumbs, had been tattooed near the second joint. It was the first time I had seen tattooed fingers. Mrs. Nakamine gave me a shy smile.

"Don't you see?" she said. "I'm from Okinawa. I got these tattooes when I was twelve years old. Both my husband and I came from near Yonabaru in Okinawa."

In Japan the inhabitants of Okinawa were not accepted as fully Japanese, and they met with strong prejudice from Japanese living in the main islands of the archipelago. Lingering prejudices were carried abroad by Japanese immigrants. Perhaps in response the Okinawan immigrants had a strong sense of community, and in Hawaii they formed one of the most active *kenjinkai* (home province association) among the Japanese immigrants.

In 1918 Mrs. Nakamine had come to Hawaii to be with her husband. They both worked cutting cane at the Waianae sugar plantation on Oahu. "I worked so hard I couldn't straighten my back," she said. Her husband's wages were seventy-seven cents a day, and hers were fifty-eight cents. After so many years at work in the canefields, her face remained deeply burnt by the sun. Even so, it had few wrinkles.

Their son, Shinei, was born a year after she arrived in Hawaii. Two younger sons born later were able to finish high school, but Shinei quit school after junior high and went to work in the canefields to help the family make ends meet. Then he got a job at a limestone quarry where the pay was better, but he was drafted on November 18, 1941. It was just three weeks before the outbreak of war. "I'll always remember that day," said Mrs. Nakamine.

She first learned that he had gone to the mainland when he wrote home from Camp McCoy. It was then that he began sending home every month a war bond bought for his kid sister, Anita Kimie, from his private's pay. The war bonds kept coming even after the unit went to Italy. Anita, now a high school teacher in Hawaii, eventually used the money to go to the University of Hawaii.

Shinei died on June 2, 1944, two days before the Allied forces entered Rome. Other Okinawans gathered at the local Honganji Buddhist Temple for his funeral. Like Joe Takata, the first Japanese American soldier to be decorated, Shinei received the Distinguished Service Cross.

As she talked to me, Mrs. Nakamine hugged close to her breast a photograph of her son, who had always worked hard without complaint since he was little, dressed in his army uniform. "It was for his country [*Okuni no tame jake ni*] . . . ," she said in a small voice as tears rolled quietly down her gentle face.

After the war ended she learned that her entire family—her elderly mother, her sisters, and their small children—had been killed in the battle of Okinawa. The civilian population of the island had been swept up in the holocaust of war as the Japanese Imperial Army fought its last desperate struggle, and tens of thousands died in the fighting. The Japanese army simply abandoned them to their fate. Some were unable to escape the concentrated bombardment of American guns; others simply killed themselves. Ushi Nakamine never found out how her family died.

On June 21, 1945, American forces finally secured control over Okinawa. A little more than a month later Truman, Churchill, and Chiang Kai-shek issued the Potsdam Declaration calling on Japan to surrender unconditionally or face utter destruction. It was then too that Truman learned of the successful testing of the new atomic bomb, dropped on Hiroshima and then on Nagasaki in early August. On August 15, 1945, Japan formally surrendered.

A special correspondent from the *Honolulu Star-Bulletin* was covering the Japanese American troops still in Italy when news of the bombing of Hiroshima arrived. "They were overjoyed," she told me. The Japanese American soldiers did not care what happened to Japan, she observed to me almost sympathetically. They were one hundred percent American, and they wanted to prove that all the time. There is no reason to doubt the impression this war correspondent received from the Japanese American soldiers. It was a matter of face for them. But their position was not as simple as it appeared on the surface.

Since Hiroshima was the prefecture from which the largest number of immigrants had come, their feelings must have been more complex. Not only did many of the Japanese American soldiers still have grandparents, aunts and uncles, and cousins living there, but not a few of the soldiers had parents who had returned to Hiroshima before the war. After learning that the atomic explosion had destroyed ninety percent of the city and taken more than two-hundred thousand lives, they must have felt differently about the bomb.

When Sergeant William Terao was two years old his whole family had moved back to Hiroshima. After he graduated from middle school in Hiroshima, William had a yearning to return to Los Angeles where he had been born. Overcoming his parents' wishes, he left for the United States by himself, hoping to enter an advertising design school there. Even by the time he was drafted a month after Pearl Harbor, he still could not understand English very well. After performing menial jobs in an Arkansas officers' club, he was sent to Alabama for retraining as an infantryman, and then he went as a replacement soldier to France just before the battle in the Vosges.

Terao was wounded in the leg during the fighting to rescue the lost battalion, but when he recovered he was not sent back to the Japanese
American unit. Instead he served with a Caucasian unit that occupied the
city of Mannheim in Germany after the end of the European war. He
learned of the bombing of Hiroshima when he opened the *Stars and
Stripes* one morning. He could not take his eyes away from the headline.
He felt dizzy as though he had been struck a blow on the head. For the
next few days he could not eat. He found it even harder to believe that he
was in Germany.

Terao's parents, who lived near the center of the blast, were killed
instantly. At least, Terao says, he likes to think that they were. His younger sister and her three children had been evacuated from the city so they
survived, but her husband had been killed. Like some other Japanese
American soldiers Terao reenlisted after the war ended and went to Japan
to work as an interpreter for the American occupation forces. It was the
only way to get to Japan immediately after the war. In memory of his parents Terao trained at a Buddhist temple in Kyoto and was ordained as a
Buddhist priest. Today, working as a graphic designer, he also serves as a
priest in Los Angeles.

At its peak strength before embarking for France the 442nd had
counted in its ranks 224 officers and 4,034 enlisted men. (These are the
figures for September 21, 1944; they include the 100th Battalion as well
as the 232nd Engineer Company and the 522nd Artillery Battalion.)
According to a War Department memo dated August 1, 1945, by that
time (nearly the end of the war) 21,102 Japanese Americans had been
drafted altogether (20,861 enlisted men, 162 officers, and 79 WACs).

In 1946 the *Pacific Citizen,* a Japanese American newspaper, reported
that the number of Japanese Americans participating in World War II in
some form or other, including the Japanese Americans sent to the Pacific
theater as interpreters, came to 33,330.[5] Of these about forty were
aliens, that is, Japanese citizens born in Japan. Whatever the actual figures, in September 1942 when the War Department was still considering
whether or not to organize a volunteer Japanese American unit like the
442nd, it had estimated that probably there were about 36,000 eligible
Japanese American youths. The proportion of Japanese Americans who
did military service in World War II was the highest of any ethnic group.

In his memoirs General Mark Clark praised the 442nd as "the most
decorated unit in the history of the United States."[6] About 8,000 men
who served with the unit received decorations, and the 100th and the
442nd were honored with seven presidential citations.[7] Five of the citations were for actions during the twenty days of fighting in the Vosges.
That was unprecedented.

On July 15, 1946, President Harry Truman, in front of an audience made up of the secretary of war and other high military officials, presented the seventh presidential citation to members of the 442nd drawn up in ranks on the White House lawn. The official repatriation of the regiment had been postponed until this ceremony could be fit into the president's schedule. Before the ceremony about ten thousand spectators had stood in the rain to watch the 442nd march down Constitution Avenue. The War Department and other government agencies had given their employees special time off to encourage them to watch.

The *New York Times* carried the headline: THE COMMANDER-IN-CHIEF HONORS NISEI HEROES.[8] The next day newspapers all over the country carried stories about the only military unit among those returning from overseas battlefields that so far had the honor of being reviewed by the president.

Sergeant Akira Sasaki, twenty-three, a native of Sacramento in Company F, and Yoshio Mamiya, twenty-six, a native of San Diego in Company F, both later recalled that they had practiced marching for the "big show" for more than six months. Sergeant Thomas Harimoto, twenty-five, a noncom in Company I who came from Honolulu, carried the 442nd regimental banner. An aide asked Harimoto and the other standard bearers to practice shaking hands while holding their flags, a difficult task at best. When the ceremony finally took place, however, Truman apparently forgot to shake their hands in the downpour.

All three men—Sasaki, Mamiya, and Harimoto—were draftees who joined the 442nd after the battle in the Vosges. More than half the Japanese American soldiers who represented the 442nd at the presidential ceremony were replacement troops. Among those honored at the ceremony were even men completely without battlefield experience who had joined the unit after the end of the war. Of the original members of the unit, who had landed at Salerno, fought at Cassino and Anzio, then from Rome to Florence, and finally in the forests of the Vosges, never turning back even as they faced the hell of battle—men who had made the names of the Japanese American units immortal in the military history of the United States—there were only a handful. Soon after the war ended most of the survivors of the original unit had returned home and were already out of uniform.

But even today at reunions the Japanese American veterans recall the words that President Truman, in his raincoat, spoke that day with feeling at the ceremony. "You fought for the free nations of the world. . . . You fought not only the enemy, you fought prejudice, and you have won. Keep up that fight, and continue to win—to make this great Republic stand for just what the Constitution says it stands for: 'the welfare of all the people, all the time.' Bring forward the colors."

On January 1, 1945, the government rescinded Executive Order 9066, under which the Japanese Americans on the West Coast had been herded into relocation camps. But the Japanese Americans still had to face many problems before they could return home. When many mainland Japanese American soldiers were demobilized, their parents were still in the relocation camps. With medals proudly pinned on their chests the soldiers returned to homes behind barbed-wire fences.

The military authorities, concerned about the complicated situation of the mainland soldiers, did everything they could to help them. The War Relocation Authority worked hard to move the Japanese Americans back to the West Coast. In September 1945 the director of the WRA informed all soldiers of Japanese American ancestry, "I want you to know that we are going to see that your families in the centers get every kind of help they need so that you can come back to find them out of the barracks and in the kinds of places which you can call home."

On October 15, 1945, Secretary of the Interior Harold L. Ickes wrote to Colonel Miller, then commanding officer of the 442nd: "The members of the combat team have made a magnificent record of which they should be proud. This record, without doubt, is the most important single factor in creating in this country a more understanding attitude toward people of Japanese descent. The goal for which they strove, acceptance for their families and themselves as loyal Americans, is being achieved."[9]

In reality, things were not so simple. In many places, especially in California, local people responded to the return of the Japanese Americans with hostility. Even though they were wearing uniforms of the U.S. Army the soldiers found that their troubles continued. Stories abounded. One returning soldier was refused at a restaurant. "There is nothing here to feed Japs," he was told. Another Japanese American veteran who had lost a leg was shooed out of a barbershop even though he was in uniform. The barber told him, "We don't serve Japs." There were even incidents involving arson and shootings. Near Sacramento the house belonging to the family of a soldier who had died in the Vosges was set afire.

In May 1945, shortly after the end of the war in Europe, newspapers across the country reported the story of how the family of Sergeant Kazuo Masuda, who had been killed in northern Italy, were driven out when they tried to return to their former house near Santa Ana, California. Mary Masuda, the eldest daughter in the family, had returned to look over the situation, but the landlord and local farmers got together to keep the Masudas out. Mary was continually harassed by death threats. The local police sat by doing nothing. Masuda's two brothers were still in the service. Six months later, in December 1945, the military authorities brought General "Vinegar Joe" Stillwell, who had been active in the China–Burma theater, to honor the Masudas. The photograph of the general standing in front of the family's small one-story wooden house while pinning Masuda's Distinguished Service Cross on his white-haired Japanese mother's chest aroused popular sympathy for the family.

In Hood River, Oregon, when the local American Legion removed the names of sixteen Japanese Americans from the Honor Roll in front of the city hall, it became national news. Messages criticizing their action came in from 12,245 branches of the organization, beginning with the national headquarters. There was no choice but to restore the names of the Japanese Americans once again.

With the end of World War II the position of the United States as the world leader of democracy was firmer than ever. President Truman's view on the relocation of the Japanese Americans was clear from the beginning. He later criticized Roosevelt's decision very strongly. "They called it relocation but they put them in concentration camps, and I was against it," he said. "It was one place where I never went along with Roosevelt. He should never have allowed it."[10] Even the army, which at the beginning of the war had thought it necessary to carry the forceful relocation of the Japanese Americans for reasons of national security, adopted a policy of helping the Japanese Americans return to their homes.

Even though more than a year had passed since the end of the European war, the ceremony at the White House had been the most effective way to publicize to the American people the heroic wartime record of the young Japanese Americans. The Japanese Americans could now justly claim the war record they had so much wanted.

Many veterans still had to face residual prejudice from neighbors and employers. Kelly Kuwayama, a graduate of Princeton and Harvard Business School, had great difficulty getting a job after the war even though he was on the East Coast where there was little history of anti-Japanese American sentiment. In Hawaii too change came slowly for the Japanese Americans.

But the young men who had survived the battlefield could thrust their chests out with pride. No matter how slow change came for them in the postwar world they would never again put up with being treated as second-class citizens. For the first time they had self-confidence to feel that they were first-class Americans with nothing to be ashamed of. Before the war Bill Kajiwara, who served as a corporal in the 522nd Artillery Battalion, was a well-known sports figure in Arizona where he had been a star football player and then a coach at his alma mater, the University of Arizona. But Bill says that his war experience made him feel all the more strongly that he was a full-fledged American. The self-confidence of other young veterans like him became the main pillar supporting the entire postwar Japanese American community.

In 1952, seven years after the war ended, Congress changed the immigration law which had prevented the naturalization of the Japanese immigrants. The change was the result of the persistence of nisei leaders who used the wartime record of the 442nd Regiment to move both the House of Representatives and the Senate to action. Often nisei leaders reminded politicians of the wartime sacrifices of the Japanese Americans by telling the story of the lost battalion's rescue. The blood the nisei had shed in battle finally won for their aging parents rights as Americans. And in 1968 Senator Daniel Inouye and Congressman Spark Matsunaga introduced a bill to abolish the Emergency Detention Act so that under no circumstances would relocation camps ever be set up again.

By the 1950s Japanese Americans were gaining new political power in Hawaii. Sakae Takahashi, who had graduated from a mainland law school, began to revitalize an almost nonexistent branch of the Democratic party. Helping him was Daniel Inouye, a veteran of Company E who had lost his right arm two weeks before the end of the war. Takahashi, who had been a patient recuperating at the same hospital in Atlanta, sparked Inouye's interest in politics, and after the war he too had gone to law school on the mainland.

In 1950 Takahashi was elected to the Honolulu Board of Supervisors. Soon afterward he resigned to accept appointment as territorial treasurer —the youngest person ever to serve in the top level of the territorial government, and one of the first nisei to do so. Other veterans were getting into Hawaiian politics too, though not all of them were members of the Democratic party. By 1950 there was one Japanese American veteran in the Territorial Senate, four in the Territorial House of Representatives, and five among the delegates to the state constitutional convention. The most successful of the Japanese American veteran politicians were Inouye, the first Japanese American ever to serve in the United States Senate, and former First Lieutenant Spark Matsunaga, who was elected to the Senate after serving in the House of Representatives.

The Japanese American veterans took advantage of opportunities outside politics as well. All were eligible for the educational benefits offered under the GI Bill. "The biggest advantage for us was the GI Bill," says Inouye. "It made possible the dramatic postwar rise of the Japanese Americans, and it changed politics in Hawaii." Many Japanese American veterans, able to graduate from college and professional schools with government financial help, went to pursue careers that their parents, who had no choice but to work with their hands, could never have dreamed of. And though many veterans had grown up in families that often had trouble making ends meet, they were able to become engineers, lawyers, doctors, dentists, and public officials.

Perhaps all this change would have come anyway. The educational level of the Japanese American community had been high before the war. But there can be no doubt that the postwar political and economic achievements of the Japanese Americans owe much to the commitment of the young men who wanted so desperately to fight for a country that had treated them at first like aliens.

Epilogue

As I pursued the story of the Japanese American soldiers who fought during World War II my travels carried me across the continental United States to Japan and Europe too. Many stops on that journey were graveyards, from northern France to Arlington, Virginia, to Punchbowl in Hawaii.

One was Pearl Harbor, even today the most important United States naval base in the Pacific. A small launch carries sightseers from the Halawa Gate on the east side of the base to the *U.S.S. Arizona* Memorial, which floats like a huge white gravestone above the waves. The bodies of 1,100 men who sank with the *Arizona* have rested there since the day of the Pearl Harbor attack.

Standing on the memorial it is possible to see the rusted body of the battleship beneath the surface. Today, forty-five years after the attack, a thin stream of oil still oozes to the surface from the fuel tanks of the sunken ship. In the clear blue of the sea the oil stain floats like a black circle. Several miles away in the national cemetery at Punchbowl in Honolulu the graves of Joe Takata and Masaharu Takeba lie not far from the grave of Ernie Pyle, the most beloved war correspondent of the Pacific War. Doc Kometani, who died several years ago, also lies buried there. Many veterans I interviewed—Hiro Higuchi, Masao Yamada, Yozo Yamamoto, Rinky Nakagawa, and others—now rest there too.

The bodies of six Japanese American soldiers who died during the war were sent to their parents who had returned to Japan. There are gravestones for Japanese American soldiers in Hiroshima, Yamaguchi, Niigata, and Okinawa.

In northern France I visited the American military cemetery at Épinal, about a thirty-minute drive from Bruyères. It is one of the fourteen American military cemeteries in Europe for American soldiers who died in World War II. On the broad and lush green lawn, so meticulously cared

237

for, stand white crosses (or Stars of David for Jewish soldiers) for 5,255 dead. After the war many families asked for the remains of their sons or fathers or brothers to be returned to the United States. The five thousand and more men interred at Épinal represent only thirty-nine percent of those killed in the Vosges and Rhone regions and originally buried there. On a wall at the Épinal cemetery are carved the names of 424 missing soldiers. Among them is the name of only one Japanese American—Sergeant George Suyama, a native of Montana and a member of Company A, 100th Battalion.

The caretaker told me that only two Japanese Americans are still buried at Épinal. The grave marker of one of them reads: "Sergeant Tomosu Hirahara/442nd Regiment/Born in Hawaii/October 15, 1944." Hirahara, a member of Company B, had lost his life in the Vosges forest on the first day of the battle for Bruyères when the battalion had been fighting to take Hill A. He was twenty-one years old. A volunteer, he had been sent to join the 100th as one of the first replacement troops. Hirahara's father was from Yamaguchi, his mother from Hiroshima. Tomosu was the last of ten children. Perhaps he got his name because it sounded like Thomas. His parents are now dead so no one can know for certain. The other Japanese American grave at Épinal is that of Pfc Edward Ogawa of Company C, 100th Battalion, another replacement from Utah.

In the Lorraine American cemetery in the suburbs of Saint Avold, Alsace, lie the bodies of two more Japanese American soldiers. They are the Akimoto brothers, who volunteered for military service from the relocation camp at Amache in Colorado. The older brother, Victor, like Tomosu Hirahara, was sent as a replacement to the 100th Battalion. Seriously hurt in the fight at Biffontaine, he was one of the party of wounded soldiers led by Lieutenant Sam Sakamoto who were surrounded by German troops while moving to the rear. He died near the French border while being sent to Germany as a POW. He was twenty-six.

His younger brother Johnny, twenty, had died in battle four months before, just after the 442nd arrived in Italy. Their mother, Mikiko Akimoto, who had come to the United States from Aomori, asked that Johnny's body be reinterred in the Lorraine cemetery beside his brother so that the two boys would not be lonely. Fifteen years after the war ended, at the age of seventy, she fulfilled her long dream of visiting their graves herself.

The mother knelt for a long time in front of her sons' graves, her hands folded in prayer. The caretaker of the cemetery, who had shown her where the graves were, remembers looking down at the figure of the tiny Japanese mother. Mikiko asked to be shown the battlefield where her second son, Victor, had fallen. She rode in a taxi to a point where she could sit quietly and look at the distant silhouette of the Vosges hills.

For a few years after the war, at the place where the memorial plaque for the 442nd now stands in the forest outside Bruyères there remained the burned-out shell of an American tank. It was here that the 100th Battalion began its battle in the Vosges. Someone had picked up a bullet-riddled helmet from the ground nearby and placed it on the tank. Several months later the present memorial plaque was erected.

When I visited the memorial in 1979, except for Serge and Monique Carlesso, who walked with me across the soft forest floor covered with pine needles, there was no one else around. The autumn sun filtered through the tall evergreens, and the heather shrubs (*bruyères* in French) were sprinkled with lovely tiny reddish purple flowers. The deadly battle fought there many years before by the Japanese American soldiers seemed like a made-up story. It was hard for me to leave the peaceful quiet of the forest.

But only a few months before, a group of five children, ranging in age from six to eleven years old, had been killed instantly by a land-mine explosion while playing in the forest. After the war was over German POWs were used to clear the area of mines, but even so nearly six hundred local people have died by stepping on undiscovered land mines since then.

Several days after I placed a bouquet at the 442nd memorial plaque, the Carlessos took me on a drive from Bruyères toward Alsace. In the midst of a forest not so different from the one near Bruyères was the site of the Natzwiller-Struthof concentration camp, where French Resistance members accused of "terrorism" were sent. The gas chamber with its little observation window, and the large white tile tub where the corpses were placed afterward, were open to the public. When I visited it I began to realize for the first time just what "liberation" meant to the people of Bruyères.

Not one of the Japanese American veterans I talked to knew about the French concentration camp where Resistance members from Bruyères had been sent. And neither did any of the inhabitants of Bruyères seem to understand very well that the families of some soldiers who liberated them had been behind barbed-wire fences in their own country.

Forty years ago Corporal Tad Kanda of Company D, 100th Battalion, wrote to his family, "Every man fighting out there has something or somebody he's fighting for, and it is the knowledge that someday when all this is over with he'll know that it was worth it that keeps a man going through all the brutalities and horrors of war. My best friend was killed a few months ago, and quite a few others with the 100th Infantry won't be going back to Hawaii, but we all know and we are proud that they did their duties as Americans looking forward to a better world to live in, hoping to bring up the children-to-come under an atmosphere of freedom where one has the same opportunities regardless of his or her racial extractions."

It was a profound and deeply moving expression of hope in the midst of war's darkness, a hope that we must constantly keep kindled.

Notes

I. The Destination of the *Maui*

1. *Honolulu Advertiser,* December 11, 1940.
2. Gordon W. Prange, *At Dawn We Slept: The Untold Story of Pearl Harbor,* p. 539.
3. Ibid.
4. From the 298th, one lieutenant colonel, one major, five captains, and eight lieutenants; from the 299th, one captain and four lieutenants (from Maui District), one captain and three lieutenants (from Kauai District), and five lieutenants (Hawaii District).
5. "Organization and Movement of Provisional Battalion of Infantry from Hawaii to the United States," Hq. Hawaiian Department, Fort Shafter, T.H., May 31, 1942. Files on organization of 100th Battalion.
6. *New York Times,* June 6, 1942.

II. One-Puka-Puka

1. *Honolulu Star-Bulletin,* obituary, October 7, 1965.
2. Interview, James Lovell.
3. "Training and Assignment of Soldiers of Japanese Descent," War Department, Adjutant General's Office, January 23, 1942. Files, Adjutant General's Office, War Department.
4. "New Americans Conference" from Takie Okumura, *Paradise in the Pacific.*

III. Go for Broke

1. Letter to the author, December 17, 1980.
2. Many Japanese Americans today object to the term "relocation camp" as a euphemism to describe what were really "concentration camps." Since "concentration camp" has other hideous connotations, I will simply use "relocation camp" to describe these detention camps for Japanese Americans.

3. Plea of the VVV, January 30, 1942. File on miscellaneous subjects, 100th Battalion.

4. "Japanese Evacuation and Relocation in the Thirteenth Naval District A8-5/EF 37/(CB-7-0)," March 25, 1943. Files, War Relocation Authority.

5. Speech by Mike Masaoka, Minidoka Relocation Center, January 23, 1943. Files, War Relocation Authority.

6. Response to letter dated June 1, 1942, from United States Citizens of Japanese Descent, U.S. Army Chief of Staff, July 18, 1942. Files, Office of Chief of Staff, War Department.

7. "Military Utilization of United States Citizens of Japanese Ancestry," Memorandum for the Chief of Staff from G-1, LHH, Br. 3329, July 21, 1942. Files, Office of Chief of Staff, War Department.

8. Letter from the Little Rock Chamber of Commerce to Hon. D. D. Terry, March 18, 1942. Files, Office of Chief of Staff, War Department.

9. Memorandum, Brigadier General F. B. Mallon to Commanding General, Replacement and School Command, Army Ground Forces, Washington, D.C., March 20, 1942. Subject: "Japanese Situation, Camp Robinson, Arkansas." Files, Office of Chief of Staff, War Department.

10. Handwritten memo to Colonel Jenkins from C.O.W. Files, Office of Chief of Staff, War Department.

11. Dillon designated Thomas Holland to present his views. Files, Office of Chief of Staff, War Department.

12. Memorandum, Adjutant General's Office, War Department to Assistant Chief of Staff, G-2, July 1, 1942. Files, Office of Chief of Staff, War Department.

13. Memorandum, Lieutenant General J. L. DeWitt to Colonel Theo. J. Koenig, War Department, General Staff, G-2, July 14, 1942. Files, Office of Chief of Staff, War Department.

14. Memorandum, Brigadier General LeR. Lutes to Hq. Army Ground Forces, September 2, 1942. Files, Office of Chief of Staff, War Department.

15. Memorandum, Assistant Ground Adjutant General to Hq. Army Ground Forces, August 4, 1942. Files, Office of Chief of Staff, War Department.

16. Memorandum, Assistant Chief of Staff to Chief of Staff, July 18, 1942. Files, Office of Chief of Staff, War Department.

17. Letter from Rev. Masao Yamada to his wife, October 30, 1943.

18. War Relocation Authority, *The War Relocation Work Force,* February 1942. Files, War Relocation Authority.

19. "Potential Number of Persons of Japanese Ancestry Available for Military Service," War Department, Military Intelligence Service, March 29, 1943. Files, Military Intelligence Service, War Department.

IV. Guinea Pigs from Pearl Harbor

1. *Washington News,* October 4, 1943.
2. Associated Press dispatch, September 25, 1943.
3. Ibid.
4. *Hawaii Times,* December 20, 1943.
5. Letter from Masanobu Mukai, *Honolulu Star-Bulletin,* January 10, 1944.

6. *Hawaii Times,* November 3, 1943.

7. *Honolulu Star-Bulletin,* October 25, 1943.

8. Letter from Melvin Tsuchiya, July 5, 1944.

9. *Hawaii Times,* February 10, 1944.

10. *Hattiesburg American,* October 21, 1943.

V. Fanatic Soldiers

1. *Hawaii Times,* January 10, 1944.

2. *Crusaders,* June 15, 1944.

3. Dated December 24, 1943.

4. Sergeant Irvin Beyl, *St. Paul Morning Tribune,* March 10, 1944.

5. At that moment all the company commanders in the 100th Battalion happened to be Japanese American officers: Mits Fukuda in Company A, Sakae Takahashi in Company B, Richard Mizuta in Company C, Jack Mizuha in Company D. Mizuha had just been wounded badly by machine gun fire.

6. *St. Paul Morning Tribune,* March 17, 1944.

7. Letter from Sergeant William Oda, September 7, 1944.

8. *Time,* July 31, 1944.

9. United Press dispatch, July 11, 1944.

10. *New York Times,* September 2, 1944.

11. Memorandum, War Department, June 26, 1942. Files, War Department.

12. Pamphlet, Headquarters, Ninety-second Infantry Division, April 4, 1945.

13. United Press dispatch, July 22, 1944.

VI. The Home Front

1. *Saturday Evening Post,* November 10, 1945.

2. *Los Angeles Examiner,* December 1, 1943.

3. Ibid.

4. *Time,* December 20, 1943.

5. *Hawaii Times,* February 18, 1944.

6. Speech by Ben Kuroki, San Francisco, February 4, 1944.

7. *Omaha World Herald,* November 11, 1944.

8. Los Angeles YMCA (Japanese Branch) to John J. McCloy, November 14, 1943.

9. Memorandum, War Department, G-1, Personnel Division, May 29, 1944. Files, Office of Chief of Staff, War Department.

10. *Heart Mountain Sentinel,* April 30, 1944.

11. Report, War Department, Military Intelligence Service, March 29, 1943. Files, Military Intelligence Service, War Department.

VII. "Little Brown Soldiers" in the Dark Forest

1. Letter to the author, May 12, 1981.

2. Letter of Bill Kochiyama, May 1944.

3. 442nd Infantry Journal, June 26, 1944.

4. Text of presidential citation to 100th Battalion for the battles at Belvedere and Sasetta.

5. *Los Angeles Times,* July 21, 1944.

6. Forrest Pogue, *George C. Marshall: Organizer of Victory.*

7. Captured documents disclosed later that the town of Bruyères was defended by the First and Second Battalions of the 736th Grenadier Regiment, but prisoners were also taken from the 19th SS Police Regiment, Second Company of the 1316th Engineer Battalion, and the Forty-Ninth Fortress Machine Gun Battalion. During the war, however, the town was under the control of the much feared SS.

8. *Notice sur Bruyères.*

9. 442nd Headquarters, Interrogation Report No. 2, October 15, 1944. Files, 442nd Headquarters.

10. Ibid.

VIII. The Battle of Biffontaine

1. This chapter and the following are based heavily on the Headquarters 442nd Infantry Journal for October and November 1944, 442nd Narrative of Events for October and November 1944, and the battalion and company monthly histories for the units within the 442nd for October and November 1944. These documents together with interviews of veterans provided the framework for the narrative of events as well as specific details such as conversations between individuals.

IX. The Rescue of the Lost Battalion

1. October 22, 1944, 1930 hours.

2. October 28, 1944, 2012 hours.

3. Mark Schorer, *Sinclair Lewis.*

4. Letter in Japanese from Sergeant Noboru Fujinaka, killed in battle October 28, 1944.

5. Dated November 4, 1944.

6. November 15, 1944.

7. October 30, 1944.

8. November 22, 1944.

X. War's End

1. The French plaque misspelled the names of Miura and Kenji.

2. Letter from Masao Yamada to his wife, January 6, 1945.

3. Letter from Colonel Miller to Colonel Dixon, April 12, 1945.

4. Letter from Masao Yamada to his wife, April 10, 1945.

5. *Pacific Citizen,* April 10, 1944.

6. Mark Clark, *Calculated Risk.*

7. Awards presented to members of the 442nd as of April 30, 1946, were as follows:

Distinguished Unit Citation	7
Meritorious Service Unit Plaque	2
Unit Commendation	1
Medal of Honor	1
Distinguished Service Cross	48
Distinguished Service Medal	1
Oak Leaf Cluster to SS Medal	13
SS Medal	343
Legion of Merit	17
Oak Leaf Cluster to Croix de Guerre	1
Croix de Guerre	12
Soldiers Medal	13
Oak Leaf Cluster to Bronze Star Medal	35
Bronze Star	807
Oak Leaf Cluster to Purple Heart	468*
Purple Heart	2,022*
Army Commendation	36
Division Commendation	84
Croce ai Merito di Guerra (Italian)	2
Medaglia di Bronzo ai Valor Militaire (Italian)	2
Total	3,915

The figures marked with an asterisk do not include Purple Heart medals awarded to members of the unit wounded in action who were hospitalized and subsequently transferred to the zone of the interior. In some cases copies of General Orders issued to the hospitals were forwarded to headquarters, but in a majority of cases no orders were received. The correct figure for the total number of Purple Heart awards should be approximately 3,600, including 500 Oak Leaf Clusters to the Purple Heart medal. The numbers indicated in this list show the actual number of awards for which orders were available at the headquarters.

8. *New York Times,* July 16, 1945.

9. Letter of Secretary of the Interior Harold L. Ickes to Colonel Miller, October 15, 1945. Files, 442nd Headquarters.

10. Merle Miller, *Plain Speaking: An Oral Biography of Harry S. Truman.*

Bibliography

Official Papers: U.S. Army

(All the following are located in the National Archives, Washington, D.C.)

100th Battalion

Files on organization of 100th Battalion
Monthly Narrative of Events, October 1943–May 1945
Monthly Casualty List, September 1943–June 1944
Summary of Events for Month, October 1943–May 1945
Unit History, September 1943–June 1945
Miscellaneous files

442nd Infantry

Monthly Narrative of Events, June 1944–May 1945
Regiment Journal, June 1944–June 1945
Second Battalion Journal, June 1944–June 1945
Third Battalion Journal, June 1944–June 1945
H Company Journal, June 1944–June 1945
G Company Journal, June 1944–June 1945

442nd Headquarters

Daily Bulletin
S-2 Periodic Report, October 1944–December 1944
S-3 Periodic Report, October 1944–December 1944
Operational Instructions, October 1944–December 1944
Operational Report, October 1944–December 1944
Interrogation Report, October 1944–December 1944
Movement Orders, October 1944–December 1944
Monthly Casualty List, June 1944–May 1945
Monthly Citations (includes 100th citations), September 1943–June 1944
Miscellaneous files

Thirty-sixth Infantry Division, Headquarters

Operational Instructions, September 1944–November 1944
S-3 Report, September 1944–November 1944
G-3 Report, September 1944–November 1944
Attack Plans

Other Units

Fifth Army Headquarters, General Orders, November 1943–August 1944
Seventh Army Headquarters, Commanding General, Assignment and Attachment Orders, October 1944–December 1944
Thirty-fourth Infantry Division, Headquarters, General Orders, November 1943–August 1944
Fourty-fourth AAA Brigade, Headquarters, Office of the S-2, Intelligence Report, October 1944–December 1944
Ninety-second Infantry Division, Office of the Commanding General (Files related to 442nd, April 1945–May 1945)
Army Ground Forces Board, Florence Area, Allied Command Material, May 1945–June 1945)

War Department

Bureau of Public Relations, Press Branch (Files on 442nd)
Office of Chief of Staff (File of G-1, G-2, and G-3 material on 442nd, 1942–1944)
Office of Chief of Staff, Personnel Division, G-1, 1942–1944
Military Intelligence Service, 1942–1944
Adjutant General's Office, 1942–1944
General Staff, Military Intelligence Division, 1942–1944
Office of the Quartermaster General, 1942–1944
Headquarters, Service of Supply, 1942–1944
Armed Service Forces, Headquarters (Files on 442nd, 1942–1946)

Official Papers: Other Government Agencies

(All the following are located in the National Archives, Washington, D.C.)

U.S. Fleet, Headquarters of the Commander-in-Chief
Navy Department, Headquarters of the Commander
Congressional Record, 79th Congress, 1st Session
Congressional Record, 88th Congress, 1st Session
Congressional Record, 91st Congress, 1st Session
War Relocation Authority (Files on 442nd; relocation centers at Poston and Jerome)
Interior Department, War Agency Liquidation Unit, 1946 (Files contain various reports, studies, pamphlets published by the WRA as well as public statements by Dillon S. Myer)

Private Papers

Letters from Reverend Masao Yamada to his wife, Ai Yamada, May 1943–August 1945
Personal letters of many 442nd veterans

U.S. Army Publications

Americans, U.S. Army, 1946.
Camp Shelby, Public Relations Office, U.S. Signal Corps, 1943.
Fifth Army at the Winter Line, War Department, 1945.
Fifth Army History, War Department, 1945.
Fighting Divisions, Infantry Journal Press, 1945.
The Fighting 36th, U.S. Signal Corps, 1949.
From Salerno to the Alps: A History of the Fifth Army, Infantry Journal Press, 1945.
From Volturno to the Winter Line, 1944.
History of the Famed 34th Division, U.S. Signal Corps, 1949.
Military Department, Mississippi, Annual Report 1980, U.S. Army.
The 92nd Division: Summary of Operations in the World War, War Department, 1945.
Nisei in Uniform, U.S. Government Printing Office, 1945.
A Serviceman's Guide to Hattiesburg and Area, Public Relations Office, U.S. Signal Corps, 1943.

Books in Western Languages

Anonymous. *The Album.* 442nd Combat Team, 1943.
———. *The Lost Years.* Manzanar Committee, 1972.
———. *Natzwiller-Struthof.* (French.) A. Humblot et Cie., 1977.
———. *Notice sur Bruyères.* (French.) Ville de Bruyères, 1946.
———. *The Varsity Victory Volunteers.* VVV, 1946.
Bloom, Leonard, and Ruth Riemer. *Removal and Return.* Berkeley: University of California Press, 1949.
Capa, Robert. *Image of War.* New York: Grossman Publications, 1964.
Clark, Mark. *Calculated Risk.* New York: Harper & Brothers, 1950.
Coffman, Tom. *Catch a Wave.* Honolulu: University of Hawaii Press, 1973.
Daniels, Roger. *The Politics of Prejudice.* Berkeley: University of California Press, 1962.
Dank, Milton. *The Glider Gang.* Philadelphia: Lippincott, 1977.
Dodin, Robert. *La resistance dans le Vosges.* (French.) Imprimerie Flash, 1980.
Domerego, Jean-Pierre. *Les batailles de Sospel et de la Roya.* (French.) n.d.
Fuch, Lawrence. *Hawaii Pono.* New York: Harcourt Brace, 1961.
Girdner, Audrie, and Ann Loftis. *The Great Betrayal.* New York: Macmillan, 1969.

Goolrick, W., and O. Tanner, eds. *The Battle of the Bulge*. Alexandria, Va.: Time-Life Books, 1979.

Grodgins, Morton. *Americans Betrayed*. Chicago: University of Chicago Press, 1949.

Hemingway, Ernest, ed. *Men at War*. New York: Berkley, 1955.

Hogg, Ian I. *Infantry Weapons of World War II*. New York: Thomas Y. Crowell, 1977.

Hosokawa, Bill. *Nisei*. New York: Morrow, 1969.

Inouye, Daniel, with L. Elliott. *Journey to Washington*. Englewood Cliffs, N.J.: Prentice-Hall, 1967.

Jackson, W. *The Battle of Italy*. New York: Harper & Row, 1967.

Japanese American Citizens League. *They Work for Victory*, 1945.

Japanese American News. *Who's Who in American Japanese*. 1922.

Keegan, John, ed. *Who Was Who in World War II*. New York: Thomas Y. Crowell, 1978.

Keylin, Arleen, and Jonathan Cohen, eds. *The Forties as Reported by the New York Times*. New York: Arno Press, 1980.

Kitano, Harry. *Japanese Americans*. Englewood Cliffs, N.J.: Prentice-Hall, 1969.

Martin, Ralph. *Boy from Nebraska*. New York: Harper & Brothers, 1946.

Miller, Merle. *Plain Speaking: An Oral Biography of Harry S. Truman*. New York: Berkley, 1973.

Miyakawa, Edward T. *Tule Lake*. Waldport, Ore.: House by the Sea Publishers, 1979.

Modell, John. *The Economics and Politics of Racial Accommodation*. Champaign: University of Illinois Press, 1977.

Mollo, Andrew. *A Pictorial History of the SS*. Briarcliff Manor, N.Y.: Stein & Day, 1977.

Motley, Mary Penick. *Invisible Soldier*. Detroit: Wayne State University Press, 1975.

Murphy, Thomas D. *Ambassadors in Arms*. Honolulu: University of Hawaii Press, 1954.

Nicolson, Nigel. *Alex*. New York: Atheneum, 1973.

Peck, Clifford, Jr., ed. *Five Years, Five Countries, Five Campaigns*. 141st Infantry Associates, 1945.

Pogue, Forrest C., *George C. Marshall: Organizer of Victory*. New York: Viking Press, 1973.

Prange, Gordon W. *At Dawn We Slept: The Untold Story of Pearl Harbor*. New York: Penguin Books, 1983.

Sheehan, Fred. *Anzio*. Norman: University of Oklahoma Press, 1964.

Schorer, Mark. *Sinclair Lewis*. New York: McGraw-Hill, 1961.

Suzuki, Lester. *Ministry in the Assembly and Relocation Centers of World War II*. Berkeley: Yardbird Wing, 1979.

Walthall, M. C. *We Can't All Be Heroes*. Hicksville, N.Y.: Exposition Press, 1975.

Weglen, Michi. *Years of Infamy*. New York: Morrow, 1976.

Books in Japanese

Anonymous. *Heiki daizukan.* Tokyo: Mainichi shinbun, 1978.

———. *Ichiokunin no Shōwashi.* Tokyo: Mainichi shinbun, 1976.

———. *Nachi-Doitsu miritari rukku.* Tokyo: Sankei shinbun, 1972.

———. *Okinawa no shōgen.* Tokyo: Okinawa Times, 1971.

———. *Shōwa rikugun.* Tokyo: NHK, 1980.

———. *Zaibei Nihonjin shi.* Tokyo: Zeibei Nihonjinkai, 1940.

Gaimusho. *Nihon gaikō bunshō: Tai-Bei imin kankei.* Tokyo: Gaimusho, 1972.

Hawaii Nihonjin rengo kyōkai, ed. *Hawaii Nihonjin iminshi.* Tokyo: Hawaii Nihonjin rengo kyōkai, 1977.

Ikemiyagi, H. *Sensō to Okinawa.* Tokyo: Iwanami shoten, 1980.

Kato, S. *Amerika imin hyakunenshi.* Tokyo: Jijitsushinsha, 1962.

Kawazoe, Zen'ichi. *Imin hyakunen no nenrin.* Tokyo: Imin hyakunen no nenrinkai, 1968.

Kihara, R., ed. *Hawaii Nihonjin shi.* Tokyo: Bunseisha, 1935.

Macksey, K. *Doitsu kikoshidan.* Translated by K. Katogawa. Tokyo: Sankei shinbunsha, 1971.

Murayama, Tamotsu. *Hawaii nisei.* Tokyo: Jijitsushinsha, 1966.

Okubo, Kiyoshi. *Hawaiitō Nihonjin iminshi.* Hilo: Hilo Taimusu, 1971.

Okumura, Takie. *Paradise in the Pacific.* Tokyo: 1927.

Ota, T. *Guntai naimuhan.* Tokyo: Toto shobo, 1967.

Soga, Yasutarō. *Gojūnenkan no Hawaii kaikō.* Tokyo: Kaiko kankokai, 1953.

Takase, Kotoku. *Ikyo ni saita hana.* Tokyo: 1972.

Taylor, A. J. P. *Dainiji sekai taisen.* Translated by K. Kato. Tokyo: Shinhyoron, 1981.

Thomson, R. W. *D Day: Normandi joriku sakusen.* Translated by R. Miyamoto. Tokyo: Sankei shinbunsha, 1971.

Newspapers and Magazines

U.S. Army Newspapers

Beachhead News, 1943–1945
Infantry Journal, 1943–1945
Rambler (IV Corps), 1943–1945
Stars and Stripes, 1943–1945
The T-Patcher, 1943–1945
Yank, 1943–1945

Relocation Camp Newspapers

Denson Tribune, 1942–1945
Gila News-Courier, 1942–1945
Heart Mountain Sentinel, 1942–1945
Minidoka Irrigator, 1942–1945
Poston Bulletin (*Poston Chronicle* after January 1943), 1942–1945

Other English-Language Newspapers

Baltimore Sun, 1942–1945
Belmont Citizen, 1942–1945
Boston Globe, 1942–1945
Chicago Daily News, 1942–1945
Chicago Herald, 1942–1945
Chicago Sun, 1942–1945
Chicago Tribune, 1942–1945
Christian Science Monitor, 1942–1945
Denver Post, 1942–1945
Hattiesburg American, 1942–1945
Honolulu Advertiser, 1942–1945
Honolulu Star-Bulletin, 1942–1945
Houston Press, 1942–1945
Klamath Falls Herald and News, 1942–1945
Los Angeles Examiner, 1942–1945
Los Angeles Times, 1942–1945
New York Herald Tribune, 1942–1945
New York Times, 1942–1945
Omaha World Herald, 1942–1945
Pacific Citizen (San Francisco and Los Angeles), 1942–1945
St. Paul Dispatch, 1942–1945
St. Paul Morning Tribune, 1942–1945
Sacramento Bee, 1942–1945
Salt Lake City Tribune, 1942–1945
San Francisco Chronicle, 1942–1945
San Francisco Examiner, 1942–1945
Santa Ana Register, 1942–1945
Washington News, 1942–1945
Washington Post, 1942–1945
Washington Star, 1942–1945

Newspapers in Japanese

Hawaii Hochi (Honolulu), 1942–1945
Hawaii Times (Honolulu), 1942–1945
Hokubei mainichi (San Francisco), 1942–1945
Rafu shinpo (Los Angeles), 1942–1945

Magazines

American Mercury, 1942–1945
Collier's, 1942–1945
Coronet, 1942–1945
Current Life, 1942–1945
Fortune, 1942–1945
Life, 1942–1945
Newsweek, 1942–1945
Puka Puka Parade, 1942–1945
Readers Digest, 1942–1945
Time, 1942–1945

Interviews: United States

Eric Abe
George Abe
Masao Abe
Irving Akahoshi
George Aki
Stanley Akita
Dan Aoki
Noboru Ashida
Tadao Beppu
Bobby Chain
Richard Chinen
Hung Wai Ching
Mark W. Clark
Howard Dehoney
Henry Dixon
Frank Dobashi
Toichi Doi
Dale Evans
Kendall Fielder
Lester Fitzhugh
Robert Foote
Fred Fujimoto
Violet Matsuno Fujinaka
Frank Fujino
Curtis Fujioka
Harold Fujita
Joel Fujita
Monte Fujita
Mitsuyoshi Fukuda
Frank Fukuzawa
Henry Gomez
Tak Goto
George Grandstaff
Roy Green
Sam Hamai
James Hanley
Tom Hara
Thomas Harimoto
Betty Hayashi
Richard Hayashi
Tadao Hedani
Hiro Higuchi
Hisako Higuchi
Yoshimi Hiraoka
Takeshi Hirata

Sandy Holck
Masaki Horiuchi
Harry Hoshiko
Bill Hull
Fred Ida
Teruo Ihara
Tak Iijima
Norman Ikari
Daniel Inouye
Richard Ishimoto
Bob Iso
Herbert Isonaga
Richard Itanaga
Harry Iwafuchi
Misao Iwamoto
Victor Izui
Walter Kadota
Robert Kadowaki
Bill Kajikawa
Margaret Kajikawa
Hiroshi Kaku
Harry Kanada
Paul Kanazawa
Tom Kanazawa
Kenneth Kaneko
Hoppy Kaneshina
Kay Kaneshina
Fumiko Karatsu
Shiro Kashino
Robert Kashiwagi
Tom Kataoka
Tom Kawano
Isaac Kawasaki
Christopher Keegan
Young Oak Kim
Sanji Kimoto
Noboru Kimura
Thomas Kinaga
Takashi Kitaoka
Hisako Kobayashi
Lily Kobayashi
Roy Kobayashi
Tom Kobayashi
Bill Kochiyama
Mary Yuri Kochiyama

Masao Koga
Etsuo Kohashi
Harry Komatsu
Kingo Kotake
Takeshi Kudo
Larry Kukita
Richard Kumashiro
Hideo Kuniyoshi
Lawrence Kurahara
Norman Kurlan
Kelly Kuwayama
Donald Kuwaye
Walter Lesinski
Emily Light
James Lovell
William McCaffrey
James Maeda
Buddy Mamiya
Masaji Marumoto
Etsu Masaoka
Mike Masaoka
Mas Masuda
Shigeto Matsuda
John Matsudaira
Mat Matsumoto
Walter Matsumoto
Spark Matsunaga
Yoshio Matsuoka
Katsugo Miho
Teruo Miyagishima
Howard Miyake
Fujio Miyamoto
Tadao Miyamoto
Kiyo Morimoto
Noboru Murakami
Slim Murakami
Yano Murakami
Kazuo Muto
Harry Nakabe
Henry Nakada
Pershing Nakada
Rinky Nakagawa
Wally Nakajima
Ushi Nakamine
Stanley Nakamoto

Herbert Nicholson
Wilfred Ninnis
George Nishi
Chika Nitahara
Teruo Nobori
David Novac
Bill Oda
Ester Oda
Richard Oda
Richard Oguro
Kiyoshi Ohkubo
Frank Ohshita
George Ohtsuka
Paul Okamoto
Eiichi Oki
Tadao Okimoto
Yukio Okutsu
Tom Ouye
Bill Pye
Harold Riebesell
Moon Munetatsu Saito
Shozo Saito
Tamio Saito
Eddy Sakai
Tad Sakai
Tadao Sakai
William Sakai
Sam Sakamoto
Stanley Sakuma
Mat Sakumoto

Kenneth Saruwatari
Aki Sasaki
Robert Sasaki
Satoru Sawai
Jack Scott
Don Seki
Sumi Seki
Tak Senzaki
George Shigematsu
Henry Shikuma
Frank Shimada
Joe Shimamura
Tamotsu Shimizu
Minoru Shinoda
Francis Shinohara
Junji Shiroyama
Gordon Singles
Lyn Crost Stern
Hiroshi Sumida
George Takahashi
Sakae Takahashi
Tom Takahashi
Russell Takashima
Michio Takata
Hiroshi Takusagawa
Ben Tamashiro
Chester Tanaka
Thomas Tanaka
Larry Tanimoto
Jim Tazai

William Terao
Takeshi Teshima
Rudy Tokiwa
Mike Tokunaga
Jyokichi Tominaga
Mel Tominaga
Taro Tsukahara
Mary Tsukamoto
John Tsukano
Conrad Tsukayama
Mike Tsuji
Helen Turner
Clifford Uyeda
Jack Wakamatsu
John Weckerling
Michi Weglyn
Ai Yamada
Henry Yamada
Masao Yamada
Yozo Yamamoto
George Yasumatsu
Feb Yokoi
Karl Yoneda
Kaoru Yonezawa
Yutaka Yoshida
Kiyoshi Yoshii
Art Yoshimura
Israel Yost

Interviews: Europe

Edouard Canonica
Monique Carlesso
Serge Carlesso
France Collin
Raymond Collin
Joseph Contes
Madame Contes
Marie Contes
Gerard Deschaseaux
Jean Drahon

Georges Henry
Gerard Henry
Romary Henry
Pierre Poirat
Henri Robert
Mary Louise Robert
Karl Schmid
Magdalena Schmid
Annie Schmitt
Jean Soulie

Paulette Soulie
Alexander Tarantzeff
Georges Tarantzeff
Jean-Marie Thomas
Josephine Voirin
Alice Zeller
Jeanette Zeller
Marion Zeller

Index

About the Author

Masayo Umezawa Duus was born in Hokkaido, Japan, and graduated from Waseda University. She has lived in the United States since 1964. The author of six books in Japanese, Mrs. Duus is also a regular contributor to major Japanese newspapers and magazines. Her first book, a study of the Tokyo Rose treason trial, was widely acclaimed by critics in Japan and won the Kodansha prize for nonfiction in 1976. The English-language edition was published under the title *Tokyo Rose: Orphan of the Pacific*. The Japanese-language version of *Unlikely Liberators* appeared first in serialized form in Japan's leading monthly journal, *Bungei shunju*, in 1982 and won its Readers' Prize for that year. Her most recent publication is *Hawaii ni kaketa onna* (the life of Tazuko Iwasaki), a biography of an issei woman who worked as a labor contractor on a Hawaiian plantation.